C000227900

WHEN HARRY MET SHEILA

Sheila Steafel

Foreword by Claire Rayner OBE

*"Harry once told me that there is a story in everybody.
This is mine."*

APEX PUBLISHING LTD

Hardback first published in 2010 by

Apex Publishing Ltd

PO Box 7086, Clacton on Sea, Essex, CO15 5WN, England

www.apexpublishing.co.uk

Copyright © 2010 by Sheila Steafel

The author has asserted her moral rights

British Library Cataloguing-in-Publication Data
A catalogue record for this book
is available from the British Library

ISBN HARDBACK: 1-906358-83-4   978-1-906358-83-9

All rights reserved. This book is sold subject to the condition, that no part of this book is to be reproduced, in any shape or form. Or by way of trade, stored in a retrieval system or transmitted in any form or by any means, electronic, mechanical, photocopying, recording, be lent, re-sold, hired out or otherwise circulated in any form of binding or cover other than that in which it is published and without a similar condition, including this condition being imposed on the subsequent purchaser, without prior permission of the copyright holder.

Typeset in 10.5pt Baskerville Win95BT

Production Manager: Chris Cowlin

Cover Design: Siobhan Smith

Printed and bound in Great Britain by
MPG Biddles Ltd., King's Lynn, Norfolk

To Tucker Ashworth, Jeanette Hurworth, D.H., and Crispin and Ben.

FOREWORD

The first time I saw Sheila Steafel perform live was at the dress rehearsal of a Charity Show being put together at a big West End theatre under the title 'Night of a Hundred Stars' in which I, for my sins, was doing a send-up of myself as an agony aunt. I knew her face from various films and TV shows in which she had appeared but had never seen her acting 'on foot'.

This is a term created in our family by one of my sons who, at the age of four, expressed an ambition to be an actor. 'What kind of actor?' his father - himself once in the business - wanted to know. 'A foot actor' the little one said. And when asked to explain what that meant he told us with some asperity, because of course we should have known, 'Well, there are actors on films and actors on television and actors on foot and. they're the best kind'.

Seeing Sheila on stage was a revelation. Her audience was just the rest of the cast - quite a lot of us, in fact - and from the moment she came on stage dressed as a very young ballerina and began to sing a woebegone song about the misery of always being cast as one of the cygnets in 'Swan Lake' and how dancing the part caused 'sweaty wings and other things - 'we were convulsed with laughter. Her timing, her ability to use the smallest movements of her body to express the little swan's feelings, her musicality which makes her voice a delight to listen to, were all great gifts which she used with consummate artistry. Here was a true clown - using the word in its best possible meaning. She was a joy, and as far as I was concerned, the best act in the show which I have to tell you included some very big names, even, I seem to remember a somewhat aged Hollywood star.

So, when she phoned me and told me she had written her autobiography and would I write the forward to it, of course I said yes. I'm her most devoted fan and always will be. But I can't deny I was anxious. There are many people who are superb performers but the most dire of writers.

I've accepted invitations like this one before from old friends and then had to struggle to come up with some sort of anodyne comments that aren't exactly lies, but aren't really true either. And I didn't want to have to do that for Sheila, and prayed that some of her theatrical talent had drifted into her ability to write.

And then the manuscript arrived and I put it in front of me on my desk and thought - well, I'll have a quick look before I get to Chapter Fourteen of the book I'm writing at present and have a quick riffle through to see what Sheila has done.

I didn't get to Chapter Fourteen that day, or the next. This is a marvellous book, an un-put-down-able story and an honest account of what life on foot, and elsewhere in the toughest of businesses, is really about. These days there has to be lots of TV and film acting, plus voice-overs for commercials and, to my personal delight, reading novels to make audio books for blind people too, to make a successful career; and I take especial. pleasure in the fact that Sheila read the texts of my six volume series 'The Poppy Chronicles' Is that a plug? Yer darn tootin' it is - for both of us.

I must be mad to say this, for heaven knows the literary world at every level, whether you write Booker prize winners or 'bodice rippers' - as a particular type of erotic pop reading is known in the trade - is crowded enough; it can be as difficult for would-be writers to get a foot on the first rung of the ladder to a career that actually earns a living, as it is for actors, and we all know how tough that is.

But I'm going to say it. Sheila Steafel can tell a story and tell it well. Her next book - and of course there must be a next book' - should be a novel. And I for one will be panting to get my hands on it.

Best wishes
Claire Rayner OBE

CONTENTS

PROLOGUE

Eisteddfod. The word transports me, not to some grand venue in Wales but to Johannesburg's Town Hall in South Africa. It is 1949, I am four years old, and my mother and I join the crush on the wide wooden staircase as children of all ages, accompanied by their doting mothers, are herded into upstairs offices adapted into changing rooms. They are pushed, pulled and cajoled into or out of their costumes, some hired but most home-made. The high-ceiling rooms echo with the racket of wailing children who have lost their minders and high-pitched irritation from the minders trying to reclaim them, bitter tears from offspring - and more often their mothers - who have failed to win a diploma, and the garbled emissions from a loud speaker somewhere, announcing the progress of various heats down in the main hall. In the jostle, torn tinsel wings are patched, intransigent zips and sagging taffeta hastily pinned, young upturned faces are rouged and half-open mouths are pulled askew and lipsticked. Then back down the staircase - "Let us through, please, my daughter's in the next group!" - and into the black-and-white tiled vestibule, side-stepping the patch of sawdust that a stoic black cleaner has scattered over the vomit of some nervous contestant (don't look, hold your breath, think of something else). Up the wide glass-panelled corridor we go, peering in at the audience of ambitious parents and anxious teachers sitting in the auditorium on rows of hard, wooden, folding chairs. At the back is a raised platform where, behind a long table, the three judges loom, pencils poised over sheaves of paper, eyes critically narrowed, concentrating on the stage ahead.

A woman standing by a heavy door ('STAFF ONLY') with a clipboard in her hand checks my age, category and name (nine, character tap, S.S.), confirmed by my mother. "Good luck, do your best!" and she is gone. Low voiced instructions – "Wait until you hear your name read out", the door is opened, and I am pushed up a short flight of stairs into semi-darkness. I stand at the side of the stage next to a young man with a list in his hand and a pencil behind an ear. He smiles at me and points to my name on the list. I nod. My heart beats faster, my palms sweat; I am nervous, excited, confident. I watch a fellow dance student in a white-skirted sailor suit shuffle-hop her way through 'On the Good Ship Lollipop', and I am sure that my tap routine is stronger, more unusual. My home-made costume is a short, tight, red-and-gold striped skirt and a red jacket with a tight waist, frilly peplum and three oversized gold buttons down the front, the long sleeves tight at the wrist and flaring into exaggerated puffs at the shoulder. My hair is hidden under a wig of tight black curls topped by a small red hat secured at a saucy angle. I am wearing shiny gold tap shoes with enormous red bows, and my legs, hands and face have been stained a dark chocolate colour, my lips exaggerated and coloured a vivid red, with circles of white painted around my eyes. I am kitted out to do my turn to the music of 'The Darktown Strutters' Ball'. The music begins. I step out, left hand on hip, right hand on hat. And STEP-KICK, STEP-KICK, STEP ...

www.apexpublishing.co.uk

PART 1:
EARLY STAGES

CHAPTER 1

I can't remember a time when this burning ambition to be an actress wasn't at the forefront of my mind. I had a gift for comedy, and as a child found I could instinctively defuse difficult moments at home (and there were many) by being amusing. But it was at the age of six I discovered the heady delight of making an audience laugh when, dressed in one of my mother's petticoats and with an upright feather stuck into an Alice band on my head, I sang Schumann's 'Lullaby' as an opera diva, 'Madame Tetra-Screamy' in my first school concert.

I never questioned why my mother enrolled me into a dance class at the early age of three, but I took to it like a duck to water. Once a week we would take a rattling tramcar with its dinging bell from suburban Berea into 'town'. I would sit clutching my precious shoe bag, which contained a pair of pink ballet slippers (held onto my feet by bands of black elastic) and a pair of red tap shoes with wide red ribbon ties and special jingle taps on the toes that rattled when you danced. Then it was off the tram, down three blocks into a dingy street, through a grimy glass door and up three narrow flights of stairs, the hubbub of children's voices and the honky-tonk of the off-key piano growing ever louder.

The studio itself was long and narrow, with on one side a row of windows overlooking a regiment of drab buildings, and on the other a yellowing whitewashed wall, into which a long wooden barre had been screwed. All the walls were marked with the scuffs of poorly executed dance manoeuvres, and the worn wooden floor groaned as it surrendered to the enthusiastic leaps and jumps of a dozen or more would-be ballerinas. A cheap, somewhat distorted mirror covered the whole of the front wall, intended for students to view themselves critically as they performed. Unfortunately it was mostly obscured, not only by our teacher, Miss Lettie, who stood in front of it, but by the group of mothers sitting on a row of chairs behind her, some knitting, some reading, and some watching and willing their offsprings' progress.

"And a ONE, and a TWO, and a THREE!"

The voice of pert, petite Miss Lettie rose high above the jangle of the piano and the thump of ungainly landings as she took the class of older pupils through their paces. To one side, Mrs Frieda Ellman sat at the game, elderly upright piano, swaddled in her all-embracing tweed coat whatever the weather, a cigarette stub glued to her scarlet lower lip, never glancing at the keys as she pounded out tune after tune, beating time with an outstretched foot.

"Thank you, class!"

"Thank you, Miss Lettie!"

Exhausted and sweaty, the class curtsied to her, then shuffle-scuffed their way to the back of the studio where their personal belongings were stacked in untidy piles. Their mothers upped and followed, scraping their chairs and scooping up their own paraphernalia, to be swiftly replaced by the next group of mothers, including my own.

"Now for my babies!"

Miss Lettie clapped her hands, and ballet shoe shod and eager I lined up with my fellow students at the barre.

"... Plié ... and down slowly ... and keep those knees out ... and stay ... and up slowly ... and arms and ..."

And no matter how much I tried, no matter how painfully I practised, the plié was beyond me; my knees refused to turn outwards.

"Don't worry about it, Mrs Steafel," Miss Lettie had said sympathetically. "Some children are just 'turned in' and Sheila's one of them. There's nothing we can do about it," adding, "Still, she does make up for it with her personality."

And it seems I did, because in spite of this handicap, at the age of four I won a Diploma of Merit in the under fives' ballet section, clad in a somewhat droopy tutu and sporting a similar pair of fairy wings.

Once the torture at the barre was over, it was time for our individual routines. Each mother anxiously watched her own child's solo dance while the other parents paid little heed, until my turn came. Down went the knitting and the magazines and up went the heads in anticipation. Adjusting my feet into 'fifth' and lifting my arms into 'attitude', I waited for Miss Lettie's command and Mrs Ellman's opening volley.

"Off you go, Sheila dear, and don't forget, USE YOUR FACE!"

And use my face I did, putting my heart and soul into my

3

performance and illustrating my feelings with my facial expressions. I didn't quite understand why they laughed but I didn't mind; the laughter was warm and approving, and I knew that they liked me. So there it was, I was a natural comic, my timing was instinctive; and once I realised I had this God-given gift, I used it whenever I could to make people laugh and like me.

CHAPTER 2

We sat, my brother and I, in the empty, darkened stalls of the Standard Theatre, having been sworn to silence and best behaviour. It was the dress rehearsal of the Johannesburg Operatic Society's production of *Iolanthe*, and several rows behind us at a makeshift table with a hooded lamp sat the director and his assistant, pencils and paper at the ready. It wasn't the first time we had been allowed to watch a dress run and we felt quite at home in this theatre with its gleaming brass and heavy chandeliers and its red plush and gilt curlicues. If we wanted we could sit in one of the 'ashtrays', the boxes at the side of the stage, from where we could see the smallest details of the set and the sweat on the upper lips of the leading singers. Sometimes we would creep upstairs to the grand circle with its distant overview of the whole stage, and on rare occasions we were allowed to sit beside the stage manager, with his copy of the text and his lighting board, in the wings, from where he ran the show. As a special treat I was allowed to sit in the orchestra pit under the stage, on the long piano stool, beside my mother, where the surge of the music swallowed me up. Before she began to play, my mother would take off her heavy bracelet of red glass lilies with gold filigree leaves and lay it carefully along the piano lid, and as she played, when she nodded her head I would quickly turn the page of her score, making sure that my arm didn't obscure the music she was reading.

But the time I loved most was when I was invited to sit with one of the actresses in her dressing room and gaze in wonder as she transformed herself into the character she was about to play. I watched the ingénue Winnie Castle, who was playing Josephine, the captain's daughter in *H.M.S. Pinafore*, opposite my father as the hero Ralph Rackstraw. She sat in front of the mirror with its surround of bright, bare light bulbs, photographs and cards tucked behind them, and stared critically at her pale, unpainted face. In front of her, neatly laid out on a faded towel, was a row of sticks of greasepaint wrapped in worn tinfoil, several mysterious tubs, a large box spilling powder, and a chipped china mug holding a variety of brushes.

Beside it stood a half-burned candle under a small round tin on a stand, and a large, bedraggled, swan's down powder puff hung from the conveniently upturned foot of a china chipped cherub. The stuffy, windowless room smelled wonderfully of talcum powder, cheap perfume, cigarette smoke, dusty carpets and sweat-stained costumes, and I sniffed it in as deeply as I could, closing my eyes to lock it into my memory.

As a child the magic of the transformation from ordinary to extraordinary never failed to fascinate me. I watch Winnie as she scrapes her hair back into a thick, tight net, then takes up the greasepaint sticks, first number five, then number nine, and draws thick lines on to her forehead, her cheeks, her nose and her chin. Swiftly, she blends the colours over her face and down her neck, and suddenly Winnie has disappeared, leaving a blank, bland mask. A small pot of dark brown paste, a flat brush and a smudged line on either side of her rather broad nose refines it, while a dab along the base of her determined chin shortens it into a more acceptable regularity. Cheekbones are boldly rouged, eyebrows strongly arched, and then, with an unladylike spit onto a solid block of black mascara and the twirl of a finely pointed brush, the upper and lower eyelids are outlined with exaggerated wings on either side and a streak of white greasepaint is applied along the lower lid. She adds a red dot to the inner corner of each eye, and then - the moment I have been waiting for - the long, thick, spidery false eyelashes! Glue is spread evenly, the lash lifted carefully between finger and thumb and with one eye shut and tongue tip protruding, comes the gentle tap-tapping along the eyelid with a small, wooden orange stick. Now a still moment to set the glue and a flutter to make sure the lash is secure, before the procedure is repeated on the other side. Then Winnie takes a box of matches, lights one, puts it to the candle under the stand, and in a few moments the 'hot black' in the tin begins to bubble and melt. She picks up a small blackened toothbrush, carefully coats the bristles and, eyes wide, binds the false lashes and her own thickly together. And, my throat tight with longing, I send up a small, silent prayer: please, God, me too.

During the runs of these performances my mother, wafting perfume and resplendent in a long, svelte black-and-red evening gown, along with my father, black tie and tailed, would set off for the theatre, leaving my brother and me safely tucked up in our beds under the supervision of our black nanny cum housemaid. She would sit in the kitchen, perhaps with a friend with her to share the tedium of the evening, while in adjacent rooms, bedside lamps relit, we would lie awake waiting for the cuckoo clock to whirr and squawk eight o'clock. Curtain up! Then together we dum-de-dummed through the overture before warbling our way through each song, la-Ia-ing when our memories of the lyrics failed, and gibberish-ing any dialogue that hadn't set in our minds. A glass of interval milk (provided by the long-suffering 'backstage staff') and then on with what we could remember of the second act. As the evening wore on, our energy and enthusiasm waned, and we seldom reached the third act. Nor can I remember ever taking a curtain call.

CHAPTER 3

My father still had traces of his native Lancashire in his speech, which he indignantly refuted, and we teased him about it mercilessly. However, because I was so keen on acting he was insistent that I should lose any trace of a South African accent and improve the timbre of my rather small, tight voice. And so when I was eleven years old I was sent to have elocution lessons with Muriel Alexander. Muriel Alexander's claim to fame was that she had once understudied Ellen Terry during her acting years in London. Arriving in Johannesburg in her middle age, she had become a doyenne of local theatre, teaching, directing and producing. Indeed, in the 1950s the Alexander Theatre was built and dedicated to her in recognition of her contribution to the city's cultural life.

Twice a week I would visit her in her penthouse studio flat in downtown Johannesburg where she lived and taught. It was a large room, a third of which had been divided off as her living quarters, and I can recall a small bedroom but no kitchen or bathroom, although, of course, these must have existed. I do remember, though, that when we students needed to use the toilet we had to climb through a door outside her flat that opened onto a tarmac roof. There to one side was an unprepossessing old flush lavatory the size of a broom cupboard.

During the first session of each week Muriel attempted to cure me of my accent and enrich my poor speech patterns.

"How now brown cow," she would roundly intone.

"Hah nah brahn cah," I would repeat in my thin voice and local accent.

But perseverance paid off, and slowly but surely my voice opened up and my drawl receded.

"High nigh brine kye," I chanted, and Muriel nodded her head in approval.

She set me pieces to memorise, and I would recite them standing at one end of the studio while 'Teacher', as we called her, sat in an armchair at the other end.

"I can't hear you!" she would call from her vantage point, even though I knew she could. "What? What was that? Speak up!"

And when I did speak up, it was received with, "No, no, don't shout! Use your diaphragm!"

My father was delighted with my progress and I was expected to sustain my newly acquired vocal skills at home. At school, however, I reverted to speaking as my peers did for fear of being teased and judged 'affected'.

For reasons I have never understood, the pieces we were set to learn were mostly silly and badly written monologues about orphans and unhappy fairies, or poems with rhymes so tortured as to make any literate person squirm. One particularly pointless piece was the story of The Three Pigs written in spoonerisms, the title thus becoming The Pee Thrigs! It is irritatingly wedged in my brain and I can still repeat it, word for nonsensical word: "In the days when there was no harecity of scam, and pork penns were a choppy a piece ..." and so on. What a pity, when it could have been some great poem or speech I could call on to quote!

The second weekly session was devoted to working on scenes from various plays with a group of other young, aspiring thespians. From time to time Teacher would put on a concert in a small theatre close by, and thrilled beyond measure, I finally experienced what it would be like when the career I intended to follow became a reality. I was in several of these one-night performances, but only two remain in my memory. In one we were dressed in Greek robes, and to the music of 'Clair de Lune' dragged ourselves round in a sorrowful circle, stopping from time to time to freeze into a picture as seen on a Roman vase. As the performance progressed, titters from the audience made me aware of how ludicrous we must appear, and I had to fight the urge to play it for laughs. The other was much more of an event. I was playing the villain of the piece, Jack Frost, who was attempting to freeze out Spring, played by a pretty girl whose long blonde hair I envied, but of whose acting skills I was scornful. Various Gnomes and Flowers pranced around, while I sat at the top of a ladder poorly disguised as a wintry tree. As the drama progressed, a particularly enthusiastic Gnome caught his foot in Spring's train of garlands, and in an effort to escape, immobilised them both. They struggled with their knotty problem as the other actors tried to maintain their sense of joy and abandon, but the choreography had unravelled and the

9

illusion was broken. One Flower burst into tears and fled the stage, others hovered with panic in their eyes, while I laughed so heartily that the ladder rocked, then tumbled backwards ripping the cyclorama, and coming to rest at an awkward angle. No one was hurt, apart from a few egos, but for a while I was firmly in Muriel Alexander's bad books.

CHAPTER 4

Once we started our schooling, my father Harold, who had always been keen that we children should be good singers, took it upon himself to coach us. This was not the best idea; he was impatient and intimidating, and I, and especially my brother Brian, dreaded these sessions. It also meant that we could never sing simply for pleasure when he was around, because he would appear and turn the casual enjoyment into a lesson. His passion was music in all its aspects, except for anything he considered modern or 'pop', which he treated with mocking disdain. As a result we would refrain from playing our records when he was within earshot so as to avoid his unkind parodies of our favourite singers. More often than not he would sing around the house or in his workshop, and whenever my mother heard him, with an expression of sour distaste on her face, she would give a slight shudder. It was upsetting, and I determined that I would never put myself into a position where I might evince that same feeling of abhorrence. As a result, I have never been able to practise singing if I thought anyone could hear me. Performances in front of the public were fine, as were rehearsals in front of fellow actors, but when I was on my own, if I thought I could be heard by a neighbour or someone in the near vicinity, I would be reduced to silence.

When my father relaxed he would invariably be found on the sofa in our sitting room, a music score on his lap and a bowl of fruit or nuts beside him, singing the notes sotto voce using the tonic solfa. He never did master transferring the notes from the page to the piano, and I remember how, almost every time my mother sat down to practice a piece of music or simply play for her own pleasure, he would appear with a score or a new song in his hand and ask her to try it out with him. Too self-effacing to refuse and fearful of the consequences if she did, she would comply. As a result it was only when he wasn't about that she felt free to let her fingers fly across the keys, eyes half closed and smiling with pleasure, but as time went by she seemed to lose interest altogether and seldom sat down at the piano to play. In later years when she openly began to resent her marriage to

Harold, she claimed bitterly that he had only married her so as to have an accompanist at his beck and call.

At the beginning, singing was for me a joyous thing. It thrilled me when my mother played the accompaniment, supporting my voice with its harmonies as I carried the melody. Later, as I became aware of her reluctance to play, I avoided asking her, picking out what chords I could find myself. More than anything I wanted a career as a singer with acting ability, and my father, whom I suspect had longed to be a professional singer himself, heartily approved of my ambition. What he didn't know was that, rather than grand opera or the concert recitals he had in mind, I ached to be in good old showbiz musicals. But then he had never seen me standing on the dining room table so that I could see myself full length in the peach mirror over the mantelpiece, gyrating and singing along with the wind-up gramophone as it churned out current popular numbers.

It was after I had won an Eisteddfod singing award at the age of eleven that my father decided I should be trained by a professional teacher.

"Her name is Madame Sokolov. She's Polish, and although she doesn't sing herself she has developed a unique singing technique," he told me with enthusiasm. "I've heard the results and they are impressive, so you'll be starting after school next Wednesday."

It was the worst decision he could have made and it badly affected my singing ability, which, to my deep regret, never recovered.

The lessons took place in a block of flats in a bleak suburb located a tedious bus ride away. The room itself was airless and smelt of cats, and was crowded with overstuffed chairs and a large, carved mahogany table. Heavy, faded green velvet drapes kept all but the merest strip of daylight out, and every flat surface, as well as the walls and the huge grand piano, was covered with framed photographs of all shapes and sizes, scrawled with signatures under effusive messages. A tall, glass-shaded lamp stood beside the piano, shedding a dull light over its keyboard and casting sinister shadows beyond.

"Leave your school hat on the sofa and remove please your jacket," Madame Sokolov instructed in a surprisingly high voice. "Now, come to me and we will see if you have good diaphragm."

With that the woman pulled me towards her, and standing in front of me, placed her bony hands around my ribcage, thumbs meeting in the centre.

"Breathe! Breathe in!" she instructed. "Push away my hands with your lungs. No! Not your stomach! Lungs, lungs! Here!" She dug her thumbs into my middle, making me gasp. "Ya, there!" she said triumphantly.

Settling herself on the elaborate piano stool, "You come sing for me," she said, and played a chord. The sound of the piano was muffled, dead. "You sing for me scales, yes? Up down, next note, up down and so on."

Dutifully I 'up-downed and so on' while taking stock of the elderly woman in front of me. She had twisted her wispy, iron-grey hair into a knot on the crown of her head held firm by an elaborate tortoiseshell comb. Her face was long with sagging jowls, her paper-thin skin made her heavy eyelids appear almost transparent, while a large mole on the side of her mouth gave the impression of a lopsided sneer.

"That's good, that's good! You have a good voice, very … precise. I can tell you are musical like your wonderful father! Now, we start here, B below middle C." She hit the note several times. "And we will see how high you can go, yes?"

"I can go to F above middle C," I told her.

"Oh yes?" Madame Sokolov seemed amused. "I think we can do better than that! Now, try, and we shall see. You sing arpeggio. You know arpeggio?"

I knew arpeggio.

She played an introductory flourish, then a chord, and nodded. Picking up the note, I sang the run. Then she produced a chord a semitone higher. I sang the next, the next and the next, until I reached what I knew was the highest I could comfortably go, and I stopped.

"I want more!" Madame Sokolov said encouragingly. "Come now, you can go higher, much higher!"

I tried the next scale but choked on the top note and smiled apologetically. "I'm sorry, I can't."

"Of course you can!" came the firm reply. "Come, the next one. You can do it. Come!" And she hammered out the next chord, her eyes hard and bright, willing me to reach it.

Taking a deep breath I started the ascent, but balked at the topmost note. "I'm sorry, I really can't," I repeated miserably.

13

Madame Sokolov stood up and, taking me by my shoulders, brought her face close to mine. The scent of stale talcum was almost overpowering.

"Your father send you here to learn. I am here to teach you. And when I tell you you can do something, you will do it! You understand?"

Her breath was sour and I turned my head away.

"Look at me!" she commanded.

Holding my breath I turned back to meet her gaze.

"You understand," she repeated slowly. It was no longer a question, but a statement.

I nodded.

She sat back at the piano and continued, "If you think you cannot sing so high, I will tell you how you do it. You scream! That is my secret. You squeeze your throat and you scream. THAT is how we train your voice to go high. NOW you understand? Ya?"

Fearful, again I nodded.

"Good. Now we go on with The Scream."

And thus began Madame Sokolov's methodical ruination of my singing career.

"What do you mean it hurts your throat?"

It was a few weeks and several lessons later. The family were sitting at the supper table and, most unusually, a conversation was in progress.

"I mean my throat gets all tight," I said unhappily. "I mean it's fine until I get to … I don't know, somewhere quite high, and then she tells me to scream, and … well, it all sort of squeezes up and it's not like singing anymore, and … well, it hurts!"

"Now listen to me, my girl." My father's voice was firm. "Madame Sokolov is one of the finest teachers I've come across, and if the exercises she gives you seem to hurt your throat, there's probably a very good reason. She knows what she's doing."

"But I can't sing the way I used to anymore," I wailed.

"Of course not!" he rejoined. "That's the whole point. She's training you to sing as a professional. That's what you want, isn't it?"

And so the weekly vocal torture sessions continued, until several months later Madame Sokolov retired to continue her destructive regime in Capetown. But by then the damage had been done; I simply could no longer sing in the upper register. And, although over the years I have taken instruction from several excellent singing coaches, I could never 'sing the way I used to anymore'.

As well as singing, my brother and I had at an early age begun piano lessons, first with my mother, who made the lessons fun as she taught us the basics, and then with a local piano teacher in order to pass our grades. Neither of us showed the talent my mother possessed, but we were both adequate enough and enjoyed playing. It was sometimes my habit to sit at the piano and see how fast I could play a piece, not only to test my skill but also because I found it interesting and amusing. One afternoon, as I was racing through, of all things, the first movement of Beethoven's *Moonlight Sonata*, my father in his work apron, his hands oily, stormed into the sitting room.

"What do you think you're doing?" he shouted angrily.

I quickly took my hands off the keyboard.

"I was just having fun."

"What you were doing to that music wasn't 'fun', it was destructive and disrespectful," he raged. "You'll have poor bloody Beethoven spinning in his grave! If you want to have fun, go outside and play with your ignorant little friends."

And, with that, he turned on his heel, slamming the door behind him.

I sat silent. My hands were shaking, and I held them together tightly in my lap, not knowing what to think or what to do. The door opened and my mother walked quietly into the room. She crossed to the piano and sat down beside me on the piano stool.

"Don't you take any notice of him," she said softly. "He doesn't know what he's talking about."

"I didn't mean to do anything wrong," I managed to utter, close to tears.

"There's nothing wrong with trying things out, and that's what you were doing. You were experimenting."

"Yes, but dad said ..."

"I heard what he said," she interjected, "and he's a great big bully. You mustn't let him put you off playing. Promise?"

"But if he hears me, he'll shout at me again."

Tears spilled down my cheeks. My mother took a small, white

15

cotton handkerchief from the cuff of her cardigan and handed it to me.

"Here, wipe your eyes, blow your nose, and then if you like we'll play one of our duets. Okay?"

"Okay," I hiccupped, blowing and wiping as bidden.

She reached for the book of easy duets lying on the top of the upright piano and, removing the heavy tome of sonatas, propped a slim volume on the music stand in its place.

"Now, how about 'The Blue Danube'? I'm the left hand, you're the right. Ready?"

I handed back the soggy piece of fabric and took a deep breath.

"Ready!"

CHAPTER 5

Had my parents set up home in England we would probably have been a 'theatrical family', but in South Africa in the 1920s and '30s there was almost no professional theatre to speak of, and plays and operas were performed mainly by amateur dramatic societies. Being steeped in music and with a pleasing baritone voice, my father Harold was also a fine character actor and was ideally suited to the operas of Gilbert and Sullivan. Over the years he not only appeared in several productions but often directed them. When I was three years old I was taken to the theatre to see the dress rehearsal of a production of *Princess Ida* in which he was playing King Gama. To make the character even more unpleasant than written he had assumed a false nose and several warts, and had padded his tights with lumps of cotton wool, making his legs look hideously misshapen. The unpleasant facial furniture didn't bother me, but as I had seldom seen or taken notice of his untrousered legs I assumed that those monstrous lower limbs were his own. Devastated and inconsolable, I had to be taken to his dressing room, where he obligingly removed the padding to prove that his legs were all they should be.

It is unfortunate that my father was so demanding and intransigent, because it made him difficult to work with, and he managed to fall out with most of his male colleagues at one time or another. Women were a different matter. Harold was a fine, handsome man with great charm, witty and funny when he wanted to be, and an incorrigible flirt. In feminine company his pale blue eyes would sparkle as he gave them his keen attention, able to make the dullest of them feel special, while my mother Eda, unimpressed, watched with a cynical eye. Yet, in spite of this, she faithfully collected all of his consistently good press notices and tidied them into a long, narrow hard-backed note book. Programmes were pasted in, dates were noted and photographs slotted in with neat, sticky-cornered brackets, and when at the age of four I won my first Eisteddfod diploma she began a similar cuttings book for me. Through the 70-odd years of my long career I continued what she started, keeping my own scrapbooks up to date, and now they sit, crammed full and the covers faded, alongside the brushes and canvases in my studio loft.

My parents met in the mid-1920s when, handsome and suave with dark Brylcreemed hair and a neat toothbrush moustache, my father arrived in Port Elizabeth from Southampton, planning to put down roots in a young and prosperous country. He had left his Lancashire hometown of Hanley to escape the cloying attentions of his mother and two sisters who, because he was the youngest and the only boy, spoilt and indulged him. His father, by all accounts, was a weak and ineffective man dominated by, and acquiescent to, the triumvirate of women. As well as his fine singing voice and passion for music, Harold was a jack of all trades. Talented in the arts and having an innate faculty for engineering, once his schooling was done he was spoilt for choice as to what career he should follow. He was offered a scholarship to an art college, but desperate to break free from the claustrophobic climate at home, he chose instead to take on any and every spare job he could in order to earn his sea ticket to South Africa.

When he finally reached Port Elizabeth he stayed with relatives, planning to settle eventually in Johannesburg, and it just so happened that at the time my mother Eda was holidaying in the resort with her mother Emily. They were invited to attend a musical evening where Harold was one of the guests. He was charismatic and charming, and Eda, though not conventionally pretty, had what would now be considered sex appeal. Although she was painfully shy, their attraction to each other was immediate. He was invited to sing, and she was persuaded to accompany him on the piano. She had, in fact, shown an exceptional musical talent at a very early age and was by this time a considerable pianist with a predictably glowing future. Inwardly, though, she seethed with frustration and resentment at the confines of her upbringing. Her mother, an overbearing woman with a will of iron, would proudly boast, "My daughter doesn't need any companions of her own age because I'm her best friend." As a consequence, Eda felt that her life was on hold, and she was waiting for an opportunity to break free from her lionising mother.

And here was Harold, who seemed heaven sent. He was twenty three, she was five years his junior. Both were from good

18

Jewish stock and they seemed ideally suited. Sadly, their expectations of what the marriage would bring were diametrically opposed. Desperate to escape her controlled and over-protected existence, she looked forward to the fun and freedom of an outgoing social life, while he, utterly self-sufficient and at his most content in his own company, simply wanted a wife to take care of him and do his bidding. He could never have guessed that under Eda's quiet and seemingly acquiescent facade, lay a will of iron.

CHAPTER 6

The house in which I was raised, number 74, stood in a row of similarly unremarkable detached bungalows on Barnato Street, in the middle-class suburb of Berea. A two-block walk down the tarmaced, treeless road brought you to the main avenue, with its metal tram tracks and overhead wires. Nearby stood a tall post indicating the tram stop, and beside it a worn wooden bench painted red carried the word 'Blankes' along its back, indicating that only white people were allowed the privilege of sitting on it. Elsewhere, somewhat sparsely, similar benches could be found painted green, with the message 'Nie blankes nie', where only black people were permitted to sit. From this stop we would catch the rattling red tramcars to make the five-mile journey into town. The green ones, old and battered, were for 'non-European' passengers and, although as a small child I couldn't understand the reasoning behind this segregation, along with my peers I simply accepted it.

Although our bungalow was the only home I knew, I never liked it nor felt comfortable in it, perhaps because the atmosphere was soured by the tense and unhappy relationship between my parents, and each room carried its own awkward or unpleasant memory. Yet there are a few comforting recollections of living in number 74, like the sound of rain hammering on the corrugated iron roof as I lay snug in bed, and the bright sunlight blazing into my bedroom as I pulled up the rattling Venetian blind. There were hot, sunny days when, as a child, I would fill a large kettle with water, and with the spout tilted, I would run and spin across the pink tiled backyard making patterns that would soon dry away, ready for the next design.

Whatever their ages, black housemaids were invariably called 'girls' by the white population and, similarly, the men were called 'boys', and all under the generic title of 'servants'. Every morning, mostly 'girls' but often 'flat boys' - black men who shopped for the residents of the blocks of flats where they worked - would be seen heading down Barnato Street towards the small nearby small huddle of shops, each clutching a list and a pocketful of small change. They carried empty bags or baskets, and once their task was completed they walked back up the road often balancing the shopping on their heads, upright and proud and graceful. Sometimes one of them would begin to sing as they walked, and another across the way would pick up the harmony. With nothing said or acknowledged they would continue the soaring duet until their paths divided, and someone else might pick up the thread.

My brother or I would often be sent to the shops on errands, a chore regarded as something of a nuisance as it took us away from our own pursuits. The fruit and vegetable shop was owned, as most in Johannesburg seemed to be, by a Portuguese family. The space had once been a garage, but now the grey plastered walls were hidden behind shelves piled high with freshly picked produce, the floor strewn with discarded leaves and skins and peelings, and the air heavy with the mix of freshness and decay. In stark contrast, next door stood the dairy. I can feel its chill embrace as I opened first one, then the second heavier door, and walked into the still, cold cleanliness of the creamery with its milky smell. The bare metal counter gleamed, and behind it the dairyman's wife stood in a pristine white overall, hair invisible under a puffy, white shower cap. She would take the large enamel jug I had brought with me, clang open the lid of a large, sturdy milk churn and, with a steel ladle pour in the cold, fresh, frothing milk. There, we would buy fresh butter cut from a large block and patted into shape with flat wooden paddles, and thick buttermilk, the creamy, tangy taste easy to recall. Then back home past the butcher's with its sawdust-covered floor the proprietors, two brothers, standing behind the blood-stained counter in their blue-and-white striped aprons, chopping and sawing at red raw chunks, and into the grocery with its decorated glass panels and jangling bell, its tins and boxes, jars of sticky sweets and snakes of liquorice, its pickle barrel and baskets of bread and rows of household necessities discreetly set to one side. Handing over the sixpence I had been bribed with, I would lift the lid of the large, square fridge by the door and pick out my favourite chocolate-covered ice cream, an Eskimo pie. Then carefully balancing the milk jug, now protected by a circle of muslin weighted with coloured beads and handcrafted by my mother, I munched my way home.

From time to time a large cart pulled by two oxen would

trundle slowly down our street. At the front, whip in hand, an elderly black man blindly ignored the accumulating irritated traffic behind him, while atop the cargo a 'pikanini' - a young black boy - would sit calling out his wares: a mountain of small, sweet yellow peaches, or a heavy stack of watermelons the size and shape of footballs. Waving them to a halt, you could bite into a peach to test the flavour, or the boy would cut a neat, triangular plug from one of the melons to prove its juicy red-ripeness, and if by chance it showed a disappointing pink, another was quickly searched out.

Number 74 had a small, square front garden, which my mother sporadically developed an enthusiasm for and tried to cultivate, but the plants seemed reluctant to respond and she would soon lose heart and abandon them. A high red-brick wall ran along the front of this uncooperative plot, and on most evenings I could be found perched on one of the columns that flanked the wrought-iron gate whose whining squeak my mother had forbidden my father to cure. "Leave it," she had said with finality. "It lets me know me when anyone's coming in or out."

From this vantage point I could view my surroundings. Opposite was a wide street flanked on either side by large jacaranda trees that bloomed gloriously for a few weeks in the late spring, then suddenly and swiftly shed their blossoms, covering the road with a purple carpet. To the right of it and occupying the whole block was a large empty expanse of ochre earth dotted with tall, dusty pine trees, and encircled by a fence of pointed iron railings. This was the so-called 'playground' belonging to the Nazareth Home, a girls' orphanage (whites only) standing some distance beyond. I would watch the children in their dark, ill-fitting uniform dresses as they ran, played games and shouted, or sat in groups, chatting or drawing in the sand. Two or three nuns - mysterious, black, shrouded creatures - would pace slowly around the perimeter, keeping an eye on their charges, until another nun appeared at the far gate and blew a whistle, shrilling the girls into an untidy crocodile. They marched across the road, through the solid wooden doors of the looming Victorian building opposite and disappeared into its tantalisingly mysterious Christian depths. Always aware and protective of her Jewish heritage, my mother openly discouraged my brother and I from forming friendships

22

with children of other religions, and she warned me of dire consequences should I make any sort of contact with the Catholic inmates of Nazareth. This caution gave them an aura of covertness and romance, and instead of the intended effect, I harboured a secret desire to run away from the emotional tangles of my family life and throw myself into the kindly arms of these compassionate brides of Christ.

But my favourite time as I sat on the wall was sunset. The African sunsets are swift; there is no twilight. The sun dips, and for a short moment the horizon brightens into gold and distant buildings become sharp and black and as flat as cardboard. And it is night; stars wink, the cicadas chirrup, and I sit quiet, feeling the warm, kindly evening breeze on my face.

CHAPTER 7

Star light, star bright
The first star I see tonight,
I wish I may, I wish I might
Have the wish I wish tonight …
I wish Uncle Geoff would come home.

I was about six years old when this incantation became part of my sunset- watching ritual and I would seek out the brightest star to ask its favour. A year earlier in 1940 at the age of 26, my uncle, Geoffrey Cohen, had volunteered to join the Irish regiment as a piper. My mother would tell me how fine he had looked in his kilted uniform, cockaded beret just so, bagpipes under his arm; how he had struggled to play them, and how she had purchased the appropriate manual, and with her musical prowess coached her youngest brother through the deafening caterwauling, the frustrations and the rages, until at last the beast was tamed and Geoff could play the pipes. And then he was gone.

My memory of him is hazy. I remember a tall, dark man with an ample moustache taking me shopping for a present for Chanukah, a Jewish festival that falls during December when the stores are full of tinsel and Christmas delights. I was hankering after one of those cheap net stockings filled with all sorts of unknown, exciting surprises, and, in spite of his attempts to cajole me into choosing something more worthwhile (and probably more suitable for a little Jewish girl), he was nagged into submission. The other memory I have is the bustle and noise of the station on the morning we waved him off to war; the shouting, the clatter of soldiers' boots, the smell and scratch of his khaki uniform as he hugged me to him, and how they all laughed when my ten-year-old brother Brian rejected his uncle's proffered embrace on the grounds of being too old for hugs. The shrill scream of the whistle, the blasts of steam and the grind of the heavy engine wheels have stayed in my mind, along with the memory of the car journey home. My grandmother Emily is sobbing inconsolably, while my

24

grandfather pats her hand distractedly as he stares unseeing out of the window. My brother and I sit squeezed in beside them on the back seat, while my father drives erratically, as is his wont, my mother grimly grasping the strap above the front passenger door, as is HER wont, in open condemnation of his performance at the wheel.

We are sitting together, Gramma and I, in a room on the second floor of the Clarendon Hotel in Hillbrow. This is where she and Grampa live, finding it more convenient than a house now that their family circumstances have altered. Also, Gramma Emily now walks with a heavy limp due to a botched hip operation executed by an inept surgeon. As a result she is slow and reluctant on her feet, and running a household would be too burdensome. The hotel room seems surprisingly small for two. It has its own bathroom and a balcony overlooking a street of busy shops. I like it here in this quiet, comfortable, safe place. Soon Grampa will arrive at exactly four o'clock, for Grampa is obsessively punctual, and if he is kept waiting, for however short a time and for whatever reason, the resulting conflagrations are a wonder to behold. So anxious is Grampa never to be late that he is almost always at least half an hour early, and by the time his appointee turns up he is in a purple rage for being kept waiting. The family has learned the trick of telling him they will meet him half an hour later than they intend to arrive.

Having appeared at exactly four o'clock, Grampa will phone down to the desk for tea to be sent up, and Benjamin, the young black waiter in crisp white jacket and a pair of white cotton gloves, will knock discreetly and carry in the usual tray of goodies. The contents never vary: a glass tumbler in a silver holder with a long-handled teaspoon resting in it, and by its side a bowl of dark red plum jam, a white china teapot with matching water jug, milk jug and sugar bowl filled with snowy cubes, and one cup and saucer. Beside the plate of sandwiches (varied) a thick, stubby glass fizzing with lemonade is for me, and as I slowly sip the warm, sweet drink I watch fascinated, as I always do, as Grampa carefully fills his glass tumbler with tea so strong it is almost black, takes the spoon and scoops up a large helping of jam, then places it in his mouth. Quickly he lifts the steaming glass and noisily sucks the hot tea through the preserve held behind his half-clenched teeth, for my grandfather is Lithuanian, and that, I am assured, is how they take their tea.

But until he comes I watch Gramma as she crochets a pair of bootees for my beloved celluloid Kewpie doll. Kewpie was given to my mother when she was a little girl and has a history of all sorts of games and adventures. I still have her. She bears the signs of an appendectomy, when my uncle Lionel painted her fat belly with iodine prior to the operation. One side of her head has a poorly disguised line of glue where a fall split it open, and the ends of her little pointed fingers are tipped with faded pink nail varnish. Kewpie has no hair as such, but instead has three moulded tufts, one at each side above her ears and one at the back, and her large, round head is topped by a pointed strand. She stands about 40cm high, and although her arms are jointed at the shoulder and move, being a true Kewpie doll her legs and feet have been moulded in one piece. The advantage is that she can stand independently, but she has to be specially shod, and Granny Emily is the one to do it. Originally Kewpie had the traditional small green wings sprouting from her neck, but at my request my father had neatly removed them so that I could dress her in properly fitting clothes. Now, here in this hotel room, she is wearing the bright blue cardigan Gramma finished only half an hour ago, and I watch in anticipation as the matching bootees grow under her flying fingers.

"Gramma, did mommy love Kewpie better than you?"

"Of course not! What a thing to say! Why? Do you love Kewpie more than you love your mother?"

"Sometimes."

"Do you? And when's that?"

I begin to regret having asked the question.

"Oh, when she gets cross for nothing and shouts and I don't know why."

Granny stops her crocheting and looks at me sitting cross-legged on the bed hugging my doll.

"Your mother ...." She stops, then continues, "Mummy sometimes gets unhappy, and when she does she says things she doesn't really mean. You'll understand more when you're older, but just remember, even if she doesn't show it, she loves you and your brother very much."

"Like you loved her and Uncle Lionel and Uncle Geoff when they were little?"

"Yes, that's right."

And then I ask, "When is Uncle Geoff coming home?"

The question is out before I can bite it back. Granny Emily puts down her crochet work, removes her glasses and places them carefully on the small table beside her. Her chin has begun to tremble and, taking a deep breath, with an effort she pulls herself out of her chair and limps across onto the balcony, where she stands, still and silent. Since he had been reported 'missing presumed dead' a year after he joined up, I had been warned not to mention my Uncle Geoff to either of my grandparents. The rest of the family had reluctantly accepted that he wasn't coming back, but my grandmother refused to believe it. Now I sit, miserably fighting back my tears and clutching Kewpie to me for comfort. All I had wanted was her reassurance that he would one day appear alive and fully recovered from whatever mischance had befallen him. The room is silent save for the rumble of distant traffic. My grandmother, head bowed, is praying. I know that, and I am miserably aware that I have entered forbidden and painful territory; I am helpless. And then Reprieve! I hear a key turn in the lock of the door.

"Grampa!"

Although my grandfather knew in his heart of hearts that his youngest son would never return, his wife's determined belief that he would kept a tiny ember of hope glowing somewhere deep inside him. He had worn a fresh white rosebud in his lapel every day of his married life, but when the news came that Geoff was missing the rosebud was abandoned. It reappeared in his lapel years later, and when it did it was no longer white, but red.

Abraham Peter Cohen (or A.P. as he was affectionately known) was a Lithuanian Jew who had fled to South Africa from his country at the end of the century to avoid conscription. There in Johannesburg he had met and married Emily Gluckman of German Jewish stock. They made a somewhat incongruous couple. Somewhat taller than her husband, Emily was a heavy woman with large breasts, a long, aquiline nose, penetrating brown eyes, and straight iron-grey haircut into a short, severe bob. She emanated strength of character and purpose. A.P. was small and dapper, always immaculately suited and with gleaming white spats over his shoes, and despite fifty or so years in Johannesburg his foreign accent was as strong as ever. In many ways this, as well as his innate charm, belied his astute business acumen and helped him to become successful. His articulation, however, had proved somewhat of a problem in the naming of their firstborn. Emily had wanted to name my mother Edith.

"Eedit," Grampa had repeated. "Nice name!"

"No, not Eedit, A.P., EdiTH."

Try as he might, A.P. was never going to master TH, and so they had compromised and settled for Eda.

In time my grandfather set up a highly successful skin and hide business, and often as a treat my brother and I were allowed to visit the store and sniff the salty pungency of the scores of animal skins drying in the heat of the African sun. They lay spread out across the vast yard that buzzed with fat bluebottles, that settled on the hides and on the chunks of meat rubbed with salt and peppercorns and hooked onto lines to dry. This was biltong, a staple food of the Voortrekkers, and now an expensive delicacy.

A.P. invested the profits of his business in stocks and shares, and the resulting gains allowed for a comfortable living. This was just as well, as it also provided him with the means to support his son-in-law, my father, a man who could do anything he set his mind to and consequently found it impossible to settle on any one thing in particular. Various business ventures had failed through Harold's restlessness and diversity of interests. At one time he had been struck by the idea of a lock that would be impossible to pick and so he set about making a prototype. Duly impressed, my grandfather had backed his project and sent him off to London to take out a patent. Ridiculous as it seems, Harold managed to leave the model, together with the only set of plans, on a London tube train. He didn't seem too bothered; after all, it was a problem solved. He paid his respects to his family in Manchester and duly returned to South Africa and the happy solitude of his workshop.

Then came the garage. As a young man Harold had done part of an engineering course until, typically, he felt he had absorbed enough to be able to read his way through any other information he might need. Measurements and draughtsman-ship he understood, but finance, figures and statistics bored him, and he left them to others more business minded than he. Ever hopeful, A.P. bought him a garage, and for a while it seemed like a good and sensible investment. Harold enjoyed working on ailing cars, and although business was slow it was steady. One day, as he was peering into the innards of an obdurate vehicle, he looked up to find a young lad watching him. Both of the boy's legs were encased in callipers and he supported himself on a pair of crutches. He said that his name was Percy, he was fifteen years old, he lived across the road with his parents, he had contracted polio when he was little, and did my father mind if he watched him. Not at all, was the reply. Over the next weeks and months my father and Percy Baneshik (who in time became a distinguished South African journalist) developed a friendship that was to last for the next fifty or so years. The boy would appear at the garage whenever he could, and Harold became interested in devising and constructing simple solutions to help him with his day-to-day living. This was time-consuming and as a consequence customers' cars were being neglected. There were also the demands of his amateur dramatic activities, what with rehearsals as well as set and lighting designs needing his attention. All these extraneous enterprises took his mind off the business in hand, and the result was a chaos of unsent and unpaid bills, an untidy stack of oil-stained paperwork, bank statements printed in red, and a lobby of enraged customers. A mere four months later the declining Essellen garage was once again for sale on the open market.

My brother and I would miss the garage. From time to time when Eda was busy with other things and Harold agreed to keep an eye on us, we had been allowed to run free in the big, echoing space with its murky corners stacked with old tyres and rusty car parts. The air smelled of petrol and oil, hot metal and sawdust, and I loved seeing the sparks fizz under the roaring blue flame of a blowtorch. I could twist for as long as I pleased on the broken swivel chair with its torn seat oozing yellowing foam in the small, messy office, surrounded by a sea of old, grease-marked motor magazines and muddled piles of papers held down by chipped mugs of cold, forgotten tea. But now I stood next to the large barrel of sawdust, shovel in hand, as Brian and I searched the cement floor for any rogue patches of shiny blue-green oil to be smothered. This was our allocated job when we visited the garage and we delighted in it.

"Can't see any more," I said, disappointed.

"I can." Brian picked up a can of oil and began to pour a thin trail carefully along the ground.

"What are you doing? Dad will kill you!"

We watched in fearful anticipation as the oil snaked along the cement floor to form an ever-widening pool. Brian shook the last drops from the empty can.

"We'll need lots of sawdust now. Come on, let's drag the barrel over!"

"If dad finds out ...."

It was too late for regrets. The barrel was heavier than we had anticipated, and puffing and panting we struggled it across the floor towards the ever-widening slick.

"What the hell are you doing?"

My father had emerged from the office and was striding towards us. He kicked at the empty oilcan.

"Which of you is responsible for this?"

His voice shook with quiet rage, a warning we had learned to dread. My heart thumped in my chest.

"Brian. Brian did it! I told him not to!"

Fear of reprisal had overcome any sense of sisterly loyalty.

"You," he said, pointing at me, "go and wait in the office."

I turned and ran, and as I opened the flimsy door I heard Brian cry out. Quickly closing it behind me I scrambled under the desk and crouched beside the wire basket full to overflowing with office detritus. Then, clapping my hands over my ears, I hummed frantically, loudly, tunelessly, to cover the sound of the cries I knew would follow.

CHAPTER 8

"Which bits of the bullets are these?"

"Not bullets, shells."

My father had been drafted in to work for The War Effort, and I am standing beside him on an upturned wooden box so that I can watch more easily. He grasps the lever of the punch and pulls it down hard, stamping out the shapes from a large sheet of metal clamped in the vice. He moves the sheet, then pulls again, and another small, round disc drops to join the growing heap on the floor.

"Can I have those?"

"If you like. What will you do with them?"

I hop off the box, crouch down and take a handful, letting them cascade through my fingers.

"I could string them together and make a bracelet. And earrings to match!"

He laughs.

"Do you think that's suitable for a ten year old?"

"I'll keep them for when I'm old enough to wear them."

Cocooned in a world of his own, this is where Harold spends almost all of his time; this is where he is at his happiest, alone and utterly content, always singing loudly or whistling under his breath. The workshop stands eight or so metres across the pink cement-tiled backyard of the house opposite the back door with its battered, swinging fly screen. It is lined with shelves that buckle under the weight of a hotchpotch of books and papers and unidentifiable odds and ends. The corners of the room are stacked with coils of wire and rope, and loops of contorted tubing dangle like sinister mobiles from large, rusty hooks hammered into the stained, whitewashed walls. On every surface stand an assortment of tools and jars and bottles crammed full of oddments, while discarded bits of metal and wood and rags that are 'bound to come in handy' litter the floor. Scattered around are parts of projects begun and typically never completed when interest waned and a new venture grabbed his attention. Small, sculpted heads, some modelled in clay, some chiselled out of wood, their faces frowning in anger or creased with laughter, lie amongst a tangle of puppets' strings and legs and arms, unlikely to dance again. There, dusty and neglected, stands the heavy iron locomotive engine, all of 40 cm high, built at the time of Harold's enthusiasm for model engineering. Fed by small shovels of real coal, it had delighted my brother and I as it chugged its way around the gleaming track set up in the yard.

Over the years there were just two things that my father made specifically for Brian and me, almost finishing them but failing at the last hurdle. One was a three-storey doll's house, which was never graced with its promised façade, the other was a model theatre, complete with a polished, wooden, raked stage, practical flies and footlights. It had a full lighting system, movable scenery, and red velvet front-of-house drapes worked by a pulley. He would place it carefully on the dining room table, pull the curtains to block out the daylight and leave us to play out our own stories. His finest work, though, was the crafting of a detailed collection of miniature musical instruments, a fifth to scale, comprising a selection of stringed instruments with delicately fretted ivory insets and minute tuning pins, as well as some percussion. These were constructed exactly as the originals, and I have them in a glass case that used to stand on an elegant, full-size spinet that he made for me in his later years. But, neglected and hideously out of tune, with guilty misgivings I sent it to auction, where at least I hoped it would be played back to life. My father would not be pleased.

"Come on, then."

With a sweep of his arm he clears a space on the workbench beside him.

"If you want to string them together you'll have to drill holes in each one, and then make little metal rings. Then you'll have to solder the joins in the rings so that they won't fall out."

"Right," I say with confidence; after all, only recently I had made a table for my doll's house under my father's supervision, turning the small wooden legs on his lathe, and although the shapes of the four hadn't quite matched, they were even in length and the little table stood firm. Now, back on my box, I listen carefully as Harold explains how to use the drill and how to mark each disc with a cross and then centre it under the fine bit that will pierce the metal.

"I want a wide bracelet, so can I have four rows all joined up?"

"I don't see why not. How do you plan to fasten it?"

"Hadn't thought."

"You'll need a clasp of some sort."

"Like a buckle on a belt?"

"Well ...." He smiles wryly. "I don't think that sort of buckle would be quite right. You want the sort of buckle that hooks together."

"Like on my elastic belt? I've got an elastic belt," I exclaim excitedly, jumping off the box and running to the door. "We could cut the elastic off!"

I run across the yard and through the back door, the screen bouncing against the house wall.

"Ow, Miss Sheila! You watch out!"

Our black housemaid Katie is in the passage heading towards the bathroom, bucket and brush in hand, and she leaps aside to avoid a collision as I hurtle into my bedroom. Flinging open the wardrobe door, I pull a wide elastic belt from the collection hanging on the brass rail, and am through the back door and over the yard before Katie can draw a reprimanding breath.

"It's not very fancy," I note uncertainly.

My father regards the metal clasp critically as I carefully scissor it off the belt.

"Can't we make it pretty?"

"Well ...." He strokes his chin. "You could hammer a design on it. I'll show you how when you've done the rest. Come on, get on with those discs."

And now the workshop is as Harold would have it, a place of industry and concentration and contentment. He looks at me, his young daughter, and I know that he is proud, but I suspect that the shadow of his son, his boy child, is never far away. He, too, should be beside his father, learning these skills from him, but Harold has had to accept that any potential has been smothered out of Brian by his overprotective mother, and any affection for his father has been metamorphosed by her into fear. Eda's unhappiness triggered her passionate possessiveness of the boy, and Harold's response had been to display either total indifference to him or sudden obsessions with his welfare. Brian was being used as an emotional football in a desperate match between his parents.

Harold begins to sing loudly, his fine baritone voice filling the workshop.

33

"*Tu pure, o, Principessa,*" he sings, and when he gets to the climax, "*Vincerò! Vincerò!,*" he lingers on the top note. Now he is quiet. He digs a large handkerchief out of his trouser pocket and blows his nose hard, then wipes his eyes, and I wonder how this man, to whom I want so desperately to show my love, can be the same man whose silences frighten me and whose presence in the family looms like a dark shadow.

"The state of your drawers and cupboards is a disgrace. I want them tidied."

My mother sat in the small blue armchair in my bedroom, her arms folded, her mouth tight. On the rug in the centre of the room were three upturned drawers, their contents spilled out. Next to them my belts lay in a jumble.

"And where's that nice new elastic belt I bought you?"

"Which?" I queried without conviction.

Oh, for heaven's sake, don't play games with me! It wasn't on your rail or in any of your drawers, so where is it?"

"It's ...."

I felt the familiar cold sinking in my stomach. I should have thought of the consequences before I had offered up the belt, but it was too late now.

"Yes?" My mother waited, stony faced.

Clenching my hands so tightly that I could feel the nails biting into my palms, I took a deep breath.

"Well, I wanted to make a bracelet out of the bits left over from dad's war job and we needed a buckle or something to hold it together and so ...." Courage deserted me.

My mother stood up and looked at me for what seemed like an eternity.

"Are you trying to tell me that you've ... cut it up?"

"Well ... yes ... sort of."

"And your father let you?"

"Yes." I could feel the tears welling up. "But he didn't ... It was my idea."

She took a step towards me and then, to my relief, turned and walked to the door.

"I'm sorry, mom," I managed to utter, tears spilling down my cheeks.

"You will be, my girl. And I want everything put back in those drawers neatly - now. I shall come and check them later, and from now on, every time I find an untidy drawer, that's where you'll find it … on the floor."

She left, closing the door behind her.

I sat on the edge of my bed, looking desolately at the mound of clothes. Why on some days was my mother so strict and so angry, while on others she was full of fun and would make us all, including my father, laugh. Those times seemed to occur less and less, and more and more there were heavy silences in the house. And now this. I knew through past experience that my father would not be confronted by the matter of the belt just yet. My mother would bide her time, adding this misdemeanour to the clutch of others that she had stored, ready to use as ammunition when the right moment came. I fished in my pocket for a scrunched-up handkerchief and mopped up my tears, then threw myself back onto the bed, staring up at the ceiling with its decorated dado and elaborate centre rose. When my brother and I had shared a bedroom at the end of the passage, this had been number 74's dining room. I must have been about five and Brian ten when one evening at bedtime Eda had discovered us playing trampoline on our beds without a stitch of clothing on. The next day the dining room furniture was moved out and into one end of the sitting room and my bed and belongings were moved in. I loved having my own space and never asked what had provoked her decision in case it might tempt her to change her mind. But I had an uneasy feeling that, as her action had been so swift, the answer might be better left unspoken.

A soft tap on the door made me leap off the bed and dive for the untidy pile on the floor, frantically pulling at the nearest garment. The tap came again.

"Miss Sheila?"

It was Katie. She spoke softly, standing close behind the door.

"Katie!" My relief was almost overwhelming. "Come in."

She opened the door and held it slightly ajar, but remained outside.

"Come in," I said again.

"No, Miss Sheila, the madam wouldn't like for me to talk to you when she's cross and makes you cry. You alright?"

She glanced nervously down the passage.

"I'm fine."

She peered into the room and then nodded in the direction of the pile on the floor.

"You want I should put those away for you later?"

"Only if you want the sack!"

I smiled at Katie's anxious face.

"You'd better go. I'll be okay," I told her.

I picked up one of the upturned drawers and slid it back into its place.

"Miss Sheila ...."

"Yes?"

Katie took a small, brave step into the room.

"Please you mustn't make your bed yourself in the mornings."

"Oh, for goodness' sake!" Irritation had raised my voice.

"Quiet, Missy!"

The urgency propelled Katie into the room.

Putting a hand on my arm, she continued, "You know it makes your mother cross, first with you, and now with me! She say to me to tell you don't do my work. She say next thing I will expect all family do my work for me and I will get lazy."

"Lazy? My God!" I exploded.

"Shhh! Please, Miss Sheila. She will hear you!"

I groaned and sat down heavily on the bed. It was true. I had recently started making my own bed.

"Oh, Katie, I'm so sorry, really I am. The last thing I wanted was to get you into trouble!"

"Why you suddenly do this thing, eh?"

"Because ...." I hesitated.

The truth was that my best friend Rhoda had been appalled when I told her that not only was our black housemaid required to make up all of our beds every single morning, but that we were instructed to strip them down to the bare mattress to ensure that they were properly made and not just tidied.

"But that's ridiculous!" Rhoda had said indignantly. "Our girl would never stand for it. I always make my own bed, except, of course, when the sheets need changing." Then, for good measure, she had added, "And sometimes I even help her dry the dishes."

Incredulous, I asked, "Doesn't your mother mind?"

"Don't be ridiculous!"

Rhoda was scornful and I felt ashamed. Although at an early age I had become uncomfortably aware that the black housemaids - the 'girls' who worked for us - had a tough work

36

regime, little time off and no personal life to speak of, there was nothing I could do about it and so I simply accepted it. After all, so did my peers at the all-white preparatory school I attended, as well as my friends at the synagogue. Now here I was with Katie, aware that my gesture of help seemed to have backfired.

"You do so much, Katie. You work so hard, on your own with no help. You start at seven and go on till whenever, and you never complain …."

"But this is what I do. This is what we ALL do!" She sounded suddenly angry. "It is what I have to do because it is my job and I am the servant here in this house. And if I lose my job," she continued bitterly, "then I must find another madam, and it will be the same in that house."

"Well, at least they might have a washing machine and you wouldn't have to do the laundry by hand!"

I tried an encouraging smile, but a short, sharp cry sprang from the depth of Katie's frustration.

"Ow, Miss Sheila? Where I get another job my age, ay? Where?"

"How old are you, Katie?"

I watched the black woman search her mind for an answer.

"I am old," she said, and she leaned towards me. "Thank you for being my friend, Miss Sheila. You be my friend and every morning, like your mother do and your brother do, you strip everything off your bed so I can put the paraffin oil on the springs and make it all nice. Jah?"

I looked up at her and smiled.

"Jah, Katie," I said. "Jah."

But it felt like a betrayal.

CHAPTER 9

Katie had worked for the family for almost as long as I could remember, but before her I could recall another black woman, large bosomed and smelling of soap and sweat, who had been my nanny when I was much younger. Her name was Sannah, and as a toddler she had been my preferred choice for comfort and companionship. During the day I would play close by her on the floor as she did her work, and it was she, generally, who put me to bed. As I grew older she often would look after my brother and me when our parents were out for the evening, and I would sit at the oilcloth-covered kitchen table listening to the round, clicking sounds of the Xhosa language as she gossiped with the friends she had invited to share the boredom. My memories of being with Sannah, though vague are happy and pleasant, and it is clear that she felt a warmth towards me, a white girl child. But even at that young age I was aware that she wasn't happy, and looking back I suspect that she harboured a bitter resentment towards her employers as well as her situation in the household. This expressed itself in a sullen negativity, and when her discontent finally became almost palpable it was decided at supper one evening that my father would have to confront her.

What followed the next afternoon is vivid in my mind. I am sitting at the kitchen table, watching Sannah iron the twice-weekly wash. She stands at the creaking ironing board using one of the pair of heavy old irons; the other is heating on the big, black, coal stove. She flicks water from a chipped white enamel basin onto the garment on the board to help ease out the creases. The iron hisses and the smell of steam fills the air. I hear the sound of my father's footsteps tramping down the dark, narrow passage towards the kitchen. The doorknob rattles, then the door opens.

"Sheila, go and play in the garden."

I slip off the chair, glancing quickly at Sannah who stands immobile, iron in hand, and hurry past him. The kitchen door slams shut behind me. I hear the key turn in the lock and my heart begins to beat faster in fearful anticipation, for although I have never been summoned to one of these secluded confrontations with my father, I have heard my mother weeping alone with him behind closed doors. I stand a little way down the passage and hear my father's voice, low and controlled, and then after a while the inevitable, expected sound of sobbing. Unable to bear it, I run out of the open front door and onto the veranda, slipping and sliding on the shiny red tiles newly wet by a sudden shower of rain, reaching at last the safety of my place on the garden wall. I wait, and after a while I climb back down and slip into the house. The kitchen door is open now and, fearful of what I might find, I creep cautiously down the passage. Sannah is at the ironing board wielding the hissing iron as before, but now her shoulders droop, and hopelessness and misery are reflected in her puffy, tear-stained face.

It was only in my early teens that I developed strong views and a conscience about the iniquity of apartheid in South Africa. Until then, even though in my early childhood I was aware of the poor treatment of the black population, I accepted things as they were. The older I got, the angrier and more disapproving I became. Brave people with ideals and courage were making their feelings felt, whereas all it did was fuel my desire to leave a troubled country, escape my unhappy home life and follow a career abroad.

Yet even as a child I felt badly for the women who worked for us. Their regime seemed relentless, with no social life to speak of. Black men weren't allowed to remain in the city after dark without special passes, which meant that the women seldom saw their husbands, and if a man dared to stay the night he risked a prison sentence. Each evening, to make sure that this law was enforced as well as to keep the house safe from marauders, my father would padlock our back gate. My mother discouraged female friends who visited Katie at any time of day, making it clear that a lingering conversation at the back door was wasting precious work time. Katie was allowed Thursday afternoons off and all of Sunday, when, dressed smartly for church, she would leave in the early morning and climb onto a battered single-decker bus for the long, dusty journey to her shantytown home outside the city. We never knew where that was, nor did we ask, and she would return late that night or in the very early hours of Monday morning.

My mother had been brought up to consider the black

population in South Africa inferior and fit only for servitude. She viewed them with mistrust and some trepidation, finding it nigh on impossible to change her attitude, and as their dissidence and dissatisfaction grew, so grew her fears. As for my father, it always surprised me that although he had been brought up and educated in England, his treatment of any black person was surprisingly harsh and unfriendly.

In the backyard of number 74, and adjacent to my father's workshop, was the servant's living quarter, and this one room was indeed a 'quarter', being about a quarter of the size of my father's own space. To the left of the room stood the lavatory, a small, dark closet with an old stained bowl and rusting chain. A hook driven into the wall held torn squares of paper, and the ill-fitting wooden door gaped above and below. Beside it was a narrow passage where, once a week, sacks of coal were emptied to feed the large iron kitchen stove, and all efforts to keep the black dust from seeping into the living space were ineffectual.

As with the housemaids before her, Katie had done the best she could with the limited area and her limited means, to create some sort of home for herself. A shabby lace curtain at the window hid the room from prying eyes. Inside, the legs of a heavy iron bedstead were supported by small piles of bricks so that boxes of her belongings could be stacked underneath. A sturdy wooden box, on which stood a candle in a holder, a box of matches and a worn Bible, took the place of a bedside table. Opposite stood her 'dressing table', another box but taller and narrower, draped with a chenille cloth that had seen better days on a side table in Granny Emily's house. On it was a collection of odds and ends, an unframed square of mirror leaning against the whitewashed wall and, in pride of place and set in a fancy metal frame, a photograph of her daughter taken at the age of six or so. In stark contrast, in the middle of the cramped room stood a low carved table that Katie had brought with her from her native village in the Transkei. On it was a paraffin lamp, while an orange box on either side supporting thin faded cushions, completed the furnishings. Her clothes were hung neatly on a wire stretched between two hooks on a wall, while above the head of her bed she had tacked a large, brightly coloured picture of the Madonna and child. Neither the room nor the lavatory were wired for electricity. My father had decided that as Katie hadn't had the use of this facility in her village, she wouldn't need it. My mother agreed, adding that if it were available she might abuse the privilege by overuse. She also claimed that electricity was too baffling for her housemaids, a view that relieved her of the necessity to buy an electric iron or a washing machine.

Each morning at dawn before the family awoke, draped in a thin towel Katie would wash herself briskly, splashing water from the outside cold tap beside the back door, hissing through her teeth with the icy shock. Once dressed, she walked around to the front of the house and knocked on the window of the master bedroom to wake my mother, who would don her dressing gown and pad down the passage to let Katie in, first unlocking the inner kitchen door and then the well-secured back door. No housemaid had ever been trusted with a key to the house, nor, for some obscure reason, with owning an alarm clock. As a result, to ensure that she roused my mother at seven o'clock sharp, Katie was 'loaned' the kitchen alarm clock each night before she was locked out of the house, and each morning, as she was let in, my mother retrieved it.

Katie started her chores as the household began to stir. She cleaned the ashes out of the stove, poking and brushing them onto sheets of newspaper, and then lit the spills of twisted paper tucked between the freshly set coal and kindling. Next the several pairs of shoes that had been left beside the stove the night before were cleaned and polished and buffed to an immaculate shine. The breakfast table was laid and the washing up, left for her from the previous night's snacks or entertaining, was done. While the family breakfasted she mopped and polished the front veranda and then, dusters and carpet sweeper at the ready (no electric vacuum cleaner to tax her abilities), she cleaned and dusted and tidied. Mid-morning, Eda would hand her a purse of small change and a shopping list for the day's food and household requirements, and after a hasty break for tea brewed in her own large tin mug and a helping of 'mielie pap', the staple sour porridge beloved by Africans and eaten from a bowl with the fingers, Katie would join the other black servants on their way to the local shops. On her return she would tackle the bedrooms, dusting and cleaning, wiping down the springs under each mattress with paraffin oil and remaking the stripped beds.

Washing days came twice a week. The large zinc tub kept

41

turtle-turned in the back yard was righted, placed over the drain under the cold water tap and filled with relays of kettles of hot water. Then, bent over a metal washboard and gripping a bar of hard Sunlight soap, Katie scrubbed the family's clothes, sheets, towels and anything else thrown into the tall washing basket in the bathroom. Rinsing and wringing, she tossed the washing into a nearby basket and then, standing up and stretching her aching back, she carried it to the two wire lines stretched across the yard, pegging out each article to dry quickly in the hot mid-morning sun. Preparing and serving lunch came next, and afternoons were filled with the chores of ironing or cleaning the silver or the windows, interrupted by serving tea to whichever of the family members were at home, on a trolley in the sitting room. Then came the evening meal and all the preparation involved, although it was my mother who generally cooked the dinners, a task she didn't relish.

We were sitting in the dining room one evening, as usual in silence, (my father considered small talk a waste of time and effort and discouraged conversation at the table) when, having cleared his plate, he pushed it away and announced, "I have decided to become a vegetarian."

After a moment, her face expressionless, my mother asked, "Did I hear you correctly?"

"I have decided," he repeated slowly, raising the level of his voice, "to stop eating meat and become a vegetarian."

My brother and I looked at one another nervously.

After a pause that seemed to last a lifetime, my mother asked, "Why?" Her voice shook with the effort to control her feelings.

My father replied, as though speaking to a child, "Because I have just read a most convincing article on how the proteins in meat can destroy the immune system and damage health, and as there is a great deal I want to do in the future I have every intention of living as long as I possibly can. And so," he finished, "as of now I am a vegetarian."

As my mother absorbed the information, we children hunkered down into our chairs. Then the storm broke.

"You selfish bastard!" she spat. "If you think I'm going to cook special food for you just because you want to live forever, you're mistaken! God knows I do enough in this house to keep things going. You do nothing to help, you take on no responsibilities, you hide yourself in that blasted workshop and leave everything to me, and now ....." She choked, tears of rage welling up. "Now you expect me to run a bloody restaurant!"

It was too much for her. She fled the table, storming down the passage into the master bedroom and slamming the door so hard behind her that the house seemed to shake to its foundations.

My father calmly wiped the corners of his mouth with his table napkin.

"Katie!" he called to the kitchen. "You can clear the table now. We've finished."

CHAPTER 10

As a schoolgirl, my mother had displayed an exceptional talent for piano playing, outclassing her contemporaries. Each day after school, aged only thirteen, she would change out of her gymslip into more suitable clothes and attend private tuition at the Witwatersrand University's music faculty. Once she had matriculated she attended the Conservatoire of Music, where she determined to fulfil her promise as a concert pianist. The inevitable isolation of her piano studies coupled with the strong will of her mother, seemed to cripple her capacity for forming relationships, and Eda became introverted and shy. As she matured, the men she met were mostly the friends of her two brothers and they tended to treat her more as a sister than a potential girlfriend. Never one for joining in their amusements, she would indulge in her favourite pastime and wander through the quiet order of stationery shops. The smell of them, the neat stacks of office equipment and school paraphernalia lined up on the regimented shelves, pleased her. She had inherited this love of uniformity and tidiness from her father, and an obsession for making lists from her mother. She told me that when my grandmother lay dying in hospital, she was still tracing out lists on the bedcover with her forefinger!

Granny Emily was a fine seamstress and an exceptional knitter, and she had handed her domestic skills on to her daughter. Eda's knitting amazed with its machine-like precision, and her embroidery was so precise it was almost impossible to tell the right side from the wrong. At school she won the teachers' praises and prizes for the excellence of her handwriting and her exemplary notebooks. So commendable was her high school botany book with its neat annotations and finely detailed watercolours, that it had been professionally bound in a stiff black leather cover, and through my childhood it sat high on one of the bookshelves in number 74, viewable with clean hands and by request only. Allied to her musicianship and masterful calligraphy, this talent meant that in later life her handwritten copies of music manuscripts were much sought after not only by musicians, but also by publishers, who would commission her to write out special documents, and it was difficult to tell them apart from print.

Before I was born, my mother had made several unsuccessful attempts to escape from her marriage. Each time she left she would take her small son Brian with her, becoming, as far as my father was concerned, a unit from which he was excluded, and that he bitterly resented. Brian was two-and-a-half the first time Eda tried to get away, but after a few days spent with her brother Lionel and his wife, her mother, whose Victorian values precluded any such demonstration of unhappiness or discontent, ordered her back to her husband, and meekly she complied. Eighteen months later, still miserable and rebellious, she begged my grandfather to send her on a trip abroad, ostensibly for a rest. In spite of Emily's energetic disapproval, he agreed, thinking that the break might bring her to her senses. Relieved to get away, once again Eda tucked her son under her arm and took a cruise ship to Egypt. The trip wasn't a success; she was a bad sailor and saw little of Brian, who was taken care of by a series of cabin stewards. In Cairo things hardly improved, for the sightseeing excursions to and from the hotel on the 'ships of the desert' made her feel even worse than she had done on board ship. Irrationally she found herself missing Harold and, confused as to what she really wanted, she see-sawed between returning to her obligations as a dutiful wife or consolidating the separation she had initiated. Conscience stricken, and baffled by her own feelings, she decided to return home, arranging to stop off on the way in Manchester to meet, for the first time, Harold's mother and his two older sisters Lydia and Dulcie.

She disliked her mother-in-law on sight. Old Mrs Greenberg was a small, birdlike woman with a tight face and strong moral convictions. She lived a life based on unbending principles and an absolute certainty that she was right about everything. She had brought up her three children with virtually no help from her husband, a tall, weak-willed but likeable man. Subdued by her bullying, he had quietly faded into the background, content to let her run the family in her own way. Lydia, the oldest of the three children, was deemed a beauty. She had a fine soprano voice and sang regularly in the local synagogue choir, where she gathered a following of admirers. Dulcie, on the other hand, was plain, but she was a jolly, warm-hearted girl, and all in all

45

the two made a highly eligible pair. However, Mrs Greenberg kept a strict eye on them, forbidding any make-up or fripperies, and allowing no social contact with men; when the time came, it would be she who would find them suitable husbands. So far none worthy enough had appeared, and it would take a brave soul to defy her.

Young Brian was afraid of his diminutive grandmother, who, hawk-like, watched his every move, as he wandered around the cold, unfriendly house, adjusting any item he touched with an impatient click of the tongue. She would constantly correct his vocabulary. One day when she was holding an open biscuit tin just out of his reach, he asked, "Please can I have a biscuit?"

"It's not 'please CAN I have a biscuit'," she reproved, "it's 'MAY'."

Confused and frightened, Brian responded, "Please May, can I have a biscuit?"

The girls exploded with laughter, but a thin-lipped Granny Greenberg snapped the lid tight shut.

Eda's visit must have seemed a godsend to the two sisters. My mother told me how the three would leave the house together on the pretext of visiting some or other local place of interest. Once out of sight, Lydia and Dulcie would rouge their lips and cheeks with the help of the contents of Eda's purse, dab Ashes of Roses behind their ears, and leave her to her own devices as they made off to whatever assignations the two had made. Later, at a prearranged time they would meet up and return home. Impatient to get back to number 74, Eda sat out the week in Manchester, and it was with a heartfelt sigh of relief that, with Brian in tow, she boarded a ship bound for her native South Africa and her future with Harold.

CHAPTER 11

Once a month at precisely seven o'clock, a group of regulars clutching music scores and manuscripts would gather in the small sitting room of number 74 for a Musical Evening. Mrs Liesel Danziger was always the first to arrive, hurling her fur coat onto the chair by the front door, leaving a heavy trace of must and mothballs that lingered for days after. Her style was flamboyant, from her vivid red hair down to her platform shoes, and her alto voice loud and as thick as chocolate. There was Mr Cooper, a strangulated tenor, short and round, and the Perry brothers, Alec and Jimmy, Scottish and as alike as two peas apart from their voices; Jimmy's baritone robust and Alec's baritone thin and anaemic. George Absalom came next, all six foot and sixteen stone of him, also a Scot, square of jaw and frame, and as fierce a basso profundo as you were ever likely to hear. He was accompanied always and everywhere by his adoring wife Ivy, small and silly, and his sister Constance, as physically similar to her brother as it was possible to be apart from her formidable, heavy bosoms. Neither of these two acolytes displayed a shred of musicality, but were content to sit quiet and adoring as he and the others performed their pieces. Sometimes new music makers were invited, scrutinised and judged, accepted or not as the case may be, and sometimes others were invited simply to listen and wonder. Needless to say, my mother was the official accompanist for all and sundry.

During these musical soirées, in spite of the sitting room door being firmly closed as well as the doors of our separate bedrooms, my brother and I could hear the music loud and clear, and on one of these nights, at the age of about eleven, I decided to risk my parents' disapproval and join the fun. Quickly donning my dressing gown and slippers, my heart quickening with anticipation, I opened the door to the concert venue. "Aaah!" and "Come in!" cried one or two, and, in spite of my mother's hasty reprimand and swift rise from the piano (which left poor Mrs Danziger open-mouthed in mid-cadenza), I was allowed to tuck myself into a corner of the crowded sofa and watch the proceedings. With a long glance warning me of future reprimand, my mother resumed her seat, the alto diva adjusted her mouth, and I took a furtive look around the assembled company. On the sofa with me were two newcomers, a man and a woman. Aware of my scrutiny, the man turned his head, winked and patted my knee, and the woman peered round him and smiled at me prettily. Constance Absalom, who was sitting opposite, was clearly irritated by this distraction and scowled before turning her full attention to the soloist, thus giving him the opportunity to wink at me again. We smiled at one another conspiratorially. The final notes caused a ripple of applause and murmurings.

Then my father rose, and to my embarrassment announced, "My daughter and I sing duets together. Would you like to hear the one from Don Giovanni?"

"Oh, absolutely!"

"Lovely!"

The captive audience seemed more than enthusiastic, but although I was ever one to seize any opportunity to perform, I was reluctant, and stayed where I was. It wasn't the invitation to perform that held me back, but the choice he had made. It was,after all a love song, and although I couldn't explain why, I had always felt uneasy singing it with my father.

"Come along, if you're going to!" my mother said impatiently, opening the score she had extracted from the pile on top of the piano and placing it on the music stand.

"I'd love to hear you sing," said the man next to me.

Unable to resist, I rose and joined my father at the side of the piano as my mother played the opening chords.

"Give me thy hand, oh fairest," sang my father, turning to me.

"Whisper a gentle yes,

Come, if for me thou carest,

With joy my life to bless."

Now it was my turn. Taking a step away from him, I began.

"I would, and yet I would not ..."

On we sang, and if any of those present had felt my apprehension it was soon dispelled by the cries of approbation and delight when the duet ended. My mother rose from the piano.

"I think it's time for some refreshment, don't you? Sheila, now that you're up you may as well come into the kitchen and help me."

The trolley had already been laid for tea with plates of small cakes and sandwiches, and as we stood together waiting for the big black kettle to boil, I asked, "Who is that nice man I was sitting next to? He's new, isn't he? So's the lady."

My mother smiled. "New to you but not to me. His name is Jack, and that's his wife Lynn. She's a great friend of Uncle Alec and Uncle Jimmy. We've met them there quite a few times. Did you like him then?"

"Yes. He winked at me."

"Did he now? You'd better watch out! His wife gets jealous."

"She's very nice."

"Mmmm." My mother sounded non-committal.

Sensing something, I asked, "Don't you like her?"

My mother flushed. "Don't be so silly. Of course I like her," she said quickly.

"Will you ask them again?"

"I don't know." She busied herself rearranging the cups on the trolley. "She probably isn't enjoying herself too much," she said, adding, "I don't think she really likes music."

"Oh no, I'm sure you're wrong," I said, determined to put matters to rights. "I noticed while dad and I were singing she was looking at you all the time, and I'm sure ...."

"I think it's time you were in bed." The interruption was sudden and my mother's voice harsh. "I'll manage the tea. No need to say goodnight to anyone. Off you go."

A few weeks later, most unusually it was my father who was sitting at the kitchen table when my brother and I came in for breakfast before school.

"Where's mom?' I asked, surprised.

"She's still in bed. Not feeling too good."

He cleared his throat, a sign that he had something important to say. Brian put down his cup and I abandoned my cereal. We waited.

"It seems your mother is finding that things are getting her down. She says she needs to get away for a few days."

My brother and I looked at each other, and sensing the question, I asked, "Is it us?"

"How should I know?" my father said, with more than an edge of irritation. "It's probably all of us, the house, everything. She says she just needs a break. Now," he continued, taking a gulp of coffee, "she's suggesting going away for the weekend. She would leave on Saturday morning and come back on Monday."

"Where will she go?" I asked.

"I believe she's been invited to stay with an old school friend of hers who lives somewhere outside Pretoria. She won't tell me where exactly because she doesn't want us to bother her."

"But what about us?" Brian enquired, agitated at the thought of being under the sole control of his father.

"That's typical of you, you selfish little so-and-so! No wonder your mother wants to get away for a while. Good God! You're both old enough to take care of yourselves. I'll be here, Katie will be here, and I'm sure your mother will organise it all before she goes."

He stood up and drained his coffee cup.

"Now get off to school. I've got work to do."

"But what about our lunch boxes?" I called, but he was already halfway across the yard and into his workshop.

Brian was close to tears. "I suppose it won't be too bad, will it?"

"No," I answered without much conviction.

As it turned out, my mother's weekend away seemed to do her no end of good. At lunchtime on the Monday when we got back from our separate schools, she smiled and joked and as a special treat made us pancakes, which we smothered in butter and maple syrup. Her good humour even rubbed off on my father, and after dinner that evening he suggested they play a game of Scrabble while we two played Monopoly on the carpet at their feet. These evenings of harmony were scarce and I relished each moment, praying that from now on this would be the norm rather than the usual after-supper routine of us all going our silent, separate ways.

"That's another game to me! So I win!" my father laughed, triumphant.

"You're just too good for me," my mother said with a smile. Then, addressing us all, she went on, "You seem to have managed very well while I was away, I must say."

"We were fine," my father responded, "weren't we, kids?"

"Yes, fine," I agreed.

"I missed you," said Brian, and I pinched his arm.

But my mother didn't seem to have heard him, for she continued, "I feel so much better having had a break. I really think I should do it more often."

My father was taken aback. "What? You mean ...."

"I mean, Harold, that it has clearly been good for all of us, and I think I should get away every weekend."

"Every weekend?" he repeated in disbelief.

"Yes, just for a while. Until I feel ... better."

There was an awkward pause before my father suggested to my brother and I that it was time we were in bed.

From my bedroom I could hear their voices through the closed sitting room door. My father's was raised, but for once my mother's was level and without tears. That night I slept fitfully, visited by a recurring nightmare in which I felt my chest being crushed by an unbearably heavy weight, yet whenever I tried to push it off it crumbled into feathery grey ash between my fingers, leaving the heaviness behind.

The next morning my mother was at the breakfast table, making out her shopping lists for the week.

"Well now," she said, "it's all sorted. I'm going away for the next few weekends. Dad has agreed, Katie says she doesn't mind taking over, and you two will be just fine, won't you?"

It clearly wasn't a question but an order.

"Where do you go?" Brian asked unhappily.

"Where I go is neither here nor there," she said brusquely. "What is important is the reason I go, and I go to get some peace and quiet and not be bothered by anyone or anything. All right?"

And that was that.

Until one Monday, when I came home from school to find my father standing in the centre of the sitting room, with my mother, pale and defiant, seated on the sofa, a protective arm around Brian, sitting beside her looking frightened. Katie stood awkwardly near the doorway, and as I walked slowly into the room it was clear they had been waiting for my arrival. Nothing was said. My father walked over to the door and closed it firmly, as though to cut off any escape and keep whatever was to follow within the confines of those four walls. Then he turned to face the room.

"Your mother," he said, "is a whore. Do you know what that is? Brian? Sheila?" His voice was quiet, dangerous. "Do you, Katie?"

Katie, way out of her depth, looked helplessly at me, and I returned her gaze with the ghost of a shrug.

51

"A whore is a woman who sleeps with men other than her husband. And your mother ...." For a moment it seemed as though he couldn't continue. "Your mother," he repeated, "has been sleeping with another man every weekend, every bloody weekend. Sleeping with that bastard, Jack! How could you do it to me? And what about his wife?" he ranted, addressing my mother directly. "What about poor bloody Lynn?"

Jack! That nice man Jack with his pretty wife! My ears began to ring. I felt faint.

"And you knew, you all knew! You all covered for her, made it easy for her to get away. Even you, Katie!"

At a loss, Katie shifted uneasily.

After a long moment he spoke again, "None of you gave a thought to me."

It was as though I was seeing my father for the first time. He stood still and silent, eyes unfocused, a figure somehow smaller, bewildered and alone. I wanted to go to him, to tell him that no, we hadn't known, that it wasn't fair to blame us, and that I was so sorry; sorry for him, sorry it had happened. Instead I began to sob. My mother got up, quickly crossed the room, and with a surprising gesture of intimacy hugged me to her.

"Don't worry, I'll get a divorce," she whispered softly in my ear.

It wasn't what I wanted to hear, and I wasn't sure for whom I was crying - my father, my mother, or myself, perhaps all three. Confused, and embarrassed by her embrace, I pushed her away, fumbled for the doorknob and fled across the passage to my room.

I don't know how long I lay on my bed, but once my tears subsided I began to try to fit together the pieces of my parents' emotional jigsaw. I remembered a day when my mother had been more than usually upset by my father. Seeing her so unhappy, I had asked, "Why don't you just get a divorce?" Her reply was unexpected. "I wish I could, but if I did, who would look after him?"

I remembered my father telling me that their marriage had hardly had an encouraging start. In lieu of a honeymoon my grandfather had bought the couple a bungalow as their wedding gift, and for the first few weeks of their marriage

Eda's mother had called on them almost every day, ostensibly to deliver household supplies, but spending the time commiserating with her daughter on the unpleasant duties expected of a wife. As for my mother, she often told us that Fate had tricked her, and she made no secret of resenting my father for cheating her out of the future she had planned and waited for. To make matters worse, he had become more and more solitary and self-absorbed, and so uncommunicative that she often taunted him, claiming that in a past reincarnation he must have been a Trappist monk!

Yet, thinking about it as I lay there, I relised I had never once heard my father say anything disagreeable about my mother. Indeed, if he did happen to mention her, he seemed proud of her achievements. Neither of them was inclined to row; instead, when there were disagreements an icy silence descended. My mother's set jaw and cold demeanour made her feelings clear, whereas my father, who surely must have been aware of the misery we children were suffering, simply continued in his usual, self-absorbed way. Often he would shut himself away in our sitting room and listen to some classical vinyl record, playing it, much to my mother's chagrin, at full volume. On one occasion - and I can't remember how or why - I was allowed to join him, and I recall sitting still and quiet on the floor opposite his armchair. As the music swelled, his eyes filled with tears, and, overwhelmed by a confusion of feelings, I wanted so much to go to him and hug him and tell him ... something, I didn't know what. But, in our family, gestures of warmth and affection were an embarrassment, and to be avoided at all costs. I stayed where I was, and the moment was gone.

It was clear that my mother was deeply unhappy, so who could blame her for seeking sympathy and affection? And when it was offered, why shouldn't she have grasped the chance of a little happiness and excitement? In spite of the enormity of her deception, it had, after all, made her happy; the difference had been there for all to see. Even my father's mood had lightened. And, because of her deception, for a few weeks life at number 74 had been wonderfully stress free. I decided that, although my father was enraged and hurt, the incident of my mother's infidelity might have strengthen their immutable devotion. And it dawned on me that she would never leave him.

The house was quiet. The cuckoo clock squawked six o'clock. It was time for me to get up. And to grow up.

CHAPTER 12

I have always been proud and grateful for having inherited a few of my parents' exceptional talents, but, conversely, confused by their individual personality traits that contradict, leaving me with a case of mild schizophrenia! In spite of the solitary and uncommunicative figure he presented I felt an affinity with my father, and although my mother was weighed down with her own dissatisfactions leaving her little emotion to spare, in a strange role reversal I felt protective and motherly towards her.

Of we two siblings, I was the luckier. From the beginning Brian bore the brunt of my parents' adversarial relationship, and in every sense suffered badly. He was a sensitive child, skinny, round-shouldered and unhappy. To add to his wretchedness, when he was seven years old he contracted a form of conjunctivitis. The local chemist prescribed the wrong drops which burnt the surrounding eye tissues and, although not actually affecting his sight, the damage left his eyelids permanently pink and swollen, making him even more self-conscious and introverted. Whatever potential he may have had was stunted at an early age. Having stoically accepted my mother's coldness, my father gave up any claim on him. Considered a 'disappointment', when my father did pay him any attention it was to criticise or chastise, and it didn't take long for the child to learn that his tears only provoked more punishment. He managed to conceal his emotions, burying them in some dark corner. But the one sense he failed to hide was fear.

I was born when Brian was five years old, and Harold made no secret of favouring me. Of course I enjoyed this privilege but I also felt a lurking guilt, particularly because sometimes I was the cause of my brother having to bear the brunt of my father's temper. One such incident occurred on our weekly Saturday afternoon trip to a local cinema. Brian wanted to see one picture, I another, and stubbornly neither of us would give way.

"Alright then, we'll just go home," he had said sullenly, and we marched back home in sulky silence, both of us angry and disappointed. My father opened the front door.

"Why are you back so soon? What's happened?"

Full of self-pity, I began to cry.

"Brian wouldn't take me to the picture I wanted to see!" I wailed.

With a swift, strong punch, he sent my brother crashing into the wall.

"She's your sister! You're supposed to look after her! Don't you ever do that again."

Slowly and painfully, my brother got up, his face expressionless. I can never recall him crying.

I sailed through the usual childhood ailments expected in those days: a feverish spell in bed with the measles, the unpleasant violation of ringworm curled under the skin of my left knee, and a bout of tonsillitis. The latter led our much revered family doctor to surgically removing the offending tonsils, and one of my most nightmarish recollections is lying on a hospital bed, restrained by a nurse, while the good doctor held a mask doused with chloroform over my nose and mouth.

"Blow it away, Sheila, blow it away!"

I blew as hard as I could and then as intended, took the deepest breath, drawing the sickly sweet, noxious fumes deep down into my lungs. With a loud ringing in my ears, reality shrank to a pinpoint and I lost consciousness.

My brother Brian was healthy enough, but he was faddy about his food. As with many children he disliked vegetables, and in spite of Harold's attempts to 'persuade' him he simply refused to eat them. Thus it was that my father decided the boy would have to ingest his vitamins some other way.

We sat around the supper table as usual in silence, but this evening the silence was different. It was the tense silence of anticipation, for on the table in front of Brian my father had placed a large brown capsule. To my childish eyes it seemed very large indeed, but how impossibly large it appeared to my eleven-year-old brother is hard to imagine, for he, like my mother, found it difficult to swallow even the smallest of pills. He sat, eyes downcast, his plate of food untouched. When at long last the meal ended, Katie was called in to remove the plates.

"Leave Brian's," my father instructed.

She did as she was told, and with an anxious look at my mother, left the room.

"Eat your food."

Brian didn't move.

My father repeated it.

"Eat your food."

Miserably, Brian shook his head.

"Alright then, get that pill down you."

Brian looked helplessly at my mother, but it was clear that she had lost this particular battle earlier and, tight-faced and grim, she looked away.

"Right."

Briskly, my father got up, picked up the capsule and, pulling Brian roughly, to his feet pushed him to the floor. With a knee on the boy's chest, he forced Brian's mouth open with his fingers, pushed the capsule far back into his mouth, then closed his jaws and clamped them together in a vice-like grip.

"Swallow!"

No response. Still holding his jaws together, he pinched the boy's nostrils shut with the thumb and forefinger of his other hand. Brian's eyes were screwed up tight, his struggles erratic.

"Stop it, Harold, you're killing him!"

My father let go and stood up, breathing heavily.

"Is it gone?"

Brian made an effort to sit up, choking and fighting for breath.

"Is it gone?"

Brian nodded.

"Good."

And, with a brief smile of satisfaction, my father left the room.

Unsurprisingly these incidents at home hampered Brian's progress at school. Although he had one or two friends he found it difficult to form relationships or concentrate on lessons, and he developed a dread of school. As time went on he began to refuse to leave the safety of his bed in the mornings and much to my mother's frustration he would feign sleep. Try as she might to rouse him he stubbornly refused to respond. One morning, having reached the end of her tether, she threw a jug of cold water over him, threatening to repeat the exercise whenever he refused to get up. It worked, but his attitude towards his schooling didn't change, and in spite of his high intelligence his grades were low, and his reports discouraging.

At the age of fifteen he begged to be taken out of school, and it was Eda who acquiesced; Harold showing nothing but disdainful indifference. She managed to find him a job with a compliant uncle who was prepared to take him on as a trainee clerk.

Always close to her son, Eda became closer still, blaming herself for his barren prospects. I suspect she felt guilty, not only that she had kept him from his father and created an unbridgeable rift between them, but also because she had failed to abandon a marriage that was damaging to all concerned.

CHAPTER 13

Being Jewish was an integral part of family life in number 74, and the first service I ever attended was with my grandparents in our local Orthodox synagogue. A dim light filtered through the stained-glass windows, and the air smelt stale. Sitting in the darkened women's gallery alongside my grandmother, I watched the men below standing in prayer, rocking backwards and forwards 'davening', large, white, silk prayer shawls draped over their shoulders, heads covered by small yarmulkes or soft fedora hats. The cantor stood by the ark where the sacred torahs were kept, swaying as he sang, his solitary voice echoing through the temple. The synagogue had a small school attached, and once a week I was sent to 'chayder' where I struggled to learn Hebrew, and the stories of the Old Testament and Jewish festivals were dryly recounted. My parents adhered largely, but not slavishly, to the Orthodox dietary laws (no pig or shellfish, no mixing of meat and milk products) as well as certain rules of behaviour. On Fridays, once six o'clock struck and the Sabbath began, we were forbidden to use either a pen or pencil, a pair of scissors or, indeed, a knife, although this didn't seem to apply at the dinner table. There would be no cutting, no sewing, no knitting and no piano playing; in fact, we could do nothing that counted as work during the twenty-four hours of the day of rest. The use of money and driving a car were included in this list of forbiddens, but judging from the number of cars parked a few streets away from the synagogue on high and holy days, that was considered a restriction too far. These restraints were frustrating, and there was a sense of relief when the Sabbath was done.

As time went on, my parents found it difficult to justify the dictates of Orthodoxy, and after Brian's bar mitzvah at thirteen, his 'entry into manhood', they shifted their alliance to a Reform synagogue, Temple Israel, where the tenets were more reasonable and relaxed, and I began to enjoy what it had to offer. The Jewish festivals were fun. Passover, or Pesach, was always difficult to keep because there were certain foodstuffs that we were forbidden to eat, and chocolate fell into this category. Easter came more or less at the same time as Pesach, and non-Jewish friends often presented my brother and I with Easter eggs. These chocolate temptations would sit in their fancy wrappings as, frustrated and impatient, we counted the days until they could be cracked open and devoured. Pesach is celebrated with a Seder, a ritualistic family meal, and at certain points during the evening glasses are raised. As a child I was allowed a couple of sips of the ritual wine, and at my first Seder. I can remember sliding slowly under the dining room into happy oblivion. Rosh Hashanah is the Jewish New Year, which culminates ten days later with Yom Kippur. This is when consciences are cleared with twenty-four hours of repentance and fasting. At first I was only allowed to fast until lunchtime, but once I turned thirteen I was expected to fast for the full twenty-four hours. My mother, now organist at the Temple, played for the all-day service, and I was charged with the task of preparing the meal that would break the family's fast. It was my first full day of fasting, and that afternoon as I chopped and carved, stirred and mixed, the temptation to lick my fingers or pop the odd morsel into my mouth became almost unbearable. Surely, I reasoned, this being my first attempt at a marathon of self-discipline, God would understand and forgive. But the still small voice of conscience intervened and, valiantly, I didn't succumb.

When they became members of Temple Israel, my mother had offered her services to the music department, much to the delight of the resident rabbi, Doctor Weiler. Soon she was invited to replace the temporary organist and taught herself to play the synagogue's Hammond organ in a remarkably short time, foot pedals, stops and all. The sheets of music used by the choir were old and stained, marked with alterations and doodles, and having always taken pleasure in transforming chaos into order, she set to work with a will. At last she had a purpose in her life, as well as earning a small but useful salary, and she began to allow herself to feel happier.

The Temple employed two choirs, one junior and one senior. The senior sang at the Friday night services and on high days and holy days. Following my mother's lead, my father took on the role of choirmaster to the older group, conducting them with a baton (self-made, of course) as he sang the baritone line. The junior choir, led by my mother, sang at the Saturday morning services, and soon my brother and I joined. We sat in the choir loft on a long, hard, wooden bench, while the congregation below, in their best Sabbath clothes, followed the service, which was mostly in Hebrew. They could probably read the Hebrew text, yet have almost no idea of the meaning unless they followed the English translation printed on the opposite page. Similarly, my mother had written the alien words out phonetically, and we sang them out with fervent conviction, not knowing or caring what commitments we might be making to The Almighty.

As I watched my mother for cues to sing, the synagogue became more like a theatre than a place of worship. Hushed and silent, I felt I was part of a backstage team, creating an atmosphere in which the audience could be uplifted. There we sat in the shabby loft with its dun-coloured partitioned walls and worn-out carpet, hidden behind the masking of the deep blue velvet curtain, and, accompanied by the rich organ tones, our childish voices would soar from the gallery above the holy ark. It was here, behind the scenes, that I felt most comfortable, and so, I suspect, did my mother, for this was her territory and here she was her own mistress. And sometimes when no one was about to my shocked delight, she would gleefully render her version of 'Tico-Tico', a popular tune played on the Hammond organ by one, Ethel Smith, in a film we had seen together,

"Well, why not?" she would call, making herself heard over the reverberating sounds. "God deserves a bit of fun!"

CHAPTER 14

Barnato Park, a high school for white girls only, was set in a large site only three blocks from number 74. The impressive Victorian red-brick building boasted a more recent science block, with several islands of formal gardens along the narrow, intersecting tarmac road, allowing access to the few authorised cars. Directly opposite the school stood a similar building, fronted by a wide fan of steps flanked by weathered griffins. Here it was that some pupils, for personal or logistic reasons, were housed as boarders. They seemed to me to be a privileged few belonging to some secret society, and I watched with envy as they disappeared through the heavy, polished doors into a world without parents. A swimming pool, several tennis courts and a hockey field completed the facilities, the whole acreage surrounded by a high, iron-staked fence with a few ornate, strategically placed gates.

The junior school, situated adjacent to the high school, was altogether smaller but just as architecturally grand, and here it was that, at the age of six, I began my formal education. I was utterly thrilled when I was fitted out with my first school uniform: a black square-necked, pleated gymslip for winter, worn over a white square-necked shirt and tied around the middle with a striped girdle of the school's colours, black and liquorice allsorts pink. Black lace-up shoes, thick, black woollen stockings held up by a garter belt, and black bloomers were de rigueur, while a black blazer and black felt hat completed the outfit. Summer wear was kinder, the gymslip replaced by a discreet, undecorated white dress, the uncomfortable stockings and belt exchanged for a pair of plain white socks, and cream-coloured panama hats. I could barely wait to join the army of uniformed pupils, and a few days before I began, in an unusual moment of compliance my mother allowed me to don my brand spanking-new winter uniform and stand outside our house as the girls walked past me on their way to school, casually pretending to be a seasoned classmate.

I may have looked forward to school, but the reality of it confused and disappointed me. To begin with it seemed that appearance and behaviour were all that mattered. On my first day in Standard One, having introduced herself, our class teacher Miss Rowse, middle-aged and prim, kindly but firm, had her new charges kneel on the floor of the classroom.

"The hem of your gymslip must be exactly two inches from the floor when you kneel," she informed us, "and I can see that many are shorter than they should be. You know who you are," she said, adding crisply, "Inform your mothers."

"Stocking seams must be ab-so-lute-ly straight!" She stretched the word, using her index finger, rather confusingly, to draw a long horizontal line in the air. "And when you bend over to touch your toes, no bare flesh must be visible above your stocking tops. "That," - her voice dropped ominously – "is asking for trouble in more ways than one!"

As we settled back into our all-in-one desks-with-seat, Miss Rowse continued.

"We will have shoe and nail inspection twice a week, and that means clean, shiny shoes and clean, non-shiny nails. You will always, al-ways wear your school hat in public, and never, ne-ver be seen eating or chewing gum. If you do, you will receive a detention. Is that clear?"

"Yes, Miss Rowse," we droned.

She perked up visibly. "Now, two of my personal tips, my little secrets. In order to keep the collars of your blazers clean, you must ask your father if he would kindly lend you one of his nice, big handkerchiefs - and remember, you ab-so-lute-ly must ask!"

She removed a large white square of fabric from under the neck of her dusty-pink cardigan, shook it out and smoothed it flat on the top of her desk. Then she picked up a piece of chalk and drew a square, corner topmost, on the blackboard.

"Now pay attention, girls! Top corner to centre, bottom corner to centre, top side to centre, bottom side to centre," she said, drawing as she spoke, "and what do we have?"

Putting down the chalk and brushing the dust from her hands, she deftly folded the piece on her desk and then came forward and held the resulting oblong aloft for all to see.

"We have a secret scarf that will keep our blazer collars clean, clean, clean and save them from wear and tear! So, fathers' handkerchiefs tomorrow, please. But ask, ask, ask! Yes?"

"Yes, Miss Rowse," came the response.

"Now my last secret. I want you all to put your elbows on your desks."

We looked at one another uneasily.

"Come along! Elbows on desks, please."

Bewildered, we complied.

"Now I want you to turn the palms of your hands towards you, close your eyes and lean your eyes against those palms."

Hiding our sniggers, we followed her instructions.

"The palms of your hands," she told us, "have soothing properties that will transmit through your eyes into your brain and thus into your nervous system, bringing comfort and calm. Sit still and quiet now, and allow the healing to work."

Peeking between my fingers, I watched Miss Rowse back at her desk carefully lifting the lid an inch or two and surreptitiously popping something into her small, demure mouth.

Miss Rowse's gentle eccentricities rather endeared her to me, and her lessons, though minimally educational, were restful. Not so with brisk, plain Miss van der Merve, teacher of geography and mathematics, whose instruction turned those two subjects into permanently anathema to me. To this day the world atlas remains a large, heavy and unopened book, and anything beyond addition, subtraction and multiplication makes me dizzy and nauseous. There were, however, two classes I relished, probably because I showed an aptitude for both subjects. Miss Parker's periods of English were enthralling, and my love for the subject as well as the language blossomed. She would quote passages filled with the wonder of words and, with an ecstatic cry, throw her head back and defy us not to share her pleasure. It was she who encouraged what writing talent I had, and made poetry, which until then had seemed exclusive and a mystery, thrillingly accessible. The other was art, presided over by Miss Dunwoody, on whom I developed a secret crush. She was tall and spare, with a pretty face framed by a halo of wispy blonde curls, and I wallowed in the glow of her approval as I produced pieces of artwork slightly better than the offerings of my classmates.

At the age of ten I graduated from the junior school and was, at last, a pupil of the Johannesburg High School for Girls, along with my best friend Rhoda. We had been pupils together at the junior school, both aged six, and we remained firm friends through our teens, until I went to university and she left for England to qualify as a florist at the Constance Spry Academy.

When we first met I had instantly admired and envied her curly black hair, her pretty face and her peaches-and-cream complexion. I longed to be like her. At night I tortured my stubbornly straight, mousy hair with iron curlers that hurt my scalp, lying awake in discomfort. As a last resort and in spite of my mother's disapproval I brought home a permanent wave kit that smelt of rotten eggs, and briefly turned my lank locks briefly into a tight, unmanageable frizz. I tried any and every cream and concoction advertised in an attempt to discourage the pimples and unsightly blackheads that cropped out on my face, to no avail. I remained my plain, ordinary, adolescent self.

In spite of the heat of the day and the ochre dust that settled everywhere, at school Rhoda remained fresh and cool. Her uniform was impeccable, her shoes spotless, and she always had a perfectly folded handkerchief tucked into the cuff of her sleeve that was, of course, never used. Her school books were neatly covered in tastefully patterned paper, and her writing was praised by all the teachers as exemplary. As regards the school's compulsory sporting activities, Rhoda's tennis technique was more than adequate, whereas I either missed the approaching ball with wild slashes of the racket or walloped it so hard it became firmly wedged in the wire netting surrounding the court. Rhoda's swimming was easy and confident, whilst I clung to the side of the pool fearful of drowning. As well as all these enviable assets, Rhoda had a strong sense of leadership and a beguiling personality, a combination that won her a posse of admiring friends willing to follow her initiative not only at school, but also at the synagogue we both attended. There was, however, one thing I had that Rhoda didn't have, and that she envied. I could sing, whereas Rhoda was tone deaf, and when she attempted to join in any chorus, the flat droning she emitted was painful to the ears and cheered me no end.

Then at about the age of thirteen Rhoda acquired what we teenage girls secretly yearned for: a steady boyfriend. Melvyn was all he should be, complimenting Rhoda's perfection. He was tall for his fourteen years, dark, slim and good looking, with a sharp sense of humour, and he worshipped at Rhoda's altar much as she expected him to. My mother disapproved of Rhoda's influence over me and not without reason, for Rhoda made me dissatisfied, not only with my appearance, but also with my surroundings, as well as my wardrobe. Rhoda's adoring mother made all of her daughter's clothes herself, and the contents of her vast wardrobe were frilly and feminine. My outfits were far fewer and leaned towards the practical, for although my mother was a fine seamstress herself, she had little time or interest in indulging my sartorial demands, not to mention the cost. Every occasion at the synagogue found Rhoda in a new and ever more flouncy outfit, and walking beside her I was only too aware that my homeliness enhanced her image.

"Can Rhoda come for lunch after school tomorrow? She's never been here for lunch and I've been there lots and it's my turn."

Rhoda, an only child, lived with her doting parents in a modern block fronted by a narrow, manicured lawn in which were set three equidistant palm trees. By standing on the balcony of their third floor flat and craning your neck to the left, you could just see the high school we attended, and each day at one o'clock sharp, as the school emptied, Rhoda's mother's black housemaid would watch out for her charge, and when Rhoda rounded the corner she would hastily put the final touches to the lunch she had prepared. Now and then, feeling greatly privileged I would be invited to join her. Having washed our hands (dried on a small individual towel) we would sit at the round dining table set with embroidered doilies and sparkling silver, a bowl of freshly picked flowers in the centre, and a small linen napkin folded into an upright pyramid on each of the two place settings. The maid would then serve us dishes that may have been ordinary enough but, dressed and trimmed, seemed exotic in comparison to the plain fare dished up at number 74.

"Can she?" I asked again, wheedling.

My mother and I were sitting at the kitchen table. She was making one of her interminable lists, while I munched on a thick sandwich filled with cheese and pickle.

"Lunch tomorrow?" My mother pushed aside the notebook, tearing off the top page and scrutinising it. "I suppose so, but don't expect me or Katie to do anything special. Neither of us has the time."

"No, no, I'll do it," I said enthusiastically, "but can we eat at the table in the dining room?"

"No, certainly not! You'll have your lunch here in the kitchen like you always do."

"But when I go to lunch at Rhoda's ...."

"I don't want to hear this. Here or nowhere." My mother was firm.

"Well ...." - I could see that particular battle was lost - "can we have a proper cloth over the oilcloth and use serviettes, and ...."

"And what else, for heaven's sake? Next you'll be asking Katie to change into a frilly white apron and wait on you hand and foot."

Oh, if only!

"If you want Rhoda to come for lunch, she'll have to accept things as they are or not come at all. All right?"

"All right," I acceded grumpily.

Attempting to make up for the shortness of her response, my mother asked, "So what would you like to have?"

"Can we have pilchards on toast?"

One of my favourite dishes was tinned pilchards in tomato sauce mashed up with a screw of black pepper and a dollop of vinegar and then spread thickly on hot buttered toast.

"Right. And for afters?"

Surprised at this sudden cooperation, I scrutinised her face for any telltale sign of a motive, but finding none I risked asking, "If you can spare it, how about one of your caramel things?"

This had been an exciting culinary secret revealed to my brother and me only a few weeks earlier. My mother had unpacked her grocery shopping and placed three tins of condensed milk side by side on the kitchen table.

"I saw these in the grocer's, and it reminded me of a pudding I used to make ages ago. You've had condensed milk before, haven't you?"

"It's that thick, white, sweet sticky stuff," Brian said brightly.

"That's right. Well, you watch this!"

She took a large saucepan off its shelf, lined it with thick newspaper 'so the tins won't rattle' and, stripping them of their labels, covered them with water.

"There!"

She placed it on the stove, telling us that it would take at least three hours for the magic to work and that we were to check it from time to time, adding more water when the level got low. After three long hours the tins were removed and left overnight to cool. The next morning before we left for school, we watched in high anticipation as my mother took one of them, carefully prised open first one end and then the other, then dipped a knife in hot water and ran it around the inside rim.

"Are you ready?"

We could barely speak as she held it over a plate and shook out a perfect log of solid caramel. We poked our fingers into the hollow, empty tin to taste what had been left behind; it was unbelievably, deliciously smooth and sweet, and that evening it was served up as dessert with a floating of single cream. Sheer heaven! I knew the last of the three miracle tins sat unopened at the back of the fridge, and to my delight my mother acquiesced.

"I've never eaten in a kitchen before," said Rhoda hesitantly as I waved her into the chair opposite me.

A small linen tablecloth covered one end of the chequered oilcloth, and on either side of the table I had put a place mat, together with a knife, fork and spoon, and a decorated glass tumbler (usually reserved for parties) filled with orange squash.

"Oh, how quaint! Snow White paper napkins!" Rhoda crowed, making me flush with embarrassment.

When presented with the main course she remarked that as they fed pilchards to her cat she had always assumed they were pet food, but I hastily assured her that these were altogether a different thing. The pudding, however, drew exclamations of surprise and relish. My mother appeared as Rhoda was leaving, and she asked if she could possibly have the recipe.

"It was soooo delicious!" she yodelled. "I'd love my mother to make it for me. It must be jolly difficult, and I bet it takes ages!"

My mother smiled.

"You're right, it does take ages," she agreed, "but I'm afraid I can't give you the recipe. It's a family secret, and I'm not allowed to tell."

CHAPTER 15

Rhoda and I were about to celebrate our entry into womanhood. We sat on a small patch of lawn in the school grounds discussing our forthcoming bat mitzvahs, the ceremony for thirteen-year-old girls equivalent to the boys' bar mitzvahs.

"Mommy is making my dress," Rhoda announced. "It's going to be white, of course, fairly plain, but with a touch of something feminine she says, like broderie anglaise." She pronounced the words carefully.

"What's that?" I enquired.

"Don't you know? It's sort of cotton, with a pattern cut out and stitched round. It's hard to describe. You'll just have to wait and see."

"My mom's going to make mine, too. She's bought the material. It's sort of wool, but thin. And it's not white, it's sort of cream." I couldn't help sounding disappointed.

My friend smiled at me sympathetically. "Never mind," she said. "Cream is nearly white. I'm sure you'll look nice. Will your mother be playing the organ or will she be in the congregation watching you?"

"Oh no! She'll be in shul with all my relatives. She's asked Mrs Froman to stand in for her."

There were three other girls in the class, and we were being taught our individual torah portions by Mr Locketz. He was a short, round, red-faced man, who spoke with a mid-European accent that was difficult to place and his bald head featured a spray of dark moles. None of us particularly liked him, and there was something about him that made me uncomfortable. I was always relieved when the class was over and I could leave the cramped, stuffy room, part of the prefabricated building attached to the synagogue.

During one of these lessons, as he sat with his head bent over his book I watched with incredulity as one of the larger moles on the top of his shiny head seemed to move. I was horrified! Was it a symptom of the disease I had always suspected he carried, and would it contaminate us all? The freckle moved again, then soared into the air, circled, and returned to land neatly back from whence it had come. A fly, for goodness' sake, a fly! Following the Hebrew script with his chubby finger, Mr Locketz was oblivious of the creature on his bald pate, and I was overtaken by a sudden bout of giggles. He looked up sharply.

"What's so funny, Sheila?"

I tried to say something, but the more I tried to control myself the more I laughed, wheezing as tears of mirth ran down my cheeks. Mr Locketz stood up, his rage mounting and his face turning a beetroot red.

"Come over here!" he managed through clenched teeth.

I walked slowly to the front of the class, who were sitting quiet and curious. Mr Locketz pulled his chair from behind the desk, shoved it to the side, then sat down on it.

"Come here." I hovered uncertainly and he repeated more firmly, "Here."

I edged closer and with a swift, surprising movement he grabbed me by my shoulders, pulled me face down across his lap and smacked me several times on the bottom with his open hand. I hadn't struggled; I had been too shocked. Now I found my feet and stood up. There was no sound except for his heavy panting. I adjusted my uniform, walked back to my seat, collected my books, left the classroom and went home. Nowadays Mr Locketz's behaviour would be considered a gross misdemeanour. As it was, my parents, particularly my father, were appalled and angry. They complained to the rabbi, whom I suppose reprimanded the man, and he turned up at number 74 full of contrition, clutching a large bunch of flowers for my mother. I completed my bat mitzvah studies with a different teacher, and to all intents and purposes the matter was closed.

Plans went ahead for the day of confirmation. Invitations to family members were sent, and a light, inexpensive lunch menu devised, but when the much-anticipated Saturday morning arrived I woke with a high temperature, a pounding headache and a blocked nose. As I was about to leave for the temple I gazed miserably at the image facing me in my full-length wardrobe mirror. My hair was lank and dull, my face pallid except for a swollen red nose, and my eyes, normally my best feature, had shrunk into puffy slits. White shoes made my average-size feet look like those of Minnie Mouse and, worst of all, the nipples of my budding breasts could be clearly seen through the thin fabric of the cream woollen dress. The service, the readings and the milling around of family and friends passed me by as I struggled to fight the temptation to curl up on the floor, any floor, and slide into unconsciousness. Somehow the day passed, and when at last I lay curled up in an early bed, aspirin-ed and hot toddy-ed, with my sore nose vaselined and a pile of tissues to hand, the stack of unopened presents waiting on my bedside table reminded me that tomorrow was another day.

"I think Martin's gorgeous!"

"What?"

The fact that Rhoda hadn't heard me wasn't surprising; the record on the turntable was playing at full volume, and the chatter and laughter of teenage couples jiving or standing in groups around the edge of the small dance floor made conversation almost impossible. It was the synagogue's monthly teenage dance, and the shul hall was draped with streamers and hung with balloons. I nudged Rhoda and pointed at a boy standing on the other side of the room. Martin was short and somewhat on the stocky side. He had blue eyes, shiny brown curls and a pleasant face, and I was in love. He had replaced the confident, brash Aubrey in my affections after I had offered to share with him my delight in a small doll I had been given, made out of icing sugar. He had taken it from me tenderly, then bitten her head off, handing back the decapitated body with a grin. As he crunched his prize, he exposed the unattractive gap between his two front teeth, which until that moment had been part of his fascination. My feelings for him evaporated, and I soon turned my attention to Martin, who had been hovering around me with interest for some time.

"Ask him to dance!" Rhoda suggested.

"Don't be silly!"

"Well, Melvyn will get him to ask you then, won't you Melvyn?"

Rhoda's boyfriend had just arrived with three paper cups of what was euphemistically called punch, a bland cerise liquid in which hovered a few chunks of tinned fruit salad.

"No Melvyn, don't!" I squeaked unconvincingly.

"Melvyn," Rhoda ordered, "go over there and tell Martin to ask Sheila to dance."

Embarrassed but willing him on, I watched Melvyn dodge

across the floor between the dancing couples. When he reached Martin I could bear it no longer and turned my back to shut out the scene about to play. What if he said no? It would be too humiliating, especially now that Rhoda knew my secret 'crush'. The dress I was wearing was new; the wide emerald green skirt swung when I walked and the white bodice with matching green piping on the edge of its puffed sleeves showed my small, pert breasts to advantage, but it had an odd smell, a sort of dry hay smell, and the hotter I got the more aware of it I became. A moment later I felt a tentative touch on my shoulder.

"Hello." It was Martin.

"Hello."

We stood facing each other awkwardly.

"Wanna dance?"

"Okay."

The music had changed now; it was slow and dreamy. "Two sleepy people ...," crooned Dennis Lotis, the current heart-throb of pop. Martin, whose dancing was disappointingly clumsy, steered me onto the quiet, cooler adjacent patio outside. The moon was high, the air warm and sweet, and I looked up - or rather, slightly down - into Martin's blue, blue eyes and prayed he wouldn't notice that smell emanating from my dress. Gently, if a little clumsily, he put his cheek next to mine.

"Mmmm," he said, 'you smell ..."

Oh God, here it comes! I thought. I stiffened, waiting for the blow.

"... lovely!" he said.

Although relief flooded through me, a part of my brain wondered whether he was a convincing liar, or had a liking for peculiar odours. He lifted his head and now our lips were more or less adjacent.

My heart began to beat faster. I think he's going to kiss me, I thought. This is about to be my very first kiss!

And our lips met. And they stayed met. Nothing else happened, no movement, no body contact, nothing. We stood together but apart, awkwardly attached at the mouth. My eyes were wide open, staring at the enviably long lashes of Martin's tightly squeezed shut lids. Then it was over. His eyes snapped open and we took a step away from one another. Well, I said to myself, at least I've finally been kissed ... I think.

For the next few weeks we hung around together, Martin and

I, by which time we were considered to be 'going steady', and at any social event at the synagogue or any outing the gang (headed, of course, by Rhoda and Melvyn) devised, we were expected to go together. I was flattered by Martin's obvious infatuation, and for the first time I started to feel confident and even attractive. Yet, although having a boyfriend was new and heady stuff, poor Martin was dull company and I found his conversation limited and uninteresting.

As teenagers in South Africa in the late forties we were obsessed with anything American, buying up everything they exported and copying their fashions, their fads and even their speech. The world of commercial radio was quick to exploit this craze, and an enterprising advertising syndicate began putting on a regular Sunday show at a cinema in the centre of town. The programme was sponsored by a firm that produced Halo shampoo, and during the hour-long performance their jingles peppered the comedy turns, wacky sketches and musical items.

"Halo, everybody, Halo!" sang the gorgeous trio of girls - one blonde, one brunette and one blue-black. "Halo is the shampoo that glorifies your hair!"

The show was broadcast live on some network or other, but, most importantly, entrance was free, and every Sunday found Rhoda and Melvyn and the gang queuing in the early afternoon for the six o'clock show. Dennis Lotis and Eve Boswell were the regular singing duo at these late afternoon events, and as I sat next to Martin, our hands clasped together in a sweaty confirmation of our mutual devotion, I felt a tingle of something I couldn't place. I gazed at the slim, handsome singer in his tightly trousered suit, tie loosened at the neck, shirt collar unbuttoned and hair carefully tousled.

"Baby, it's cold outside ..." he moaned, swaying sexily, the microphone almost touching his lips.

I glanced at Martin sitting beside me, and I was suddenly gripped with a fear of the dullness, the ordinariness of a future I had at all costs to avoid. I wanted to be there on the stage. I wanted to prove that I could be special, too. Withdrawing my hand from Martin's clammy clutch, I pretended to fish for something in my handbag and then held my hands firmly together in my lap. Aware of his hurt, questioning gaze, I pretended to concentrate hard on the entertainment on stage. I knew I was being unkind, but the fear I had felt was overwhelming. I had looked over the edge of a precipice and I had to distance myself from it. As we left, jostled by the noisy young crowd, I tried to get ahead of Martin, who struggled to stay by my side. I couldn't bear to look at him.

"Wait, Sheil!"

How I hated being called Sheil.

It was dusk, and I scurried towards the tram stop, Martin panting behind me. All I could think about was the future I was determined to have.

We stood side by side at the stop, Martin confused and miserable,

"Sheil ...."

When I became famous I would call myself by my middle name, Frances. Or perhaps Steve. I had always liked the name Steve for a woman. There was a character in a radio detective series called Steve. She was the hero's wife.

"Do you like the name Steve?"

Martin hesitated.

"Steve who?"

"Oh, never mind!" I snapped, hating myself.

As the tram approached, I turned and looked at him, grateful for the half-light.

"I'm sorry, Martin, I don't want to see you anymore."

He watched me jump aboard the tram, his face slowly crumpling. I threw myself into the nearest available seat, my mind a muddle, guilty at the churlish way I was treating him, remorseful at hurting him, but angry with him for being weak and inept. Strongest of all, though, was the feeling of dread that I might be sucked down into a dull, domestic future with someone like him. A sense of relief flooded through me, dousing the pang of regret that I no longer had a boyfriend. I was free, I was unshackled, and my future was my own.

CHAPTER 16

It was my final term at school. I had turned sixteen, applied to the Witwatersrand University, and been accepted by the Fine Arts faculty to study for a B.A. However, although I was proud and excited, my heart wasn't in it. What I desperately wanted was to travel to London and audition for the Royal Academy of Dramatic Art (RADA). My mother, my father and I had spent many hours discussing this and, although my parents weren't entirely against the idea, the feeling was that I should have a degree 'to fall back on". I didn't understand what they meant. I certainly didn't want to teach and, although my drawings and daubs were passably good, I knew I could never earn a living with my pencils and paints.

One morning at the school assembly the headmistress, Miss Langridge, standing on the stage at one end of the wood-panelled hall with its high arched windows, made an announcement that fired me with enthusiasm.

"Girls," she said, projecting as best she could in her high-pitched, bronchitic voice, "as you know, this is the final term of the year, and the staff and I have decided that, instead of the usual Christmas concert, the leaving class will perform a pantomime."

The murmur of interest that ran round the two hundred girls seated on the floor in front of her was brought to an abrupt halt by the blasting voice of Miss Hutton, our busty, burly sports mistress.

"That will do, school!" she barked, coming forward to stand next to the headmistress, who dabbed at the corners of her lips with a crumpled white lace handkerchief. She mouthed a grateful "Thank you," and Miss Hutton, flushed and rewarded, returned to her seat on the platform behind Miss Langridge with the rest of the teaching staff.

"And so," continued the head, "we are going to hold a competition for the best pantomime written by one of the girls who is leaving. Their English teacher Miss Parker will be the judge, and the winning script will be performed here," - she waved the handkerchief around vaguely – "in our splendid hall.

This year it is our turn to invite our brother school King Edward's, to a ... er ... function," - she dabbed at the corners of her eyes – "and this would seem an ideal ... er ... opportunity." Her voice faltered with the effort of expressing such unusually permissive plans to an audience of strictly governed girls.

Sinking into her large, throne-like chair, she waved a weak hand in the direction of Miss Stark ('The Lark') sitting at the piano, and thus commanded, she began thumping out the introduction to our school song.

"And did those feet in ancient times
Walk upon these out mountains green ..." (we sang).

It was Miss Stark herself who, when she had joined the staff as music teacher three years earlier, had suggested that the school song at the time ("Barnato Park the finest/All aspects good combinest") should be replaced by 'Jerusalem', pointing out that the only change needed to its stirring lyrics would be to substitute "England" with "these our". Miss Langridge, it seems, had agreed that it certainly outclassed the existing piece, ignoring the fact that Johannesburg, set in dry, flat veldt, boasted no "mountains green" or "pleasant pastures", although "dark satanic mills" might just pass muster. Certainly patches of "green and pleasant land" could be found, particularly in the more elite suburbs of the city and in the sprinkler-watered lawns surrounding our school grounds. Nonetheless, when on academic occasions we were called upon to support our school, our scalps would tingle with pride as we sang our way towards the crescendo of the final phrase. Sports days, though, were a different matter. It was impossible to cheer our teams on with a rendering of 'Jerusalem', so we resorted to our primeval instincts and simply and gloriously screamed, as only adolescent girls can.

"A pantomime!"

It was break time, and Rhoda and I were sitting side by side on our favourite spot in the school grounds, sheltered by a large weeping willow.

"I'm sure I could write one, and of course I'd produce it as well."

"I thought what you wanted was to be an actress," Rhoda countered. "You couldn't produce it AND be in it."

"Oh yes I could!" I said defensively. "My father does both sometimes when he produces Gilbert and Sullivan."

76

"So you would."

"What?"

"Be in it as well!"

I considered for a moment before responding, "No, I'll just write and produce it this time. It'll be good experience for when I go to England and study ..."

" ... At the Royal Academy of Dramatic Art and become a star!" Rhoda interjected, finishing the mantra she had heard me recite so often. "You seem pretty sure that Miss Parker will choose your pantomime."

"Well, I'm pretty sure she will," I said. It hadn't occurred to me that there would be any doubt. "After all," I added, "theatre is in my blood."

After school I ran home and in through the back door, flung my school hat onto the kitchen table and rummaged in my bag for an exercise book and my pencil case. Then I pushed aside the plate with its waiting sandwich to clear a space.

"Ow, Miss Sheila, what you doing?"

Katie stood at the sink watching me.

"I'm going to write a pantomime," I said, kneeling on the hard wooden chair and turning the leaves of the notebook to find a fresh page.

"No, first you eat your lunch. Then you write."

"Alright, I'll do both."

I took a hasty gulp from the glass of milk in front of me.

She came over to the table and stood beside me, watching as I picked out the sharpest pencil and smoothed the page flat.

"What is this thing you write?"

"A pantomime. It's a play for Christmas."

"For Christmas?" Katie chuckled. "But you a Jew girl, Miss Sheila. You can't write about the good Lord Jesus. Ow! Your parents will punish you!"

"No they won't, Katie. It's not religious!" I explained. 'It's ... well, it's entertainment ... fun! It's to do with fairy stories and things like that. You know? Like Christmas trees and presents. They're not religious."

"Then why your parents they not give you and Master Brian Christmas present? Why your mother she shout at you when you put coloured paper on the tree outside?"

There was logic to Katie's question. The previous December my brother Brian and I had indeed draped a few leftover party

77

streamers between the fronds of the tall palm tree in the front garden, and although it looked rather pathetic, it had been an attempt to join in the festivities we viewed every year with envy. Returning from shopping that morning, my mother had hastily dumped her packages on the steps of the veranda and pulled down the offending decorations. This was followed by a lecture reminding us of our Jewish heritage, and making it clear that we were to avoid any temptation to join in Christian celebrations. She warned us that, had our father been the one to discover our blasphemy, there would have been darker disciplines. But surely, I thought, writing a Christmas pantomime had nothing to do with religion? After all, over the years we had been taken to see several. Still, illogical as it seemed, I supposed there might be a possibility that actually creating one was a different thing altogether.

"Sheila? You back?" My mother's voice triggered Katie's hasty return to the kitchen sink where she began the clatter of dish-washing.

"I'm in the kitchen," I called.

She appeared at the door. "Homework?" she queried.

"No, not really." I took a deep breath. Much depended on her answer. "Is it alright if I write a pantomime?"

"A pantomime?"

She sat down on the chair beside me.

"Yes. Is it alright?" Keen to explain before she vetoed the idea, I went on quickly, "They're having a competition at school for the girls in my class to write a pantomime and the best one will be put on at the end of the term and I know it's alright to go and see one because we've been, but I just wondered if actually writing one is … I mean, is it alright?" bravely adding by way of explanation, "Being Jewish?"

She looked at me for a moment, then threw her head back and laughed as I had seldom heard her laugh before. She removed her glasses, retrieved a handkerchief from the pocket of her cardigan, wiped her eyes and sat back with a sigh.

"You're a funny girl," she said. "I don't know where you pick up some of your ideas. Of course you can write a pantomime. Which one are you going to choose? *Cinderella*? *Aladdin*?"

"No! I want to do a brand new one!"

"But aren't pantomimes supposed to be traditional? You know, based on stories everyone knows?"

"Oh." I was momentarily perplexed. Then I had what I thought was a really good idea. "I know," I said excitedly, "I'll write one with lots of different stories that everyone knows and mix them all up together!"

I finally settled for three: *Jack and the Beanstalk*, *Cinderella* and *Ali Baba and the Forty Thieves*, which is how the highly original pantomime entitled *JACINDERALI* came to be written and produced by Sheila Steafel, a pupil in class 5b at the Barnato Park High School for Girls. It was performed in the school hall by her fellow students to celebrate the end of their final term, and according to the outraged head, Miss Valerie Langridge, had she not been leaving anyway, she would probably have been expelled.

As far as I know, no script of the evening's entertainment remains, and I have thankfully expunged from my memory the machinations that wove the three storylines into one confused whole. I do, however, have an entrance ticket giving the date, time and place and ticket price (children one and sixpence, adults two and sixpence). At the top of this small square card is printed 'IN AID OF EKUTELENI', an Anglican Missionary for black children. I also have a faded pink programme with the information that the three acts of the pantomime would be prefaced by a first half of short 'entertainments', and these were what primarily triggered Miss Langridge's fury.

We performed three blackout sketches that were plagiarised by me from a thin volume culled from the bookshelves at home. I can't bring to mind the plots or dialogue, but the titles and characters imply a certain degree of innuendo that was bound to please the younger members of the audience and make the teaching staff more than a little uncomfortable. According to the programme 'THE DOCTOR SAID ...' involved The Maid, The Plumber and Sir Roland, 'LOVERS (K)NOT' had a cast of five which included three pretty girls, an Office Boy and a Travelling Salesman, and 'HELPING THE WAR EFFORT' revolved around a German Spy, yet another pretty girl, and a Curious Bystander. Between these items 'A TAP DANCE' was performed by Joanna Dee, and Gillian and Sandra Mackie along with Lynda Ferreira gave us a 'MEDLEY OF SONGS'.

Although the plot and the deathless dialogue of the pantomime itself may be lost to future generations, I have a photograph of the cast in their splendid costumes, made by their doting mothers. Yashmak-ed and turban-ed, draped and bejewelled, they stand and sit, kneel and crouch, a huddle of happy school leavers literally caught in the final act before wending their separate ways. And I wonder what happened to them? Where are they all? And, indeed, ARE they all? My eye is caught by the bulge of a cushion stuffed under Myrna Berg's satin coat to give her depiction of a potentate credible gravitas.

"Get that protuberance removed!" Miss Langridge hissed.

The afternoon performance now over, I stood in front of the headmistress having been peremptorily summoned to her office.

"It's disgusting. The girl looks pregnant!"

"But she's playing a fat man!" I countered.

"Quiet!" she thundered. "Just get rid of it. Furthermore ...."

Speech seemed to fail her. She slumped into her high-backed chair, then dabbed at her brow with the ever-present handkerchief. After a moment she gathered herself with some effort into an upright position.

"I suppose," she continued, "we must give the audience some value for their money, otherwise I would insist on the first half being cut altogether. However ..." she paused, "we will have none of those disgusting, lewd scenes and nasty characters. You will replace them with other forms of entertainment. Surely amongst your classmates there must be one or two who can recite a poem, or ... fill in the gaps with ..." - she waved a weak arm – "... something. Whatever it is, you will search them out and send them to me within the hour to show me what they intend to do, and I will decide whether it is suitable for tonight's concert or not."

"Yes, Miss Langridge."

I rose quickly, anxious to begin my search for talent.

"Sit down! I haven't finished."

I sat.

"The tap dance, though unexceptional, can remain. As for the songs, the skirts of those three girls must somehow be lengthened, and their necklines filled in. Which brings me to your ... pan - to - mime." She rolled the word out as though it tasted unpleasant. "Bosoms and midriffs will be covered, earrings and lipstick will be removed, and you ... you will remove every rude and lewd word spoken in that travesty of your so-called entertainment."

She picked up a notebook from her desk and seemed about to read out what was written. Instead, with a weary frown, she shook her head and passed it to me. The list read as follows:

God
Blimey
Blast
Bloody
Blooming well
Crikey Moses
Ass
Schweinhund [clearly the German sketch]
Himmel [also]
Ach [similarly]
Oy Vay [not the German sketch]

I handed it back with a nervous nod.
"Keep it to hand."
She waved it away and then levered herself out of her chair.
"I suggest you get yourself and the rest of your class to the art room. I have instructed Miss Dunwoody to have ready a large supply of crêpe paper and a quantity of glue and safety pins."
I rose.
"Yes, Miss Langridge. Thank you, Miss Langridge."
"You may well thank me," she snorted. "You're a nasty girl with a nasty mind, and I would have expelled you from this school. Fortunately for you ... and for us ... you will be leaving anyway."

CHAPTER 17

The first thing I did at university was to join the dramatics society, the second was to head for the Fine Arts faculty and meet my fellow students. They turned out to be a disparate lot, two men and seven women, ranging in age from the youngest - me and Maggie, both sixteen, and Myrna aged seventeen - to Tyler, the oldest, a twenty-seven-year-old sculptor who had "come to freshen his bones". As the term progressed, Myrna, Maggie and I gravitated towards one another and soon became an almost inseparable trio. Whether it was the similarity in our ages that drew us together I don't know, but a more unlikely alliance it would be hard to imagine. I was a 'nice Jewish girl' educated in a school for nice middle- to upper-class girls, while Maggie, an orphan brought up by a fervent Catholic grandmother, had attended a co-educational school on the outskirts of the city. Myrna, a quiet, introverted girl, had been in the same class at my school and matriculated at the same time.

I was fairly outgoing, clothes conscious, boy conscious and, as I have said, a fairly talented painter. In contrast, Maggie was soft-spoken and sensitive, and the quality of her work marked her out as a gifted painter with a future. Her face was square, her jaw determined, her eyes bright and intelligent, and her enthusiasm when she spoke about art or poetry or literature was infectious. My own interest in these subjects had so far been peripheral educational necessities rather than pleasures, but Maggie's passion fed my curiosity. She made me aware of the works of French writer Andre Gide, and obscure poets like Lorca and Rilke... Heady stuff.

Myrna's ambition was to be an industrial colour consultant, but she was persuaded by her elder brother, to whom she was devoted, to start her studies at Wits and move on to a commercial art course later. As a young child she'd had tuberculosis and lost the use of one lung. Consequently, this pale, delicate Jewish child with large dark eyes and a mane of black hair had been excused any strenuous activity at school, and while her classmates sweated on the sports field, she sat in the shade, textbook in hand. This sedentary lifestyle added to her weight, and by the end of her schooling she regarded herself as obese, although in truth she was only somewhat over the average. This obsession with her weight made her painfully self-conscious and shy, and once she shed her school clothes she always wore ample smocks or all-embracing duster coats. No one, not even her mother, was permitted to see her without them.

Many of the Fine Arts lecturers and instructors that came and went were somewhat eccentric. Charles Gold, Professor of Life Drawing and Anatomy, was a large, paunchy man with an oddly mincing gait for one of his size and shape. His balding head showed wisps of fine ginger hair, and he wore a full, flowing red beard through which his bowed lips protruded like the petals of a snapdragon. Notable, though, was the inch-long nail on the small finger of his right hand. This was his 'tool', his weapon for correcting any drawn line that offended, leaving behind a scored mark on the unfortunate student's block. Charles had a lover, a pasty man in his thirties, who would turn up to model for our life class. Mervyn (for it was he) would strip off behind a screen in the corner of the studio, and I always wondered why the models we drew needed the discretion of a screen when they were about to reveal all to us. Wrapped in the faded dressing gown kept for these occasions, Mervyn would mount the low platform in the centre of the room and Professor Gold would arrange him into a pleasing pose. Once set, we would shuffle our easels around our subject, attempting to find some interesting angle of his pale, shapeless mass, while his lover stood by, eyes shining with blind love and admiration.

Nellie van Outen, a woman of uncertain age, could at first sight be mistaken for a down-and-out, and only on closer inspection did it become clear that the layer upon layer of ragged-edged and faded fabrics she wrapped herself in were expensive, and carefully contrived. When she leaned over your shoulder the better to judge a canvas, instead of the anticipated smell of earth and sweat, a subtle aroma of some exotic perfume would engulf you. Not much was known about Nellie, though her cut-glass English accent seemed genuine enough, and it was believed she had studied at the Slade School of Art in London. She was always late for lectures, in spite of living in a small boarding house near the campus, and every day her diminutive, birdlike figure could be seen scurrying towards the university, clutching several plastic shopping bags. Others in the department seemed keen on conformity, whereas Nellie encouraged individuality. However, although I tried hard to spread my artistic wings, my representations stayed deeply mundane. Typically, the first subject she gave our group to paint was 'Yellow'.

"Yellow?!" I had snorted with derision, as we three sat on the wide steps of the main building during a lunch break. "How can you paint yellow, for God's sake?"

The other two seemed quite sanguine about the project.

"I don't see why not," Maggie said. "It's just a matter of lateral thinking."

"What does that mean exactly?"

"It means," Myrna interjected, "that instead of painting the obvious you look for a different approach … a different meaning."

"Oh really?" I countered sarcastically. "So I've got to think of yellow not as the colour yellow but as something else entirely?"

"Exactly," replied Myrna.

"Quite," echoed Maggie.

"Of course," I said. "Silly me!"

"Well, let's see what we have."

It was a week later and our easels had been placed side by side along a studio wall. Myrna had opted for what appeared to be a yellow fog through which strange shapes appeared, while Maggie had painted a seated figure with a severe case of jaundice. I had considered painting the head of a Chinese woman, but thought that giving it the title 'Yellow' might seem racist, so I settled rather unimaginatively on a modernistic bunch of marigolds. Nellie van Outen slowly crabbed her way along the line, now peering closely, now stepping back, eyes narrowed, brow furrowed. Finally she was done, and, placing herself in front of an easel second from the left, said, "This is yellow."

And yellow it most certainly was. The artist had placed a bleached white canvas board on the floor, squeezed a large dollop of bright yellow acrylic paint onto it and then stirred it vigorously, sending spatters and streaks skidding across the surface. This masterwork was completed by wiping a palette knife loaded with the same paint along two of the canvas's edges, then leaving it undisturbed to dry.

"Straightforward, simple and honest. Well done."

Lynda, an intense woman with acne who was responsible for it, simpered with delight.

"As for the rest …" Nellie van Outen began, then shook her turbaned head and left.

Eccentric she may have been, but Nellie van Outen was an astute critic and teacher, and it was largely through her that I became aware that I was out of my depth in the world of Fine Arts.

The theatre productions put on twice a year by the drama society were semi-professional affairs, and each time I offered my services to help backstage, making props and painting sets, but I was desperate for an opportunity to act. Just as I managed to scrape into my second year, auditions were held for a production of Ben Jonson's *The Alchemist*, and to my utter amazement I was cast in the part of Dol Common. It was to be directed by a professional, Minna Milstein, with a two-week run in the large, modern, well-equipped university theatre. I was over the moon!

I spent the rehearsal period neglecting work in the art studio and attending lectures with the script hidden under my notebook, and I talked of nothing else. My parents put up with me, stoically assuming that once the run of the play was over I would get back to normal and resume my studies. How wrong they were! I soaked up the whole experience hungrily. Minna helped me to create the character of Dol and understand her role in the structure of the play. She taught me to grasp the meaning of the lines and speak them with relish, and reassured me when I doubted my ability. But it was only when I was shown the designer's sketch of the costume I was to wear that the full implication of being in a serious production hit me. It was a watercolour of a young woman in a low-cut, laced bodice with a gaudy, multi-layered skirt, the top one looped up and tied with a rope. She wore a pair of high, buttoned boots and stood squarely confident. As I looked at her, my own confidence drained away. I realised that this was the real thing.

As the final curtain fell on the first night, I felt exhilarated and somehow fulfilled; I had found my niche. Notices of the production appeared in several newspapers during the next few days, and my performance was picked out and praised. By the end of the week I knew that this was what I absolutely had to do, and that I had no interest in finishing my degree. Besides, there were subjects in the course that left me behind: draughtsmanship defeated me, and I was at a loss with statistics. However, psychology, which for some obscure reason was included in the syllabus, absorbed and interested me.

Late one summer's night I sat on one of the tiered seats overlooking the campus sports stadium next to Don, the hero of the football season. He had just taken me to the annual university ball, and I was still unsure as to how I had managed the 'coup' of Don asking me to be his date. In spite of his jug ears he was good looking, athletic and much sought after, and there was a gaggle of pretty and desirable girls in the sorority available to him. However, I did know that he had seen the production of *The Alchemist*, so I decided that the mystique of the theatre had probably done the trick.

"Did you really enjoy the play?" I asked yet again, trying to edge him towards complimenting me on my performance.

"Loved it."

Don nuzzled my ear.

"What about me?" I asked, twisting my head slightly out of range.

"Oh, you were great."

He shuffled closer and put an arm around my shoulders, trying his subtle best to slide a hand down the front of my evening dress.

"Really?"

I picked his hand out of my cleavage.

"Yes, really. Great."

Again, he groped his way towards my décolletage.

"Oh, that's so good to hear, because I want more than anything to get to England and study to be a professional actress."

"Uh huh?"

Don's response was muffled, his head in my neck.

"I've told my parents and they want me finish my degree, but I don't want to wait."

He grunted something unintelligible as his tongue explored my ear. I pulled my head away as politely as I could.

"What do you think I should do?"

"I think you should take it easy and relax," he said in a low voice.

Turning my face towards him with both his hands, he aimed for my lips.

"Don, stop it!" I got up angrily, and adjusting my dress, went on, "You haven't heard a word I've said, have you?"

"Oh, I have, every single boring word!" Frustrated and furious, he swung his jacket over one shoulder and continued, "And if you're so damned keen, why the hell don't you stop talking about it and just go?!"

Now why hadn't I thought of that?

Whether it was the nosebleed, or whether my parents were grateful to grasp at any excuse to put an end to the display of misery that had engulfed me for weeks, I can only guess. The three of us were slumped around the dining table - my father, my mother and I. We had reached an impasse yet again. I wiped my eyes, swollen and red with crying, and blew my nose hard, so hard that it began to bleed, first a trickle, then a flood.

"Look at that! See what you've done?"

My mother retrieved the handkerchief from the cuff of her cardigan and held it out to me.

"What I'VE done?" blustered my father. "It's you who's been so insistent that she finish her degree."

"So have you!" countered my mother.

"Not if it's going to upset her like this."

They glared at one another as, head tipped back, I held the scrap of fabric to my nostrils. Then my father spoke.

"I don't know anymore," he said, defeated. "Up to you."

If I hadn't been handicapped by a nosebleed, I would have held the breath I was already holding. Instead, I straightened up and waited for my mother's verdict. She sighed.

"If she wants to go that badly, let her go."

I burst into a noisy Niagara of tears, my father heaved himself out of his chair and fled to the sanctuary of his workshop, and my mother retrieved her bloodstained hankie and disappeared to soak it in the bathroom basin. And thus it was, after a fortnight of sulks and tears and heavy sighs, it was agreed that I could abandon my degree and pursue my ambition to become a professional actress.

The next day I walked into the studio and found Charles Gold critically surveying a batch of our most recent offerings pinned up in front of him.

"Can I have a word?" I asked.

He frowned, and without breaking his concentration, gave a slight nod of the head.

"I thought I ought to tell you I'll be leaving at the end of the term."

For the first time ever, he looked at me with some interest.

"Really?"

"Yes," I said. "I've applied to the Royal Academy in London."

Beneath the jungle of red beard his face froze, then he spoke slowly and with some difficulty.

"You've applied ... to the Royal Academy?"

We stared at each other for a long moment. Then the penny dropped.

"Of Dramatic Art!" I cried.

Unable to speak, he gripped my hand and shook it much too enthusiastically.

CHAPTER 18

Throughout my stint at university I had kept up my coaching with Muriel Alexander, and at my next session I asked her to help me with my audition for RADA. She wasn't enthusiastic.

"I'm not at all sure you'd get in, dear," she said, smiling to soften the blow, "and it's a very long way to go to make such an expensive and heart-breaking mistake. Why not stay here, dear, and see how it goes? I mean, look what happened to dear Vivien Martin. She was one of our leading actresses, off she went to London thinking she'd make it over there, and now she's back, grateful to be in our repertory company. You don't want to make the same mistake, do you?"

"But it's what I want. It's what I have to do."

More people were sent to warn me against this foolhardy move and try to persuade me to stay, but it only made me more determined. Finally, with a defeated shrug, Muriel sent off for an application form. It arrived two weeks later, and, with a sympathetic smile, she handed me copies of the two set pieces I was to learn.

My mother had made one stipulation when she agreed to my abandoning my university education: I would have to earn my boat fare to Southampton. She had decided she would deliver me to London herself, and, as I would be taking all my worldly possessions with me, the journey would have to be made by sea. After some searching in local papers I answered an advertisement for a receptionist who was willing to take on a few simple tasks that were usually performed by a dental nurse. The dentist, Mr Potter, was a pleasant, slightly overweight young man, who informed me he had only recently qualified and couldn't afford a nurse. He assured me, however, that my nursing duties would be simple and undemanding, and I agreed to start the following day.

The newly decorated surgery was part of a small block of offices within walking distance of number 74. The morning I arrived he proudly showed me around the premises. Leading off the reception area with its desk, chair and switchboard, was a small, empty room 'for future use'. The kitchen was even smaller, but somehow a second-hand dental chair had been manoeuvred into it. That, he told me conspiratorially, was for Africans.

"I can't see them in the main surgery - my patients wouldn't stand for it," he told me, "and we'll have to smuggle them in and out when no one's looking."

The surgery itself was impressive, gleaming with glass surfaces and chrome fittings, and Mr Potter, in his high-necked, short-sleeved white jacket, spent the morning showing me how to mix fillings, sterilise instruments and use the small switchboard in reception. At lunchtime he sent me off to buy myself a starched white nurse's uniform with a matching cap, together with a few magazines to keep waiting patients occupied, and by the afternoon we were all set to go. Mr Potter lolled in reception, paging through the new glossies, while I paged through his large, empty appointment book. Time crawled by. Once or twice we heard footsteps in the corridor outside and he darted into the surgery as I adjusted my face into what I thought was a businesslike but welcoming expression. Each time, the footsteps passed by. At last, much to Mr Potter's nervous relief, a woman clutching a handkerchief to her mouth pushed open the door and demanded instant attention. Mr Potter obliged, and during the next half an hour or so we proved our worth as a team. As he scrubbed his hands at the basin, I ushered the patient into the chair, clipped a paper towel around her neck, popped a pink tablet into the adjacent water glass and stood back, watching with some distaste as Mr Potter poked and probed inside her mouth. Now and then he asked for an instrument, first by name, then by description, and finally by pointing, and I handed it over with an air of professionalism. The sound of the drill had me chewing at the inside of my cheeks, but fortunately neither the patient nor Mr Potter seemed aware of my little phobia, and my first amalgam mix was masterly.

As the days went by it became clear that it was going to take longer than Mr Potter had anticipated to accumulate a regular clientele. I felt embarrassed for him when the few patients he did acquire asked for appointments and I opened an empty diary, so I began to fill in other names to make him seem busy. Unfortunately, I failed to mark which of these were genuine and which were not. Mr Potter was not best pleased, although I did point out to him that he had to wait around anyway.

"I suppose so," he admitted gloomily, "but it's not knowing whether next is next or whether what isn't next actually is or isn't that's getting me down."

I more or less understood exactly more or less what he meant.

He started to spend time out of the surgery, and I began to amuse myself by surreptitiously making up small batches of dental plaster in the kitchen and sculpting figures using his nifty dental implements. I was just beginning to show some promise when one afternoon my employer walked in on me. Shamefaced and apologetic, I cleared away the remains of my artwork, returned his instruments to their rightful place and was banished to the chair by the silent switchboard. I had been with the practice for three weeks when Mr Potter broke the news that we were to be joined by a doctor, a GP who would occupy the small, empty room. He, too, was freshly qualified, but he had several patients already, and Mr Potter hoped that this might benefit him. Dr Fellows, over six feet tall and broad shouldered, had a friendly, sunny disposition, and he dwarfed the room he had rented. He accepted me quite happily as his receptionist cum nurse until the matter of the specimen beaker. Needing to collect a sample of urine from a patient, he searched high and low for the receptacle, eventually chancing upon it on my desk filled with flowers. I still think it looked quite charming.

Although I could hold the fort as a receptionist and mix a mean filling, I wasn't much good with nervous patients, particularly where needles were involved. As the victim offered an arm or presented a rear for an injection, I had to look away, hissing through my teeth until I guessed the procedure was done. One day a middle-aged woman with time on her hands who paid well and promptly for Dr Fellows attentions, asked to have her ears pierced, something well outside the usual demands made on him. Wishing to do as good a job as he could, he nervously called me in to help, requesting I bring a tape measure and a pen. He measured one ear lobe carefully to find a central point, asked me to mark it, and then painstakingly matched the other side. Satisfied at last, he asked for the hypodermic syringe.

"I'm going to deaden your ear lobes," he told her, "so that you won't feel the needle going in."

Thus the poor woman endured her ear piercing twice over. I left after six months. I believe the doctor's practice grew and flourished, while the dentist turned to pig farming, hopefully through no fault of mine.

But I had earned my boat fare, and along with my chaperoning mother, two large tin trunks, and a head full of dreams and ambitions, I set sail on the *Capetown Castle*. It was 1952 and I had just turned seventeen.

PART TWO:
WHEN HARRY MET SHEILA

CHAPTER 1

18th November 1952
Dear Maggie
We're here!
The voyage aboard ship was glorious and I loved every minute. My poor mother is a bad sailor and was seasick for most of the time, so I was virtually left to myself. A nice, elderly German man who sat at our table spent each mealtime explaining the menu, recommending what went with what (and how to eat it), and tried to teach me a little about wine. I now feel a lot more sophisticated! The young officers flirted with me, and I got to know a frightfully British young man in his twenties with a frightfully British accent. We were quite friendly until one evening he invited me to his cabin for a nightcap, then retracted his offer when he asked me how old I was. Can't imagine why!

We are staying in a bed and breakfast place just off Baker Street, and I must confess I find it odd and a bit of a trial sharing, not only a room, but whole days and nights with my mother. Both of us are making an effort to be on our best behaviour, but it isn't easy, particularly as we are both stressed, I, because of the RADA audition next week, and she, not only because money is tight, but also I suspect she feels somewhat out of her depth and can't wait to get me sorted and return home.

Yesterday she took me shopping for sensible clothes for the winter to come ... I believe it's likely to be very cold and that it might even snow ... can't wait! A few weeks ago the clocks had been put back an hour, so now it gets dark surprisingly early. There was something very cosy about wandering through the West End of London at four o'clock in the afternoon and feeling it was night-time. I loved it, particularly as the Xmas lights and decorations can be seen at their magical best. Xmas makes much more sense here than in the baking African heat with its sweating Santas and limp cotton wool snow.

After a lot of tryings-on and a few disagreements, I am now the proud owner of my first ever winter coat. It's a sort of sludgy green, one of my favourite colours, and has long wide sleeves and a high collar that buttons up into a sort of muffler. A pair of lined black leather gloves came next, and then ... oh, the excitement ... a pair of winter boots! Also black leather, they have low heels and they zip up the side, reaching halfway up my calves. They're lined with sheepskin, and are so comfortable I was reluctant to take them off in the shop. It was decided I would need some really sensible shoes, and now, as well as the wonder boots, I have a pair of brown leather brogues with thick crêpe soles that make me walk noiselessly and feel inches taller. Next on the list was to be a hat of some sort, my mother insisting on a practical knitted pull-on thing, while I'd set my heart on a chic little black beret. A heated argument ensued with neither of us prepared to give way, until the saleslady, whose patience and temper were wearing thin, suggested we leave it for another day. Which we did.

That's all for now. Off to rehearse my pieces for next Wednesday. Wish me luck!

Love
Sheila

P.S. The most extraordinary thing. Yesterday we took a bus tour around the city just to get our bearings, so to speak. London is glorious and I can't wait to get to know it properly. Londoners must feel so grounded, being part of all this history. When the trip was over we stood in Trafalgar Square; it was late afternoon and the grey November day was chilly. The roaring traffic circled the square, groups of tourists wandered about, beady-eyed pigeons waddled, Nelson stood atop his column, and there and there and there and there were the four massive stone lions, and something came over me that's hard to describe: I felt at home. I really felt I'd come home.

2nd December 1952

Dear Maggie

Well, the audition's over. Now I have to wait a week or so to hear whether I've been accepted or not.

It was exciting and pretty scary. The Royal Academy of Dramatic Art isn't quite what I was expecting. I thought it would be a big, grand edifice set in grounds of some sort. Instead it turned out to be one of a terrace of similar buildings in a one-way street in Holborn. Admittedly it was old, and it did have a small flight of steps leading up to the door, but the entrance hall itself wasn't particularly imposing. I gave my name to a rather disinterested woman sitting at a table and was ushered into a waiting room.

There were nine others waiting to be seen, seven girls all about my age except for one who looked older (so I suppose I should call her a woman), and two boys (do you call seventeen-year-old boys, boys?) Anyway, no one seemed inclined to talk. Some were mouthing their lines, eyes tight shut, others stared vacantly at the floor or into space, some shifted in their chairs, but I'm sure we were all of us feeling much the same, confident yet uncertain, resolute yet faint-hearted, desperate to be there but just as desperate to be gone. Having sized up the competition I tried to relax and control my nerves with a blast of Teacher's recommended deep breathing, to no avail. One by one the candidates were summoned, and now and again a new one appeared.

At long last my name was called. I wiped my clammy palms on the new tartan skirt bought for the occasion and followed the young man across the hall and into a room opposite. Behind, a table, side by side, sat two women, and a man. All were of a certain age, all were trying to look kindly, and all were failing. The man rose and held out his hand.

"Miss Stifle," he said, attempting a smile.

"Steafel," I corrected, attempting one, too.

"So sorry, Miss Steafel. STEEfill," he repeated. "Unusual!"

He turned to his fellow adjudicators. They nodded and murmured in agreement.

"Not English, then?"

"No, I'm from South Africa."

"We know that, dear," said the larger of the two, picking up a sheet of paper and waving it at me. "He meant the name. Didn't you, Mr Crossbeam?"

Unusual name? HE can talk, I thought.

A momentary flash of irritation passed across Mr Crossbeam's face.

"That's right, I meant your name. STEEfill."

"Oh, it's Austrian."

"Austrian!" he repeated.

"Austrian!" repeated the women.

I nodded, and then decided that to establish a more personal bond between us would be no bad thing.

"It's Austrian," I continued, "for boot. A stievel is a boot in Austrian. A sort of Wellington boot. So I could always change my stage name to Sheila Wellington Boot!"

I waited for the laugh.

Instead, "Hmmm," rumbled Mr Crossbeam, exchanging 'looks' with the others as he resumed his seat.

"My name is Crossbeam," he said. "I am here to assess your acting ability. Mrs Jameson here," - the larger of the two woman waggled her pen at me – "will be listening out for your vocal potential, while Miss Pettigrew," - the other woman forced a narrow smile – "will be assessing movement. Now, Miss Steafel, what are you going to give us today?"

"I've chosen the maid Violet's speech from Terence Rattigan's THE WINSLOW BOY, where she rushes in and describes the scene in the court ..."

"Yes, yes, we know it well ..." said Mr Crossbeam.

"Only too well!" said one of the Mrs's.

"In your own time," said Mr Crossbeam.

I moved to the middle of the room and, with my back to the trio, flapped my hands vigorously as though I had just washed them and was trying to shake them dry. Oddly, I hadn't planned on doing this, but suddenly remembered seeing an actor at university perform this trick in the wings each night before he made his entrance, "in order," he expounded, "to relieve the tensions in my body". This must have lurked in my subconscious, waiting for an opportunity to surface at a time of need, and there it was! Having performed this ritual, I turned to face the adjudicators, took a deep breath, and launched into the rest of my life.

"Oh sir, oh sir, oh Miss Kate, what a shame you missed it ..."

I gave it my all; no, more than my all. I gave it my heart, my soul, my eyes, my teeth, and my liver. Every part of my body went into it. All except my feet. I seemed rooted to the spot. I had rehearsed the words, the meaning and the passion of the speech with Teacher, but we had never actually plotted 'moves' as such. Now here I was,

97

horribly aware that the lower part of my body was not cooperating. I tried a tentative step forward, but it seemed a pointless move so I retracted, and to make up the deficit began windmill-ing my arms and punching the air to emphasise my feelings. At last, at very last, I was done.

The Triumvirate were ominously silent. Then they lowered their heads and, after a short spate of mutterings, the Pettigrew (or it might have been the Jameson) spoke up.

Ye-e-es." Whichever she it was sounded equivocal. "Some nice things there. Your cockney went a bit Australian from time to time, but I expect that's due to your Austrian background." [Pardon??] "That will need sorting. By the way," she went on, "may I ask, do you have some sort of problem with your legs? You were very … what's the word …"

"Static," said Mr Crossbeam helpfully.

"Yes, I noticed that," agreed the other Mrs.

"Well, you could hardly HELP noticing it." There was acid in her voice. Then she addressed me again, "Well, do you?"

"No no, it's just that …" I had to think fast. "I felt Violet was so excited and so desperate to tell them exactly what had happened in court that she put all her energy into the words and it left her with no energy to move about, so … I didn't," I concluded lamely.

Another lowering of heads, another muttering, and a shuffling of papers as they resettled into their chairs.

"What else have you brought?" asked Mr Crossbeam.

"Portia's speech from Shakespeare's The Merchant of …"

"Oh God, not another Portia!" Mr Crossbeam was not best pleased. "I wish we'd never put it on the list," he grumbled. "Alright, off you go."

Alright, I thought, I'll show 'em. As I began the speech I took several swift steps forward, found I was too close to the table for all our comforts, and stepped back to base. Through the rest of my rendition I strode purposefully around the floor with now and then a small leap to emphasise a point. I felt empowered, my vocal energy matched my physicality, and I believed utterly in all I said. I finished and waited, and finally got my laugh.

"Nothing wrong with those legs, that's certain!" crowed one of the ladies.

"Pity the performances weren't reversed. I prefer my Portia static!" agreed the other, dabbing at her eyes with a handkerchief.

"Well, it certainly was different." Did I detect the ghost of a smile on

Mr Crossbeam's lips? He sat back in his chair. "You'll hear from us one way or another in about ten days or so. Thank you, Miss Steafel."

"Thank YOU, Mr Crossbeam."

"Crosby!"

Oh God!

"Crosby!"

I hope that won't count against me!

Ten days to wait! Sitting it out is going to be hell. Do I count today as day one, or day minus one?

Watch this space.

Love

Sheila

CHAPTER 2

Aunt Eileen and Uncle Bernard featured in a list of relatives and friends that my mother had brought with her to contact, either as a matter of familial duty or for help and advice. While we waited anxiously for the result of my audition she made a few phone calls, and Eileen invited us to join her and Bernard for lunch the following Sunday. Strictly speaking, Aunt Eileen wasn't an aunt, nor was she a blood relation. In the thirties she had married a distant cousin of mine, Bernard, on the rebound, I was told, from a love affair that had all the trappings of a Mills & Boon novel. In her late teens, strikingly pretty with curly auburn hair, she had fallen in love with the son of a well-to-do Jewish family, and he with her. For over a year their love had flourished secretly until it came to the notice of his family. They had other plans for his future that precluded marrying a girl from a socially inferior background, and further contact was forbidden. He acquiesced without protest, and, furious and broken-hearted, Eileen agreed almost at once to marry Bernard, who had been waiting in the wings. He was a bluff, plain-speaking North Countryman, kind-natured and generous, and well established as a travelling salesman with an office in Nottingham. He could barely believe his luck at marrying this beautiful young woman, and, constantly trying to please her, he indulged her every whim. But Eileen's affections could not be bought, and she spent the rest of their life together punishing him for not being the man she had loved and planned to marry. Eventually, Bernard conceded defeat, and taking the path of least resistance, spent his working weeks in Nottingham, returning to London each Friday evening to follow Eileen's strict weekend regime. On Sunday nights he would retreat back north, leaving her to the ministrations of her housekeeper and the blind affection of whichever dog she owned at the time.

When my mother and I arrived in Hendon for lunch that weekend, I couldn't have guessed that this would be the first of what was to become a regular obligation, and whenever I was in London it would be considered mandatory that I turn up on the

100

dot of twelve-thirty for lunch each Sunday. The menu never varied, roasted, boiled and baked by Amy, Eileen's Irish housekeeper of many a long year. Small, slight and sallow, Amy was a quiet creature with few friends. She had been taken on by Eileen shortly after her arrival in London, since when she had developed a fierce loyalty to her employer and a marked indifference to poor Bernard. At Eileen's behest, she served the Sunday luncheon at one o'clock sharp, and woe betide anyone, visitor or family, who for whatever reason missed this deadline. Eileen's disapproving silence would be palpable, casting an icy pall over the diners around the table, who, as soon as protocol allowed, fled.

Unsurprisingly Bernard and Eileen never had children, and when my mother arrived on the scene that afternoon with me in tow, Eileen saw a golden opportunity. Here, without the nuisance of giving birth or nurturing, was a ready-made surrogate daughter. She offered to watch over me, and if my mother agreed, she would make sure that she saw me on a regular basis (there went those Sundays!) and would keep her informed of anything she needed to know. That night in our digs in Baker Street we discussed Eileen's offer and decided that if I did get into RADA it would be a perfect arrangement, relieving my mother of the burden of worry, responsibility and, I daresay, guilt.

11th December 1952
Dear Maggie
A quick note to let you know The Letter with its distinctive logo arrived today. Don't know whether to be miserable or pleased, but at least the waiting's over.
I haven't been accepted into RADA, but they've offered me a three-month term in their preparatory academy, PARADA (Preparatory Academy), after which I can audition again. Knowing I'm not resident in this country, they've also offered me accommodation in their hostel, which is just opposite the school in Highgate.
Of course I'm going to accept both, and I'll just have to work double hard. I've got over the initial disappointment and am starting to get excited; butterflies in my stomach when I think about it. I'll be moving in next week, after which my mother will fly home.
More soon.
Love

Sheila
22nd December 1952
Dear Maggie

As you'll see by the address I am now resident in the hostel in one of the more salubrious suburbs of North London, and independent at last. Well, almost, because the place is run by a Matron. As you can imagine, this pleased my mother, but filled me with some trepidation until I met her. Carrie (she likes us to call her by her first name) is not at all what you would expect. She is in her thirties, stylish and friendly, and she managed to charm my mother and win me over at one and the same time.

The last term finished on Friday and I moved in on Sunday, by which time almost all the previous boarders had moved out. My mother, who was due to catch a flight home that afternoon, saw me in, and was in a remarkably good mood, looking more and more relieved by the minute. She refused to let me see her off at the airport, which was somewhat of a relief, as I still find the transport system confusing, and the cost of a taxi would have been prohibitive.

I've been allocated a room that I'll be sharing with another 'foreign' student when she arrives later on this month (the term begins on January 4th). It's on the second floor, and I know you'll think I'm pathetic but this has added to the thrill of it all. I've only ever lived in a bungalow, and the double storey houses I visited in Jo'burg (but never actually stayed in) belonged, along with the tennis courts and swimming pools, to my rich friends' families. Now that I have to climb flights of stairs to my bedroom I feel like one of the elite, all the more so because the hostel building itself is old and rather grand. I'll be here over the Xmas holiday, but, as I explained to Carrie, it's not a holiday that we, as a Jewish family, ever celebrated, so there's nothing for me to miss. Nevertheless, she's insisting we (she and I along with the other early arrivals) have Xmas lunch with her and 'a friend' (I'm guessing her boyfriend) in a local restaurant. She said she'd already booked it, and when I questioned her about the cost she told me she had put the plan to my mother before she left and she had readily paid up, saying how glad she was that I wouldn't be alone while others were out having fun.

Talking of money, before fleeing the country, it was with an audible sigh of relief that my mother handed over the reins of responsibility to my 'Aunt' Eileen, plus a cheque for my future keep. Eileen (more of her later) has taken on the role of guardian with zealous enthusiasm, and for the present I'm quite happy to fulfil the role *allotted me. However today, having undertaken the hazardous bus journey from Highgate to Hendon in order to collect my weekly allowance, much to my chagrin 'Aunty' insisted I give up a half crown piece and slot it into a specially purchased large, round earthenware moneybox with no visible means of withdrawal! This, I was informed, was a lesson in frugality, and the money would be saved until such time as she decided it was appropriate to be used on something worthwhile! A whole two and sixpence taken out of the ten pounds a week I have to live on! Not the greatest start to our future collaboration but there's nothing I can do about it, and telling my mother would only rock the boat. Or do I mean 'cradle'?*

Love
Sheila

Christmas passed, and I spent the days before the academy opened walking around Highgate in my new boots and cosy coat, venturing on tubes and buses while clutching an ever more dog-eared A to Z, and getting to know my fellow students staying at the hostel. The day before classes began my room-mate arrived, having travelled down on a coach from Edinburgh. Emma was blonde, about my height but athletic, and spoke with a soft Scottish accent. I loved the lilt of it but wondered if that was the reason she, rather like me, had been rejected by RADA and sent here to be taught to 'speak proper'.

By now I was getting into the routine of looking after myself, having to make my own bed, clean my room, and wash my own clothes. I felt rather proud of these achievements and wrote to tell my mother, expecting praise and admiration. Instead her reply was full of sympathy and commiseration, ending with a message from our housemaid.

"Katie says you shouldn't have to do your own clothes, and wants you to send your washing back here so that she can do it for you!"

Days in the academy were full and diverse and fulfilling, covering every aspect of the career in which I was determined to succeed. I bought a cheap tape recorder and sat alone in secluded corners whenever I could, listening to myself in order to hone my accent into acceptable 'Received Pronunciation'. There were lines to learn, routines to rehearse and lectures to attend, leaving little time to form friendships. Even my room-mate Emma, whom I seldom saw except at bedtimes when we were both too tired to say anything but 'goodnight', was almost a stranger.

CHAPTER 3

At the end of the three-month term at PARADA, we students were called in one by one to receive a verbal report from the head of the academy. Although I can't recall his name, I can still see him behind his desk: a small, thin man with small, thin hair, who tapped his teeth with a chewed yellow pencil. He gestured me to sit, then sighed heavily.

"Well, Miss Stayfill," - I winced but resisted correcting him; in fact, I was getting used to the odd permutations of my name, the most bizarre so far being Sheena Strepsil! - "what can I say?" He paused and tapped. "The thing is, you're not ... how can I put this? Usual. You don't fit into any category. You've certainly got something, otherwise you wouldn't be here, but at the moment it's hard to define what it is. Do you follow me?"

"No, not really," I replied, and meant it. What I DID know, or rather what I was becoming aware of, was that I felt awkward and out of place in a group and found it difficult to socialise. I was only comfortable and happy when I was at work, so to speak, and I can remember thinking, absurdly, that it would suit me best if I could be tidied away in a cupboard when the day's tuition was done, then taken out and shaken into shape ready for work the following morning.

The head put down his pencil and leaned forward.

"I have a strong feeling you will come into your own in your thirties. As a character actress. Nothing wrong with that. You'll need patience, and in the meantime any experience you gain in any ..." - he searched his mind for the word – "field ... yes, any field will benefit you when you ... if you ... eventually ..."

His voice trailed off. We sat and looked at one another. I wasn't sure whether to laugh or cry.

"So, the audition for RADA ...?"

"Oh, by all means go in for a re-audition, it can't do any harm. And, well, you never know, do you? It's a funny old business."

No, it wasn't, not remotely funny. I was seventeen and he was suggesting I put my life on hold for ... how many years? I got up and turned to go.

"By the way, that name of yours," he said. "Stayfill sounds

foreign, probably is. The British public are pretty jingoistic, you know? Favour their own? So I would change it if I were you. Eventually," he added helpfully.

I re-auditioned, but my second attempt to be accepted by the mother academy was equally unsuccessful, and it was suggested that I return to PARADA for yet another three-month stint and then try again. And on and on until I turned thirty? I didn't think so! I was hugely disappointed, but I was angry. How did the head have the right to judge my future? I'd show him he was wrong. I didn't divulge the news of my rejection to my mother or Aunt Eileen. Instead I begged the matron Carrie for her help in searching for an available place in some other drama school in London, and, after an exhaustive few days spent mostly on the telephone, I found a school with one vacancy left: the Webber Douglas in South Kensington. A hasty interview, a successful audition, and with the start of the term only days away, I presented Aunt Eileen with a fait accompli and phoned my mother. She was, of course, disappointed, and confused by my sudden change of schools. Once more she allowed Eileen to take charge, and it was arranged that I would stay with her in Hendon until I had found some digs nearer the school. Although I wasn't keen, there was for the moment no other practical solution, and so I moved my sparse belongings into Hendon.

Serendipitously Alida Barlow, also a new Webber Douglas student, was looking for someone to share her bedsitter, three blocks from the school. She was in her late teens, a tall, gangling American who was mad about all things Spanish. She wore ethnic skirts and espadrilles, scraped her long black hair away from her face into a bun at the nape of her neck, and peppered her speech with *olé*'s and *hola*'s. Fringed shawls were thrown over the back of anything that had a back, and our shared bedroom cum sitting room was dominated by a huge poster of a bullfighter, red cape flared, about to run a rampant bull through for the kill. During the holiday break in our first term we went for a week to Barcelona, my having read, on her recommendation, Hemingway's *Death in the Afternoon*. Of course we attended a bullfight, the sole objective of her visit, and she was almost orgasmic with pleasure and excitement. Catching her mood, I became almost as exhilarated by the smells, the noise and the atmosphere, and as she explained each moment, each pass and each gory detail, I cheered and shouted with the rest of them.

Back in London, each Saturday Alida would collect her weekly subsistence cheque from the post office, and I would bring out nine crisp pound notes, one ten shilling note and three half crowns. Pooling our resources, we did the weekly shop for our Saturday night treat, which never varied: a bottle of Martini mix, a jar of olives and a tin of Nescafé (which is where of necessity I learned to take my coffee as I do now, black and sugarless). We bought the ingredients for her special spaghetti sauce and a long, oblong, purple packet of dried spaghetti, along with an extravagant tub of grated Parmesan cheese. This shopping spree left us with just enough to pay for the frugal lunches and dinners we lived on during the rest of the week, and each Friday, when funds were drained and strained, I muttered silent imprecations against Aunt Eileen and her earthenware savings bank.

Tucker and his friend Dan had both won Fulbright Scholarships in America to continue their drama studies in London, and it was my good fortune to be a student at Webber Douglas at the same time. Both were dedicated Anglophiles and loved the school and its rather precious atmosphere, largely due to the staff who were mostly middle-aged or older; wonderful, memorable individuals whose ideas and techniques were worthwhile but somewhat dated. A few students in our class, including Dan and Tucker, were frustrated by the lack of tuition on film, television and contemporary theatre. Method acting was the thing in the States, and we young British students were keen to know more, so Dan suggested some of us get together for a couple of evenings a week to explore and study texts and improvise. He was staying close by the school in a rented room in a mews cottage that belonged to Peter B., one of the younger and more innovative lecturers. When the idea was put to Peter he was as enthusiastic as the rest of us, and agreed not only to host the evening sessions, but to supervise and direct them.

There were six of us in all: a Chilean named David; Leonard, an East Ender; Liza, a splendid Israeli actress; and Dan, Tucker and me. Those evening workshops were more useful and more illuminating than the days spent at the school, and after almost a full term of these seminars Peter decided to hire a small local theatre for three nights and direct us in a production of Henrik

Ibsen's *Ghosts*. Dan would play Oswald, I would play Regina and Tucker was to be assistant director. Dan was dark, good looking and intelligent, with a warm, vibrant voice, and I had watched for the slightest indication that I might get to know him better, but it never happened. It was while we were rehearsing *Ghosts* that I began to take notice of Tucker, who stood in for Peter when he was busy elsewhere. Tucker's general appearance was dishevelled, his straight, brown hair unruly, and his round-rimmed glasses constantly slipped down his nose, to be reinstated with an impatient flick of thumb and forefinger. He was bright and talented and fun. His profound passion was poetry, and his intelligent, sonorous readings taught me not only to appreciate it but also to love language. The more I got to know him, the more I liked and admired him, and the more time I wanted to spend with him.

Webber Douglas had an annual competition to find the best pupil in various categories, and I decided to try for the Margaret Rutherford Award for Comedy. At Tucker's suggestion I chose Sabina's opening speech in Thornton Wilder's *The Skin of Our Teeth*. It's addressed directly to the audience, and although we were told not to get any help in preparation, I persuaded Tucker to sit in front of me so that I could get used to talking to an audience. He sat there dutifully saying nothing, but I could tell by the odd wince, or the ghost of a smile, whether I was failing or succeeding, and much to our mutual delight I won the award. One of the judges was the actor cum songwriter Hubert Gregg, who sent me a note of congratulations, along with an invitation to visit him if I felt I needed advice about my future career. Naturally I was thrilled and accepted, but all I can remember of my visit is that he accompanied me as I sang some popular song or other, told me I had a useful voice, and then criticised the rather gaudy skirt I was wearing.

By now my friendship with Tucker was growing ever stronger. He was living in a bedsitter around the corner from mine, and I would visit him whenever I could and listen to him talk, strum his guitar or read poetry. One of our favourites, Edna St Vincent Millay's Recuerdo about a young couple crossing the Hudson on the Staten Island ferry, later became a symbol of our lasting friendship. We both enjoyed limericks hugely, and Tucker's fund of them, naughty and witty and sometimes wise, seemed endless. It became a standard joke between us that each time we parted company he would turn to go, then dart back and proclaim the first line of one limerick in particular, before disappearing.

"My dear Mrs Ormesby-Gore," and - slam! - the door would shut behind him, leaving the unfinished stanza hanging in the air. My frustration at not knowing the rest of it grew, but Tucker was intransigent, refusing disclosure.

One day I arrived at his digs just as the landlady was leaving, and taking advantage of the open door I ran up the stairs to his room. After a peremptory knock I burst in and found the room in darkness, curtains drawn. Tucker was standing with his arms stretched out in front of him.

"What on earth are you doing?" I asked, bewildered.

"Practising being blind," he said, with a short, dismissive laugh, crossing quickly to the window to pull the curtains open.

"Is it an acting exercise?" I asked, ready to join in.

"If only!" he exclaimed wryly, before throwing himself onto the bed, crossing his legs and folding his arms behind his head.

Unsure of what to do or say, I stood and watched him staring at the ceiling.

After what seemed an age, he said, "I guess I might as well tell you. Come and sit here." Swinging his legs over the side of the bed, he patted the space beside him. Then, in a matter of fact way, he told me that his sight had always been poor, and that his left eye had been badly damaged in a childhood accident. That eye was now all but useless, his other eye was deteriorating, and he was preparing himself for the worst scenario. Words of comfort seemed trite; instead, I hugged him hard and we sat side by side, close and silent.

"My dear Mrs Ormesby-Gore ..."

It was the last thing I had expected from him and I was taken aback. I searched his face, unsure of how to respond, and suddenly we began to laugh. We laughed so hard that we fell back on the bed, and then we laughed some more until, wheezing and panting and wiping away the tears, we sat back up again.

"Okay. Ready? Want the rest?" he asked, gasping for breath.

"You mean ... Mrs Ormesby?"

"Gore. Yes. The rest."

"You'd do this for me?"

"I'd do this for you," he said theatrically, "because you," - he placed a firm, dramatic hand on my shoulder – "are my true and trusted friend!"

He got to his feet, gave a slight bow, and was about to give me the complete and unabridged limerick when I yelped , "No!" and covered my ears with my hands.

"Good Heaven's, why ever not?" Tucker was totally baffled.

I said the first thing that came into my head. "Because it would ruin your exits!"

"Aha! True, dear lady, true!"

I'm still not quite sure why I stopped him. Perhaps my view of him had changed so suddenly and so radically, I wanted everything else to remain the same.

Whenever we could outside school hours, we met up to stroll through London in true tourist fashion, or take bus rides, getting acquainted with the city. We queued for cheap theatre tickets and viewed productions from up in the gods, sitting uncomfortably on seats you felt would tip you out if you leaned too far forward.

One evening, sitting in the Everyman cinema in Hampstead about to see *Les Enfants du Paradis*, Tucker began to quote some lines of verse that fitted exactly with the music playing in the auditorium.

"What's that?"

"… and the chimes remind us of sweet birds singing …"

He went on reciting, and the more I heard the more intrigued I became. When the piece ended I asked again.

"It's *Façade*," he told me. 'William Walton wrote the music and Edith Sitwell wrote the words. It's one of my favourite things. I've got a recording of the music back at the digs and I'll play it and read the poems to you. You'll love it!"

I did, and *Façade* was added to the list of requested readings in Tucker's room. Only I wanted to master this one myself, and in time. I got to know it almost by heart.

At school one day, Tucker told me he would be picking me up at six o'clock the following evening, and that I was to promise, on pain of death, to keep my eyes closed from the moment we left until he told me to open them.

"And no questions!"

As promised, he picked me up and, as promised, I did as I was

110

told, keeping my eyes tight shut as he led me onto a bus, off a bus, along pavements, down flights of stairs, and after some time into a noisy foyer, or so I assumed. He guided me up several levels of stairs and eventually sat me down.

"Can I open my eyes now?" I really hadn't cheated and I was beginning to feel impatient.

"No, not yet," he insisted. "I'll tell you when."

After an interminable wait, the noise in the auditorium died down, followed by a storm of applause.

"Now!"

I was sitting in an upper tier in the Royal Festival Hall. On stage was a large screen with an art deco design with the title 'FAÇADE' painted on it, while standing in front of it and about to take their places behind it were Dame Edith Sitwell and the tenor Peter Pears.

(Much later, when I had an established career, I was invited as a guest on the BBC's programme *Desert Island Discs*, and *Façade* was one of my choices. Jane Glover, then resident conductor of the Mozart Players, heard the broadcast and invited me to perform *Façade* in a recital at the Queen Elizabeth Hall. It is usually performed by two readers, one male and one female, and several actors were approached to join me, including Sir Michael Hordern, but he declined.

"It's not the first time I've turned it down," he told me. "John Gielgud and I were once asked if we would do it together and we both refused. Much too difficult!"

Eventually I performed the piece alone and, I hope, relatively well. At any rate, Tucker would have been pleased.)

Classes continued at Webber D. I moved out of Alida's bedsitter and into a basement flat in Chelsea with Liza, the Israeli student who shared our evening acting sessions. She was a large girl with a handsome face and thick, hennaed hair. Matriarchal, down to earth and forthright to the point of embarrassment, she spoke her mind loudly, indifferent to anyone around her. She was considered sexy, and it wasn't unusual for her to bring one of her many conquests home for a night of passion. The following morning I would hear her send them packing with an earful of invective. I pretended to be as worldly as she, laughing conspiratorially at the foibles of the male sex, although I was in fact still pretty naïve and fairly shocked at such goings on.

111

The room I occupied was cramped and dark and smelt of damp. It had a single window that looked out onto a small, walled-in, concrete yard that housed an old outdoor toilet. There was only space for a folding bed and a small side table, so my belongings were stored in the narrow corridor leading to the kitchen. Each night the bed would be opened out, and once extended it filled the space almost entirely. One night Tucker came to eat and to talk, staying longer than he intended. He missed his last bus home, so we agreed he might as well stay the night, and we pulled open the creaking, iron frame and made up the bed. Tucker, wearing his shorts and singlet, trampolined over to the other side, while I stood on my side and reached for the switch. As the light went out there was a hefty thump on the door.

"Good for you, Sheila!" came Liza's happy shout. "You teach him how!"

We tried to settle down for a night's sleep but were both restless, disturbingly aware of one another. After a while we cuddled up, and sleep solved any dilemma that may have lurked. The next morning after he had left, Liza came into the kitchen as I was making coffee.

"Well? Was it good? You have converted him?"

"What do you think?" I answered, with what I hoped was an enigmatic smile.

But I didn't like myself for the implied deception; I felt I had betrayed a trust. Tucker was my dearest friend and he was gay, and that was okay because I loved him for who he was, and as he was. I had never shared a bed before, and I confess I had wanted him to hold me, but nothing more. Anything else would have been too much to contemplate.

And so the course at Webber Douglas ended. Dan and Tucker left the term before I did, heading back to the States, and one blustery autumn afternoon I saw Tucker off at Waterloo station. The solitary bus ride back to South Kensington was bleak and lonely, and I felt wretched and bereft.

CHAPTER 4

It was my last term, and for the final concert I had been cast in three different scenes due to be performed in front of agents and casting directors. My parts were strong and I was sure I would find someone who would take me on. My mother arrived from South Africa to see me launched as a professional actress, and the day before the show I felt confident and happy ... and itchy. I had begun to itch. Angry red spots appeared on my chest and spread to my neck and arms. Somehow or other I had caught chickenpox. I was infectious and was bundled into an ambulance by two white-coated, masked medics and delivered to a local hospital. Instead of watching the fruition of two years' training in the dramatic arts, my mother sat dismally at my bedside in a children's quarantine ward wearing a gown and face mask. There was nothing for it but to sit it out, surrounded by fellow patients a third of my age or less, and note how much keener the young trainee doctors were to inspect the spots on my chest than on theirs.

Spotless, I returned to my digs, and my mother, anxious about my future prospects, left for home. I was frustrated and angry; it seemed to me that by missing the end of term shows the two-year training had come to nothing, and I would now have to find an agent through perseverance and a large amount of luck. I bought a copy of *Contacts*, "the essential handbook for everyone working in the entertainment industry", and set about writing letters randomly to any agent whose name appealed. The replies were sparse and mostly discouraging.

One of the pieces of information I had picked up from other students at Webber Douglas was about an agency in Soho that cast film extras, as well as small productions with budgets so low that no other agency would handle them. All you had to do was go along and sit in the crowded room until either you were called into the inner sanctum or sheer boredom and a numb backside propelled you back out into the street. However, this information came with a warning: Mr Marsh who ran this casting office had a slight squint in one eye, and it was often difficult to tell whether he was looking at you or the person sitting beside you. This caused a certain amount of confusion and disappointment.

One day, as I sat yet again in one of those interminable waiting sessions, Mr Marsh appeared at the door of his office, but instead of his usual perusal followed by confusion, he asked, "Anyone here want to go on a schools' tour of Wales? There's no money. The kids pay, you get paid; no kids, no pay. Anyone interested?"

There were five of us, all females who put up our hands.

"You might as well all come into the office and meet the writer, director and producer," he said, and he stood aside as we followed one another into his office. Instead of the anticipated team of three, one anxious-looking man in his mid-thirties rose from his chair.

"Here you are, Richard. Managed to get you five." And, with other things on his mind, Mr Marsh returned to his desk and his telephone.

The man Richard had written a half-hour version of *Hansel and Gretel*. He needed, he told us, two actresses - one to play Gretel, and one to double as The Witch and The Good Fairy. He had been hoping for an actor to play Hansel but was prepared to let a girl to take the role if one of us was willing. He gave each of us a script (handwritten in lined exercise books) and asked us to read for him to the accompaniment of Mr Marsh's voluble telephone dealings. We had a go at each part, trying to inject some life into the pedestrian dialogue.

Thank you, that didn't sound half bad," he declared, surprised and rather pleased with himself. "Wish I could take you all, but I can't, so it's you," pointing at me, "and you," pointing to the short, round girl with dark, bobbed hair, "and …" - his finger hovered between the three remaining actresses, then settled on the tall, expressionless blonde – "you."

The two rejects left and he explained he was not only the writer but also the producer of the project and he was planning to direct it, manage it on the road and drive the van in which the cast, the set and the props would travel. We were to rehearse for a week in the front room of his suburban house, during which time his wife would make our costumes, then we would set off on a tour of small village schools in Wales. He would pay us a small amount to cover expenses while we rehearsed, and once on the road he would pay for meals. Accommodation

114

would, he assured us, be provided by the generosity of the schools' staff, eager to instil a love of the arts in their young scholars. As for pay, after each performance he would collect a shilling from each child in the audience and we would split the takings.

Well, I had to start somewhere.

We rehearsed for the week, and then crammed ourselves and our minimal personal belongings into the battered old van, along with all the show's paraphernalia, and headed north to entertain the natives. Strapped to the roof were struts of Dexion, a sort of light-weight plastic, and at each venue we hauled them down and struggled to form the frame of a box, draping a square of canvas with a badly painted gingerbread house on it over the back end, and a red bedspread, 'the curtain', over the front. When the piece began, whoever was 'offstage' would give the spread a hefty tug, setting the Dexion frame rocking. Before each performance Richard would beg several slices of bread from the school kitchen, which we used as the crumbs that Hansel and Gretel left as a trail. These slices were often already buttered, and as the days went by the residue, insidious and rancid, slowly worked its way into the set, the costumes, and ultimately the van itself.

There was no mother in Richard's version of the story, and he had cast himself as The Father. The dark-haired actress who was a good bit shorter than me, played Hansel, I was cast as Gretel, and the large blonde, who was slow of speech and of a grumpy disposition, doubled as The Witch and The Good Fairy. Her fairy frock had been made out of a flesh-coloured petticoat sprayed with glitter and wired around the hem. As we travelled the glitter wore off, percolating (along with the butter) into every corner of the van. The wire in the hem became twisted and misshapen, as did the net-covered wire wings she wore strapped to her back. It was November and chilly, so to keep out the cold our Fairy often draped an acid green cardigan over her shoulders, covering the wings, and gaving her the appearance of a hunchback. This apparition terrified the children a great deal more than her depiction of the black dressing-gowned Witch.

We had been on the road for five days but it felt like fifty, and the prospect of two-and-a-half weeks more was depressing to contemplate. The plan that we would be accommodated singly at each venue by the generosity and goodwill of the teachers was failing. We had spent the first night in a cheap bed and breakfast on the outskirts of our village of attack. We three girls had squeezed into a single bedroom, drawing straws for sharing the narrow single bed or sleeping on a thin mattress on the floor, while Richard suffered the discomfort of a double room with bath. The next morning we played to our first school audience, a bunch of twenty or so noisy, disruptive kids averaging around nine years of age who showed little interest in the story, but found it hilarious to see a well-developed girl dressed as a boy in a pair of revealing lederhosen. At the end of the performance (if such it could be called), as we deconstructed our stage, our writer/ producer/ director/ manager/ driver walked along the restless rows collecting their money in a small canvas bag. The goodwill of the staff at that school, as well as the school we visited that afternoon, was in short supply, and we headed back to the bed and breakfast to rest up while Richard counted the meagre takings.

Our routine for the next three days never varied. We performed two shows a day, and although the reception by the pupils was invariably raucous and derisory, the staff were sometimes more magnanimous. I spent one night on the comfortable couch of a dinner lady whose husband, she told me, had abandoned her and run off with the wife of Jim, the local 'chippie'.

I didn't mind nearly as much as Jim did, poor fellow," she told me. "And his wife must have known he'd be devastated and close the shop down. Now we have to drive to the next village for our fish and chips. No consideration, some women!"

One night, when all else failed, we three spent the night in the van parked on the forecourt of a local pub. We huddled under coats alongside the tea chests of impedimenta, taking turns to curl up foetus-like on the marginally more comfortable, battered front seats. Richard had taken a room in the pub.

At a school in a village outside Abergavenny, the headmaster and his wife invited me to stay overnight in their small cottage. They were more than welcoming and invited me to share their evening meal. Curious to know more about me and my fellow travellers, I explained the hows and whys of our odd touring company, and when they began questioning me about my family background, I mentioned I was Jewish.

"We've never met anyone Jewish on a social level before," the wide-eyed headmaster admitted. "I would have expected someone more … how can I put this? Well, different, but you seem much the same, just like one of us, in fact."

They seemed surprised and delighted that I appeared unexceptional, and I felt it may have been only one small step for a nice Jewish girl, but was possibly a giant step for Judaism!

Early the following morning the headmaster left for work and I waited for the van to pick me up, but as time dragged on it was clear something was amiss. My two fellow actresses had spent the night at the house of one of the teachers, and the headmaster phoned to inform me that they, too, had been waiting and were now with him at the school. His wife drove me to join them, and by lunchtime it was clear that our writer/producer/ director/ manager/driver and his van had evaporated into thin air, as had our scant takings.

Exactly how we returned to London remains hazy. My recollection is that we phoned Actors' Equity and told them of our plight, whereupon they instantly wired us the money for our train fares, we all got home safe and sound, and Richard was blacklisted. The more probable version is that I phoned an anxious Aunt Eileen who listened, appalled, demanded to speak to the headmaster and asked him if he could possibly …

But no, I like my first version better.

CHAPTER 5

On my first day back at Mr Marsh's casting suite luck smiled on me: I landed my first (and last) job as a film extra. Luck, in fact, smiled on everyone in his waiting room that day, because Mr Otto Preminger needed at least a hundred peasants to witness the burning at the stake of Jean Seberg, starring in his film Saint Joan. Arriving at Pinewood Studios at seven o'clock the following morning, I joined the long queue of men and women waiting to be handed a bundle of clothes – "What size? Shoes? Next!" - and followed them into a marquee set up on the lot. I had been given a rough skirt, a shabby blouse and shawl, and a pair of shoes that pinched. Not fancying leaving my own clothes on the dress racks provided, I decided to wear them under my costume, and I abandoned the tight shoes in favour of my own, figuring it unlikely that my feet would be spotted in the crowd. Once changed, a megaphone instructed us to file past the make-up department - a trestle table overseen by several indifferent girls who dabbed fake dirt onto our faces and hands and checked our hair, handing out hats, scarves, or gel when considered appropriate. The stage itself was vast and the village square set was impressive, featuring an enormous pyramid of logs, in the centre of which stood a sturdy wooden beam.

Instructed by several harassed assistant directors clutching megaphones, we were marshalled here and herded there, and soon what I had anticipated would be an interesting and exciting day became a long, hot and uncomfortable slog, and boring beyond belief. From time to time, as the crane swung over our heads, I caught a glimpse of Mr Preminger sitting beside the camera with the operator. We had a short respite from the tedium when we broke for lunch and queued, yet again, to be handed an anonymous wrapped sandwich and a paper cup of something lukewarm and brown. By mid-afternoon I was exhausted, hungry and depressed and seriously contemplating slinking away and forfeiting the fee, when it was announced that Ms Seberg was about to take the place of her stand-in for the final rehearsal. As per instructions, we jeered as the cart in which she stood shackled, was dragged into the square, we jeered some more as she was manhandled out and tied to the stake, and we dutifully cheered as a flaming torch was held high for all to see and then lowered to light the pyre. But, to everyone's horror, instead of the anticipated gradual spread, a sudden blast of flames shot high into the air. The star screamed and collapsed, hanging limply on the post as fire hydrants foamed, and a crowd of technicians rushed to her aid. She was quickly carried off the set, conscious but in shock and, as far as I could tell, unhurt. A jabber of excitement was hastily silenced by the blast of a megaphone. We were to break, we were dismissed, and we were to return our costumes and collect our pay.

As I joined the final queue of the day, I noticed several extras abandon their positions as they neared the pay desk and rejoin the queue at the rear.

"What are they doing?" I asked the woman ahead of me.

"Collecting more time. We're paid depending on how long we've been here, so when those at the back of the queue reach the money they'll have earned a bit more."

"What about you?" I queried.

"Me?" She managed a weary smile. "I just want to get home. I've had enough."

Me too. It was definitely time to get an agent.

I set to work with a frenzy, writing shoals of letters to any and every agent in *Contacts* whether I had approached them before or not, and to my relief it paid off with three proffered appointments. At the end of two of these I was informed that they would "keep me in mind", but as luck would have it, during the third the agent's phone rang, and after a short conversation he replaced the receiver.

"Fancy a summer season in Blackpool Rep?" he asked. "They're looking for an assistant stage manager who can play small parts. You'd be on the standard Equity minimum plus subsistence. I take ten per cent. Starts next week. Interested?"

Was I?! At last I was on my way and, as it turned out, thrown in at the deep end.

I was offered shared accommodation in a flat that had been rented for the season by one of the two directors and his leading lady wife. It was rumoured that it had been vacated recently, by Diana Dors. Blackpool Rep was twinned with a small theatre in nearby St Anne's, so the company of actors would rehearse two plays with different casts concurrently, one for each theatre. Once the plays were up and running they would swap theatres midweek, which meant the summer visitors could see two plays a week, thus keeping the money rolling in. Meanwhile, the actors would be rehearsing the next couple of plays during the day, except, of course, on matinee afternoons.

I made lists of the props for each play, then scuttled around the town begging shops, hotels or any other likely source to lend the theatre whatever was needed, promising that whatever it was would be returned promptly and in pristine condition. Sometimes an object couldn't be found, and I would set about making it out of bits and pieces rooted out from the dusty collection of bric-a-brac crammed into the dark and daunting prop room under the stage.

Before each performance I set the props needed on stage and laid the rest on a prop table in the wings. If the script called for drinks I made up bottles of cold, weak tea for whiskey, water for gin and Ribena for wine. Tea or coffee had to be hot and ready on cue, and any food to be eaten during the play, after long discussions with fussy actors ("Crumbs will make me cough", "That would take too long to chew", or "I'm allergic to ..."), was prepared in an offstage room on a primitive gas ring.

From time to glorious time I appeared in a play, usually as the maid, and I would have to fit my stage managing chores around rehearsals and learn my lines on the wing. One never-to-be-forgotten day I was given my first comedy role, Poppy Dicky in the classic Ben Travers farce *Rookery Nook*. I struggled through rehearsals, not sure how to play the part, but on my first entrance something extraordinary happened and I connected with the audience, knowing instinctively how to control their laughter. Although I was unaware of it at the time, I had discovered my natural gift of timing.

During that energetic season in Blackpool and St Anne's I celebrated my twenty-first birthday, saw a ghost in the boiler room under the stage, became addicted to custard tarts, and fell asleep one afternoon, coming disastrously close to missing the train to St Anne's. I painted sets as well as a few portraits of company members, and had to inform my mother that, no, they wouldn't give me the day and evening performance off in order to keep a Jewish holiday. And on my return journey to London, as I sat on a train surrounded by a disparate collection of bags and baggage, I made up my mind that I had done my apprenticeship, and I would never stage manage again.

CHAPTER 6

The year or so that followed is a jumble of memories. My agent found me two repertory jobs: one in Lincoln, in which I was painfully miscast as the elder sister Meg, in a production of *Little Women*; and the other in Hunstanton, a small town on the Norfolk coast, where I did two consecutive productions – *The Hollow* by Agatha Christie and Terence Rattigan's *Separate Tables*, though I can't recall which part I played in either of them. Jobs came and went, and I packed and unpacked my belongings, moving into and out of several bedsitters and also Aunt Eileen's house in Hendon.

Whilst waiting for work I applied for regular jobs, but these never lasted long because if an interview or audition came up I would have to plead sickness or family problems, excuses that were acceptable only once. But I enjoyed these forays into the real world, probably because I knew they were temporary and saw them as opportunities to observe people. I temped as a filing clerk at Sainsbury's, where I was obliged to cover my hair with a net cap on the grounds of hygiene even though I worked in an office. I was employed as a sales assistant on the glove counter in the venerable old store Derry & Toms, but within an hour of starting I was called to the phone by a sour assistant. It was my agent who had lined up an interview for that afternoon. As there seemed little point in asking for time off, I made some lame excuse and left then and there. Possibly the most enjoyable job was serving on the chocolate counter in Piccadilly's Lyons Corner House. The white overalls and perky little hat were, I thought, quite fetching, and the chocolates were utterly delicious and irresistible. I was caught with a mouthful of coffee creams and sacked on the spot.

An advertisement for a night chef in a small bar off Kensington High Street caught my eye. Since the licensing laws forbade drinking alcohol after a certain time unless food was served with it, the owner had decided to legalise his after-hours drinking by serving steak sandwiches. The job didn't seem too onerous, although the working hours - 11 p.m. to 2 a.m. - were hard for me to sustain. I found it difficult to stay awake until I went to work, and getting to bed at three in the morning left me exhausted and useless the next day. Cooking steaks on a small electric grill in the windowless kitchenette behind the bar became uncomfortable and hot, while the fumes made my eyes water and the smoke made me choke. After five exhausting nights I handed in my notice on the grounds of imminent asphyxia and seriously considered becoming a vegetarian.

A more straightforward job was the answer, so, giving the number of the public telephone on the landing outside my room in the digs, I advertised my services in a local newsagent's window as a babysitter. I hadn't too long to wait before a well-spoken man rang in, asked a few questions, and arranged to send a taxi to pick me up in order to continue the interview in more depth. Half an hour later the cab arrived, and I found my potential employer sitting in the back. He was a middle-aged man with receding grey hair, and as he asked me a barrage of questions, he picked distractedly at the sleeve of his expensive coat. He was looking, he said, for someone rather special, and that the remuneration would be substantial. Was I a patient person? Had I dealt with awkward or unruly children? Was I physically strong enough to control a child with a fierce will of its own? To begin with I answered straightforwardly, but the more he probed the clearer it became that the young person he had in mind had difficulties that I was thoroughly unqualified to handle; it wasn't a babysitter he needed, it was a minder. I blamed my own inadequacies for declining his offer, and, apologising, slipped out of the taxi and scuttled to the newsagent's to remove my advert from the shilling-a-day display case.

I was determined, though, to stay in London and rejected the few offers made by my agent of interviews for plays in obscure provincial theatres or tours. She was losing patience with me. Then one rainy afternoon she sent me for an audition at London's Old Vic Theatre. It was to understudy two different parts in Shakespeare's *The Tempest*, and I could hardly believe it when they accepted me. The production was a late seventeenth-century adaptation of Shakespeare's play by the poet John Dryden, in which he had added characters as well as a few masques, augmenting the piece with incidental music composed by Purcell. This meant that two casts were called for: one of singers and the other, actors. It was opulent and stylish, with colourful baroque sets, extravagant costumes and Purcell's glorious score. During the play the plot would be suspended while soloists, small of neither musical nor physical stature, rendered the arias. For example, when Ariel, played by a slim, boyish actress, had finished her dialogue she would stand close to a large polystyrene rock, and as the orchestra played the introductory notes of the aria that followed she disappeared swiftly behind it. At once an identically dressed but much larger Ariel emerged from the other side, sang her piece, and to the thunder of appreciative applause stepped behind the rock, quickly replaced by the slimmer version, and the plot resumed.

The evening ended magnificently with a musical triumph, *The Masque of Neptune*, and whenever I could I would creep through the pass door at the side of the stage and tiptoe behind the audience to listen and watch. The short, stocky tenor singing the part of Neptune was blessed with a stunning voice but little stagecraft. His wig was bright red and styled like the knave in a pack of cards, and he was dressed in a baby blue mini-tunic edged with white marabou, making the skirt stand out like a ballet dancer's tutu. His sturdy legs were encased in a pair of gleaming white tights, and he sported Greek-style gold sandals, cross-gartered all the way up his chunky calves. As the finale commenced, Neptune descended jerkily from the heavens on a swaying cardboard cloud. Having recovered his balance, he was helped onto terra firma by three buxom handmaidens draped in filmy georgette, and strode purposefully to the front of the stage to perform his piece. This was the moment I waited for each night. Keeping a keen eye on the conductor, our tenor began to beat time to the music with his dazzlingly white, Lycra-sheathed sizable left big toe. Its flexibility was riveting, it was compelling, and it mesmerised the audience. The glorious music, the soaring voice and the splendid set and costumes faded into nothing as we marvelled at this remarkable feat of foot.

I was understudying Ariel as well as Dorinda, one of the characters not in Shakespeare's version. These two had several scenes together, which meant repeating each of them twice over during understudy rehearsals, which became thoroughly tedious. Understudying was not only frustrating but also boring beyond belief, and sitting backstage each night in the company of similarly bored and frustrated actors exacerbated the tedium.

Nevertheless, although I longed for the opportunity to appear in the play, it was something of a relief when that particular terror didn't materialise. On the plus side, I did learn to do cryptic crossword puzzles and knitted a couple of rather stylish sweaters, and at the end of the run I was delighted when the director, who had watched one or two of our rehearsals, offered me a small part in his next production.

CHAPTER 7

Landscape with Figures was the first, and probably the last, play written by the eminent photographer and film and theatre designer Sir Cecil Beaton. It concerned the artist Gainsborough, his life and times at home and ... well, not at home. It seems he frequented a euphemistically named Temple of Health, searching out young 'models' to sit for him, and the late, great actor/manager Sir Donald Wolfit had agreed to play the lead. Sir Cecil would, of course, design the sets and costumes, and when I realised I would have a costume especially created for me by the great man himself, I couldn't believe my luck. The play would tour the provinces for nine weeks and then, depending on the notices it received, open in London's West End.

There were three of us cast as the Temple's so-called 'demi-reps': myself, Paddy, a jolly Australian redhead, and a strikingly pretty young woman, Samantha Eggar. She was to play Emma Hart who later became the infamous Emma Hamilton, and, although our three parts were equally minimal, the fact that Samantha was playing someone with an historical pedigree set her apart. That wasn't all that set her apart, as she clearly wasn't relying on her weekly salary alone, and during the tour, while Paddy and I searched out the cheapest theatrical digs, Samantha would be staying in the same hotels as the leading actors. Often we would arrive at the stage door to find a pile of exciting looking packages waiting for her, and although we tried to appear indifferent we seethed with envy.

As is the way with most beginnings, the rehearsals started well enough, with everybody being excessively nice, treading carefully and sizing each other up. But, as the rehearsals progressed, it became clear that Sir Donald was having problems with the script. He would read out a line, pause, roll his eyes heavenward, and shake his leonine head.

"This," he would intone, "is not a good line. It is a line one cannot speak." Then he would add wearily, "No one could."

He would drop a heavy arm, allowing the offending pages to slip from his fingers, and Sir Cecil would visibly grind his teeth, while the director nervously tried to cajole the great man to "give the script a chance". In an attempt at diplomacy, the poor man would corral the two titans into a corner of the rehearsal room. There they would hiss at one another, only emerging once Sir Cecil had sourly agreed through gritted teeth to rewrite the offending lines. Each day the performance was repeated, at first about single lines, and then about whole scenes, and the cast would be sent away for an hour or more. When we reassembled, Sir Cecil's rewrites, amended by the other knight, would be handed out to us. The atmosphere was becoming tense, company spirit began to disintegrate, and the director was losing his grip. Then came the day when yet another batch of Sir Cecil's exacted rewrites arrived. Sir Donald glanced through them, flung them into the air with a derisory "Hah!" and, as the pages floated to the floor, marched out of the building. We were sent home. The next day, to everyone's relief, the great man turned up. He appeared to be in a calm, almost benevolent mood, but when Sir Cecil, smoking nervously, attempted to hand a clutch of rewritten rewrites over to him, Sir Donald moved him gently aside, and from his copious overcoat he took out a sheaf of paper.

"Listen to this!" he commanded, waving them above his head. "This, this is true dialogue."

Then, settling himself in a nearby chair, he proceeded to read out his own rewrites of the rewrites that Sir Cecil had already rewritten. As he lowered the last sheet, he smiled benignly while we waited, hardly daring to breathe, and the silence in the room was deafening.

At last the strangulated voice of the director called, "Take a break, everybody!" and with much scraping of chairs and embarrassed glances we shuffled off to congregate around the coffee-stained table where the hot water machine hissed and gurgled, trying to gauge the measure of the council of war at the other end of the room. It was a long wait and what was said we never discovered, but, despite the ostensibly insurmountable battle of personalities, the project resumed its lumbering course. And I still had my costume to look forward to.

I was summoned to Bermans the costumiers for my first fitting, to be overseen by Sir Cecil Beaton his very self. I was excited and nervous as I mounted the narrow staircase, for although I'd been in the rehearsal room with this legendary being he had never acknowledged my existence, so this was to be my first personal encounter. A woman on the first floor ushered me into a large curtained-off area full of rails of costumes and stacked high with cardboard boxes, and there, leaning casually against a mirrored wall, cashmere coat thrown casually over his shoulders, hat tipped at a rakish angle, and a long cigarette holder held between his even white teeth, was Sir Cecil Beaton CBE by Royal Appointment of HM the Queen. He looked at me blankly and with some distaste.

"Which one is this?" he asked of the three subservient young minions waiting to do his bidding. They looked at me with disdain. One of them took a step towards me.

"You're?"

"Sheila. Sheila Steafel," I managed, smiling weakly.

Another began to page through a pile of sketches lying on the seat of a nearby chair.

"No," said he, "no sketch. Now …"

He stood back, surveying me through narrowed eyes.

"Yellow," he said, followed with some irritation by, "Come along, get those clothes off."

I complied. Embarrassed and chilly, I stood there in bra and pants while another young man wrestled a roll of egg-yellow fabric down from an upper shelf, reeled off a length, and waited, poised for his next instruction.

"That will do."

It was snipped across with a large pair of scissors. Under the guidance of The Master's eloquent hand, the lackey wound the fabric around my waist, tying it into place with a measure of tape pulled from a handy spool. Then a second length of cloth was snipped off, tucked into the tape around my middle, thrown across one shoulder, around the back, under the other arm, and over the other shoulder. I couldn't move. I was trussed.

"Fine," said Sir Cecil. Then, standing back to survey his creation, he added, "Perhaps something around the waist?"

A bulging drawer was winched open, and after some scrabbling about a thickly padded, ridged cummerbund of worn gold lamé was produced and fastened around my middle. I looked as though I'd been clamped into an old pumpkin that had seen better days. Sir Cecil was contemplative, and at last he spoke.

"Makes her look rather shapeless. Paint black stripes down the seams, that'll help. Now, a little decorative something on the shoulder to finish it off?"

A trio of large red paste beads discarded from something else was retrieved from the floor and pinned into place.

"Headdress," ordered The Designer, and he pointed to a large glass jar on a nearby shelf that held a variety of feathers. An eager courtier leapt to attention and held it out to him. He picked out three and handed them to one of the other young assistants, watching apathetically as he tied them together with a small piece of something handy and held them against the back of my head.

"That'll do," said Sir Cecil. "Good afternoon." And out he swept.

As they struggled to extricate me from my yellow cocoon without disturbing it too much, my eyes pricked with tears of humiliation and disappointment. It hadn't quite been what I'd expected. Things didn't improve when I was given a tall, narrow, powdered wig to wear. It sat on top of my head, echoing the rather long oval of my face, so that I looked like a caricature of myself. As the tour progressed I managed to squash it down until it looked like a very messy bird's nest. As it happened, it didn't matter. The production had seemed doomed from the start and, like so many touring plays that were to come my way, once it had limped its weary way around the provinces it faded quietly away.

CHAPTER 8

Ridiculously dressed in a sari, a red spot in the middle of my forehead, I sit at the bar of Rahji's Kismet club and listen as a pair of feet descends the narrow stairs of the dark, cheaply decorated basement. Too nervous to meet the gaze of what I assume will be my very first customer, I fix my eyes on my tightly clasped hands. Rahji, a small, ferret-like Indian with small, dark eyes and a wide smile full of teeth, stands behind the bar. He is effusive.

"Welcome, welcome! Good to see you!"

"Evening, Rahji." The man takes the tall stool next to mine. I look up briefly.

"Want a drink?" he asks rather gruffly.

I'm about to refuse when I catch Rahji's eye, and his meaningful stare reminds me of our arrangement ("You ask for whiskey, I give you cold tea, we share the money"), so instead I smile cautiously at the man.

"Yes, why not? I'll have a small whiskey."

"Ice?"

"No thanks."

"Give the lady a small whiskey, and I'll have a double. No ice."

We sit in awkward silence, watching Rahji dispense our drinks. I sneak a sideways glance at the man beside me. Perhaps he's shy. I look harder. Nice looking, a strong face, about thirty-ish I'd say. An actor? Probably. After all, I was told this is somewhere actors hang out.

This was my first evening working at the Kismet. The day before I'd been sitting in the downstairs coffee bar of the Arts Theatre club in Great Newport Street, where out-of-work actors would accumulate on weekdays after signing on for the dole. Here the grapevine for rumours of possible jobs flourished, and as I gloomily stirred my coffee and waited for any crumb of information to fall my way, a tall, gaunt young man approached me.

"How're you doing, hen?"

I've always been a sucker for the lilt of a Scottish accent, so I smiled.

130

"At the moment I'm not."

"Aye, it's a lousy business. I'm Ian, by the way. Ian McNaughton."

"Sheila Steafel," I responded.

"Well listen, Sheila, there's a very nice club opposite here called the Kismet. Do you know it?"

"No." I must have looked a bit wary.

"Don't get me wrong!" he laughed. "It's a really nice little curry house run by Rahji and his Irish wife Monica. He's just got a club licence so that folk can drink in there for longer, and just now they're looking for someone to take coats, serve curries, and be nice to the customers."

"How nice is nice?"

"Well, they got rid of the last girl they employed because she was nicer than nice. They want someone reliable and sensible."

"How do you know I'm any of those?"

He smiled. "I'm a great judge of character. Anyway, there it is. If you're interested, go over and see them."

So I did, and they took me on. At the time I was once again temporarily boarding in Hendon, and, knowing Aunt Eileen wouldn't approve of my working in a club, I told her I'd taken a job as a waitress in a nice little restaurant in the West End. She seldom moved outside her social circle of rubbers of bridge and dog charities, so it was highly unlikely she would search me out. And now here I was, gainfully employed for the first time in three months.

Rahji places the drinks on the bar in front of us. "Two whiskies, no ice," he announces. "Oh, let me introduce you. This is my new hostess. Her name is Sheila."

"Nice to meet you," the man says. "I'm Harry. Harry Corbett. Harry H. to my friends."

"What does the H stand for?" I ask.

"You remember the film about Harvey, the invisible rabbit?"

I nod.

"Well, I had to think of something that would make people realise I didn't earn a living sticking my hand up a glove puppet. Hence my invisible difference!"

As we chat on, I have the strangest feeling that somehow I recognise him, that I know him. It is something indefinable, and it makes my heart beat faster.

That night Harry stayed drinking with friends, and later on

Ian, who, as it turned out, was one of Harry's closest friends, arrived and gave me a friendly thumbs up. As I served curries and drinks to other customers, I was aware that Harry was watching me, and I found myself searching him out. That night, as I lay wide awake in Aunt Eileen's spare bedroom, I replayed my encounter with Harry over and over again in my mind. Had he really been interested in me? Perhaps I'd misread the signs. I wondered if I would see him again, and so hoped I would, but the next evening there was no sign of him, and by ten o'clock I was disappointed, gloomy and angry with myself for seeing possibilities where none existed. Why did I never learn? Well, at least, I told myself, it was only my pride that was hurt, and I hadn't made a fool of myself.

When I got back to Hendon that night I was tired and miserable and wanted to get to bed, but, unusually, Aunt Eileen was waiting up for me. She sat on the hard-cushioned sofa in the sitting room under the light of a single standard lamp, upright and prim in dressing gown and curlers.

"Are you going to be back this late every night?" she asked, tight lipped.

"Well, the restaurant is in the West End," I reminded her, "and people come in after they've been to the theatre. It's all part of the job," adding for good measure, "and the late night buses are few and far between."

"I see. Well, I may not be your mother, but if I was …"

"Look, I'm really tired," I said, trying to curb her attempt at surrogate parenting. "Can we talk about it in the morning?"

She hesitated for a moment. "Alright, tomorrow."

"Goodnight, then."

As I turned to go, "What's that on your forehead?" she asked.

My hand flew up to the smudge of red I'd inexpertly tried to rub off as I changed out of Mrs Rahji's sari. I clicked my tongue in mock irritation.

"Must be lipstick," I said. "It's the restaurant owner. When I left tonight she insisted on giving me a kiss on the forehead! She's Polish and very effusive. And she's the boss!"

I lay in bed, still thinking of the previous evening with Harry, but this time searching for anything I might have said or done to have changed his mind about me. Yet why should it bother me so much? After all, I had spent the shortest time with him and knew nothing about him; he may well be happily married with several kids, and the other evening nothing more than a harmless flirtation. Married? With a groan, I knew this was going to be a long, sleepless night.

"I know this sounds ridiculous, but I've missed you!"

It was approximately ten minutes after opening time and I was sitting at the bar in the Kismet with a glass of fake whiskey in front of me and Harry H. beside me. I wondered whether I had heard him correctly.

"What did you say?"

"I said I've missed you!"

"But we only met the night before last!" I tried to sound flippant, but the blood was singing in my ears. "Mind you, I did look out for you last night." I said, realising as I did so that this was a giveaway on my part. Harry was quick to take it up.

"So you missed me too?"

"Well ..." I could feel myself blushing, and took a quick sip of Rahji's watery drink.

Harry went on, "I had to go to a read-through last night. I'm an actor ... or did you know?"

"I guessed."

"Some friends wanted my opinion on a production they're planning," he told me. "Joan Littlewood and Gerry Raffles. They run Theatre Workshop ..."

Theatre Workshop! A few weeks back I had auditioned for Joan Littlewood, one of the most innovative and celebrated theatre directors in the UK, and I desperately wanted to join her company of actors. Walking out onto the stage of the Theatre Royal in Stratford, I had faced a darkened, empty auditorium.

"Hello there!" a voice had called out from the gloom. "Who are you?"

"Sheila Steafel."

"Okay, Sheila. I'm Joan. I want you to imagine you're the only person here, that you've come out onto the stage, no audience, no one else in the building, and I want you to enjoy yourself, improvise, show off. Anything. Off you go."

I can't remember what I did, but by the time she called out, "Thank you," adding, "Very well done!" I had felt that maybe, just maybe, I stood a chance.

"Theatre Workshop?" I said excitedly to Harry. "I auditioned for them a few weeks ago!"

"Really?" It was as though he hadn't heard me. "Now, you and I have got at least twenty-four hours of catching up to do. Cheers!" And he knocked back his double whiskey, no ice.

Harry turned up at the club almost every night and stayed late, watching me, calling me over if he thought a customer was paying me too much attention, and dutifully downing a dishful of curry. His arrival became the focus of my evening, and I felt safe and happy under his guardianship. I thought about him almost all the time, and there was no doubting it, I was head over heels in love. During the brief spells that we snatched together when my duties as a hostess allowed, I learned a little of his history. He was born in Rangoon in Burma in nineteen twenty-five, his father had been an army officer, his mother had died when he was three and he had been sent to Manchester to be brought up by an aunt. He had joined the Royal Marines, which explained his slightly rolling, and, to me, endearing walk. During his stint in the Navy he had contracted malaria and suffered shell shock, the results of which I was to witness during our time together. As for his career, he was well on his way up the ladder, a serious talent to be reckoned with.

Most of the members of the Kismet seemed to be actors, some of them well-known celebrities, but not to me. Working out of London I hadn't watched much television, and having little money to spare meant that visits to the theatre were out of my range. Patrick McGoohan was intrigued that I didn't know who or what he was, and, lingering over his meal, he kept me chatting whenever I served him. Harry had left earlier, and, having established that I was living in an area 'on his way home', there seemed no reason to refuse when Mr McG offered me a lift in his taxi. I realised my folly as he moved closer to me in the cab, put a casual arm around my shoulders and nudged me towards him. How could I have been so naïve? As we chatted inanities I felt stupid and angry for accepting the lift more or less under false pretences. No doubt he would assume that I was a calculating manipulator, but that couldn't be helped. As we approached the house I pointed it out.

"This is really kind of you," I said. "My aunt will be so pleased to see a cab draw up. She really worries about my coming back this late on public transport."

"Your aunt?" The hand on my shoulder slackened.

"Yes. She'll be waiting up for me." I slid from under his arm, picked up my bag and opened the door of the now stationary taxi. "Would you like to come in for a coffee or something? I know she'd be thrilled to meet you."

The response was a low and, fortunately, indecipherable growl. The door slammed shut and the taxi accelerated away.

"Thank you so much for the ride, much appreciated!" I said softly, not wanting to disturb the neighbours.

CHAPTER 9

I could scarcely believe my luck when one morning I had an unexpected phone call from Gerry Raffles. He and Joan had enjoyed my audition and were offering me the opportunity to join Theatre Workshop! I couldn't wait for Harry to arrive at the club that night to tell him the thrilling news, but when I did his response was not at all what I had expected. His face grew dark.

"What's wrong?" I asked apprehensively. "Is there a problem? I thought you'd be pleased!"

"Let's sit down," he said, and taking my hand he drew me to a table in a quiet corner.

"Look, there's something I haven't told you." He paused, then choosing his words carefully he continued, "I don't live alone."

"You mean you ..." I stopped, uncertain, dreading what he might say.

"I don't live alone," he repeated almost angrily, then continued in a softer voice, "What I'm trying to tell you is that I live with someone. Her name is Avis Bunnage and she's a member of the company."

"The company?" My mouth was dry.

"Theatre Workshop. She's an actress with Theatre Workshop. That's where I met her."

He paused, waiting, but all I could do was sit very still.

"I should have told you before. I'm so very sorry. Avis and I have been together for quite a while now," he went on. "She's older than me, and in a way I suppose she's been a sort of mother figure ... the mother I never had."

My life was falling apart.

"Why didn't you tell me?" was all I could manage.

"I wanted to clear the air first, tell her about us when the time was right, and then leave. I thought doing it that way round would avoid hurting you. Like ..." he shrugged, "like this."

Glancing round the room at the few early punters tippling and joking together I thought what a miserable looking pair we made. Harry reached for my hand. 'You must know how I feel about you, and it was stupid and selfish of me not to tell you, but now it's out in the open it's a huge relief. I just hope you understand. I will tell her about us soon, I promise. Trust me?'

I nodded hesitantly.

"Forgive me?"

Once again I nodded, and the tears I had been holding back spilled down my cheeks. Releasing my hand, he moved his chair closer and leaned towards me.

"There's something I have to ask you to do for me, and I know it won't be easy." He paused, watching me carefully

"What's that?" I asked, fumbling in my pocket for a tissue.

"It's about Gerry's offer. You'll have to turn it down. You can't join Theatre Workshop."

I looked at him aghast.

"But it's what I've been waiting for! It's such a great opportunity, and I may never ..."

"Don't you see?" he broke in. "It would put me in an impossible position, having you both in the same company, working together. It would be awkward and difficult not only for you, but also for ..." He stopped.

"Avis." I finished his sentence for him.

A kaleidoscope of thoughts spun around my head. I felt almost dizzy. It was a long moment before Harry spoke again.

"You'll have to choose. It's me, or Theatre Workshop."

I looked at the man beside me and there was no question of choice. After all, other career opportunities were bound to come my way in the future. (Indeed they did, and almost invariably my heart would rule my head and I would yet again lose my foothold on the ladder to success).

I had been working at the club for three weeks when Rahji informed me that the following Saturday was designated a colour festival in the Indian calendar and he was planning a special evening.

"I want you should wear a very fancy sari," he informed me, "and you will stay late, yes?"

When I mentioned this to Harry he wasn't best pleased.

"There's bound to be too much drinking and a lot of testosterone around. I think I should stick around, don't you?"

"It'll go on until quite late," I told him.

"Well, in that case ...' - he paused for a moment – "why don't I book us into a nearby hotel for the night?"

I caught my breath, for although I was all of twenty-two and

I'd had several struggles in the backs of cars and, indeed, in bedrooms other than my own, I was still a virgin. Then I nodded, aware of the giant step I was agreeing to and shocked at my easy acquiescence.

I told my aunt that my fictitious restaurant proprietor was planning a birthday bash, convincing her that it would be wise for me to spend the night with a fellow waitress who lived in town rather than try to get back in the early hours of Sunday morning, and on the Saturday in question, excited and apprehensive, I set off, clutching my overnight bag. The club was crowded and noisy, and while I took orders and served drinks, to the dismay of guests who knew him as an actor of some repute, Harry checked in hats and coats and handed out numbered tickets. Later in the evening, ignoring the joshing, he carried trays and dispensed drinks, keeping an eye on me to make sure I remained unmolested. The evening was long and tiring, and at 2 a.m., footsore and weary, we left the Kismet and walked towards the small hotel on the corner of Leicester Square where Harry had booked a double room for the night. I slipped the cheap gold wedding band I'd purchased that week in Woolworths onto the fourth finger of my left hand.

The hotel foyer was bare and brown.

"Breakfast in your room, sir?" the tired hotel clerk queried.

"Yes," said Harry, "we'll have tea ..."

"No, coffee. I don't drink tea."

Harry tried to bypass the interruption.

"Juice."

"Can I have prunes?"

"Prunes?"

"Yes, prunes. I like prunes."

Harry's discomfort was beginning to show, as was the clerk's interest.

"Why don't we just have the continental breakfast ... for a change?" he added pointedly.

"Oh, continental! Lovely!"

"Continental it is then, sir and ... madam?" He just managed to tip the word into a question. Then, as we walked towards the lift, he called out, "When would you both like it? Breakfast, that is."

"I'll ring down," Harry answered, as the lift doors opened and I hurried in, hoping the clerk couldn't tell from the back of my head that I was blushing.

The room was small, the double bed didn't look big enough for two, and I hurried into the bathroom, closing the door behind me. A peremptory shower, then out of my small overnight bag I took the short, frilly, watermelon-pink nylon nightie I had kept aside, but had never had occasion to wear. Until now. I checked myself in the mirror above the washbasin and then nervously opened the door. Harry was sitting on the side of the bed wearing only his shorts. He smiled and held out his hand, but I stayed where I was.

"Harry, there's something I ought to tell you. I haven't done this before."

He dropped his hand, clearly amazed.

"Are you telling me …?"

"This is my first time."

"Come here," he said.

As I reached him he took my hand in his, sat me down beside him and then, kissing me gently, turned out the bedside lamp. For a long while we lay quietly together side by side holding hands, talking a little and dozing from time to time. As the dawn light crept into the room Harry turned on his side to look at me.

Are you sure?" he asked me.

"Yes, I'm sure."

We left the hotel without room service, breakfasting instead at a formica-topped table in the Golden Egg opposite. I felt mature and safe and cared for, and happier than I could ever remember. Harry leaned back in his chair and looked at me for a long moment.

"Well," he said matter-of-factly, "I'm just going to have to marry you."

At Harry's behest I moved out of Aunt Eileen's house and into a tiny bedsitter in South Kensington. The space had been cunningly split in two lengthwise, one side converted into the narrowest of bathrooms, while the other housed a single bed, a tall wardrobe with shelves and a mirror, and a small table. On it sat a Baby Belling cooker, and under it lurked a minuscule and fairly useless fridge. In spite of its limited size, I placed as many of my paintings as I could on all the available surfaces, much to the loud disapproval of the housekeeper, a small, unpleasant creature in her forties, whose face wore a permanent expression of reproof.

"They're obscene," she muttered acidly one day as she collected the weekly rent, her eyes fixed on a particular sketch I had done of Harry as he lay stretched out on the narrow bed. "And don't think," she added, "that I don't know what nastiness goes on in here of an afternoon."

At the time Harry was rehearsing a play for television, and on most late afternoons he would come to my digs. I would walk down the Old Brompton Road to meet him, and my heart would leap with pleasure as he came towards me. We'd hug, then walk back to the cramped little haven and make love. Later, as Harry dozed, I would prepare some simple dish on the valiant little cooker and wait for him to surface. One afternoon, as Harry lay dozing, the housekeeper beat on the door with her fists.

"I know what you're doing in there," she shouted, her voice high and penetrating, "and it's disgusting! You should be ashamed of yourselves. Do you hear?"

We heard, as did everyone in the vicinity. The following week I moved out and into yet another bedsitter located not too far away, but considerably larger and more spacious.

At that time an incident occurred that turned out to be significant of things to come. I had gone to meet Harry as usual, and happened to be wearing a pair of figure-hugging imitation leopard-skin trousers; not, I admit, in the best sartorial taste, but much in fashion at the time. As I walked towards him his expression changed from pleasure to one of shock and embarrassment. He grabbed my arm and hurried me away saying, "You can't possibly wear those! People will look at you!"

I laughed it off, but it was an indication of something that would contribute towards our eventual break-up: Harry's almost Victorian attitude towards women.

CHAPTER 10

Ibrahim, the Indian chef at the Kismet club, had taken a shine to Harry and me as a couple. He was a man somewhere in his forties, happily married he assured us, with two teenage sons and a six-year-old daughter.

"I am very lucky man," he told us. "Lovely house, wife very good woman, children good also. You must come to visit, yes? I will cook for you very special curry, my own very special. You come, yes?"

He had watched with delight as our relationship blossomed, nodding and smiling his approval whenever he caught our eye, and handing us small parcels of neatly wrapped leftovers as he finished his nightly shifts. He repeated his invitation to visit him so frequently that it became clear we would have to accept.

"But I really don't want to go," I said testily.

"Why not? You like him, don't you?"

"Of course I do! But Sunday's our only day together."

"It's only for lunch," Harry said. "He just wants to show off his house and his family. And he wants to cook up something amazing especially for us. Anyway," he added with finality, "we've got to go because he'd be so disappointed."

Sunday was chilly and dull with clouds that promised rain. We had been given directions, and as we trudged through the east of the city I became ever more apprehensive. The street name printed in pencil on the back of a Kismet bill heralded a row of shabby terraced houses. Weeds had nudged their way through the cracked cement stairs of number twenty-three, and as we were about to climb them a voice from below called, "Harry! Sheila! Down here!"

Ibrahim emerged from the flight of basement steps, panting slightly from the effort.

"You are most welcome. Please to follow me!" Gesturing for us to join him, he turned and led us into the narrow, gloomy yard below and through a glass-panelled wooden door. The room we stood in was bare of furnishings apart from a large, low, round table covered with a brightly patterned cloth. Four small, faded rugs had been placed around the table, and a neat row of cushions sat along one of the walls. A small woman dressed in a sari stood by the door opposite, while at her side a young girl wearing a pretty, flowered dress tried to hide in the folds of her mother's costume.

"This my wife, Sumitra!" Ibrahim announced.

She folded her hands in front of her face and briefly bowed her head.

"And my lovely little daughter Kaya. Come!" He gestured to her to join him, but she retreated even further behind her mother's skirt. "She very shy but she very clever ... like school very much. Eh? Kaya? You like school?" Giggling, the child nodded. "Come then, come and meet my friends,"

Quickly, she ran across to him, hiding her face as she hugged his knees.

"Now you meet my boys," said Ibrahim as he stroked her hair. "My boys here today instead of football practice because I say more important you meet my friends. My boys, they love football. You think they go to school for to learn classes? No, they go for to learn football!"

Pleased with his joke, he threw his head back and laughed heartily, displaying a set of uneven teeth and a glint of gold I had never noticed before.

"Oh, that's a shame, you really shouldn't have made them ..."

I tried to catch Harry's eye to stop him, but fortunately Ibrahim wasn't listening.

"Tadi, Som, come!" he called through the open door. "My friends they are waiting! Come now! Come!"

The second command held a tinge of impatience, and almost immediately two young boys shuffled into the room, eyes down, mouths sullen. They were close in age, I guessed eleven or twelve, and both wore football shirts and boots, in protest, I surmised, at their father's ruling. As Ibrahim introduced them they looked at us briefly, muttered a few unintelligible words, and were waved towards the cushions on the floor.

"Now please," - he gestured for us to sit on the rugs at the table - "you sit, then you eat. Sumitra!"

With a polite nod in our direction his wife left the room, her daughter scampering after her as we took our allocated places. I could think of nothing to say, and neither, it seemed, could Harry, clearly upset by the ordered presence of the two sons. We sat in awkward silence, Ibrahim standing over us beaming his pleasure, his boys glowering from the sidelines.

"Have you lived here long?" Harry eventually dredged up the question.

"Oh, long time, long time now," Ibrahim replied.

More silence.

"How old is your daughter?" I asked, realising as I spoke that he had already told us she was six.

"Six years, she is six," he volunteered enthusiastically.

Silence fell again.

Then, just as Harry drew breath to speak, Ibrahim's wife called from what I supposed was the kitchen.

"My wife Sumitra, she calls me," he said needlessly, and he left the room. Harry grasped the opportunity.

"Look, lads, I know how you must feel. I love football, and I don't blame you. I'm really sorry your father …"

The two stared at him stoically, but Harry was undeterred.

"The last thing …"

Just then, Ibrahim's wife emerged holding a steaming saucepan of rice. Behind her came the young daughter with two empty bowls and two spoons, followed by Ibrahim carrying a covered metal bowl I recognised as coming from the kitchen in the club. He placed it reverentially on the table beside the rice and, lifting the lid, sniffed it appreciatively. I sniffed and glanced at Harry. The familiar aroma told us that the contents, too, had come from the kitchen in the club.

"Not too much for me, please, Ibrahim!" I exclaimed, but he had already filled the bowls. He handed them to us, and then joined his wife and daughter standing on the other side of the table.

"Aren't you eating with us?" Harry asked, surprised.

"No, no. You eat, you eat," said Ibrahim, with an encouraging smile.

We struggled valiantly to swallow the food set before us, our five observers hungrily following each spoonful from bowl to mouth and back again. Pleading a small appetite, I managed what I could, and once the bowls were cleared and compliments and thanks delivered, we hurried home through the drizzle.

As we sat on the bus homeward bound, Harry asked, "Do you know what the worst thing was?"

"You mean apart from those poor kids being made to miss their football practice?"

"Yes. Apart from that," he said, "the worst thing was that we were probably eating their dinner, and they'll go hungry tonight."

CHAPTER 11

"Sorry, kid," Harry said bleakly, pushing his bowl aside, "you're going to have to get yourself another job or I'll die of curry poisoning."

It so happened that a friend of mine, also a struggling actress, had found a job as an usherette at the Players, the Old Time Victorian Music Hall theatre under the Arches in Charing Cross, and the following week I started working there too. Joining the staff was like becoming a member of a large family, and I loved it. What's more, because my father had sung music hall songs around the house when I was growing up I felt quite at home in the genre. Each night, once the curtain had gone up, I would stand at the back of the auditorium and watch wonderful actors like Hattie Jacques and Clive Dunn perform their solo pieces accompanied by the pianist, who sat at a grand piano that stood just below the stage, level with the audience. Don Gemmel, who ran the Players alongside his partner Reggie Woolley, was usually 'chairman'. He sat on the side of the stage at a table covered with a chenille cloth, holding a pewter mug of beer in one hand and a gavel in the other. Keeping the audience in check, he announced each act with an astonishing display of verbal gymnastics, heralding the performer with a great thwack on a conveniently placed wooden block.

Don and Reggie were the antithesis of one another. Don was a large, barrel-chested, avuncular Scot who generated warmth and a kindly authority. Reggie, half British, half Chinese, was slim, elegant and lithe, and looked for all the world like one of his Mandarin antecedents. He had always worn a carefully trimmed moustache and goatee beard, which, along with his head of abundant silky hair, had turned a sleek silver. Reggie was a theatre designer of repute, not only for his work at the Players but also at several opera houses at home and abroad. The Players, though, was his first love. Here he directed actors, produced Victorian plays and pantomimes and, with his extraordinary talent for lighting and hand-painted sets, created remarkable depth and atmosphere on the surprisingly small stage. Artistic down to his marrow, Reggie did not suffer fools gladly. He was impatient, easily riled, and could be cuttingly acid-tongued when he chose. At these times it was Don alone, with his matter-of-fact wisdom, who could persuade Reggie into a calmer frame of mind. As far as the presentation of the artistes was concerned, Reggie ruled, and woe betide the performer who crossed him. They would find their costumes less than flattering, and the lighting they appeared in atmospheric to the point of obscurity. He had a small and exclusive coterie of actresses whom he liked and whose talents he rated, referring to them affectionately as his 'sluts', and I'm proud to say that I eventually qualified as one.

I was told that once a song had been performed by a particular artiste it became theirs … until, I supposed, they relinquished it through boredom or demise. Desperate to swap my job from usherette to performer, I decided that rather than looking for any old obscure song I would search for one I could perform as an appropriate character, making it particular to me. The Players' archives were kept in a small, cramped loft in the eaves over the office, and I wheedled the elderly secretary to let me to look through them. It was bursting with stacks of yellowing, dog-eared music manuscripts, and after much searching I came across a saucy Marie Lloyd song entitled 'When I Take My Morning Promenade'. Having established that no one claimed it, I learned it with the help of a pianist friend. Actors seldom dressed up for the Players' auditions, and I decided that Reggie and Don might take more notice of me if I wore a costume of some sort. The Wardrobe Master, also a Reggie, was a delightful man with a wry sense of humour who over the years became a devoted friend, and I persuaded him to lend me a cheeky Victorian outfit for the occasion. Thus it was that one Tuesday afternoon at approximately 3.40 p.m., wearing a tightly laced corset, a pair of high buttoned boots and a large ostrich-feathered hat, I performed for the first time on the Players Theatre stage. And at approximately 3.47 p.m. - or possibly 3.48 - Don Gemmel and Reggie Woolley offered me a spot in the following week's 'bill'.

I couldn't wait to tell Harry my thrilling news, but when I did his response threw me completely.

"Don't expect me to come and watch you. I'll just wait for you in the foyer after the show."

We were sitting in a coffee bar in the Earl's Court Road, a

stone's throw from my relatively new accommodation. I was speechless.

"Look," he said, making an effort to sound reasonable, "I don't mind you doing this sort of thing for the time being, but I don't want to be married to an actress. I don't want you going away on tours or filming with a bunch of blokes who'll be after only one thing ..."

"But Harry, I wouldn't ..."

"No, listen!" His temper was rising. "Whatever you say, that sort of thing is on the cards, and I haven't the time or energy to waste worrying about you. I want a proper wife who'll look after me and my children, and let me get on with my job."

It seemed so unfair! I wanted a future with Harry, but why should I have to make a choice? As always when confronted with a crisis, I sat still and silent, my heart beating fast.

Harry spoke again, his tone kinder.

"If it makes you happy and it'll help you to get this acting bug out of your system, then go ahead for now."

Well, I reasoned, I couldn't entirely blame him. After all, he had met me as a waitress-cum-hostess, and now I was an usherette. There was no reason for him to think that I had any particular talent, nor have any idea of the dedication and aspirations that had motivated me ever since I could remember. For the moment, then, I would hold my peace, convinced that in time Harry would get used to the idea of having an actress wife. And of course, when he realised how talented I was, he'd be proud and delighted, we'd become a celebrated showbiz couple, and might even start a theatre dynasty of our own!

And so each night, when the show was over, Harry waited for me, sitting in the foyer on the elegant red plush sofa opposite the box office. Reggie clearly found him attractive and would invariably be sitting beside him, keeping him company. One night Reggie suggested that the three of us might go out for dinner after the show. Harry agreed, and a few nights later we were sitting at a table in L'Escargot, a fashionable restaurant in Soho. I wasn't used to dining in smart, sophisticated restaurants, let alone drinking wine, and I was well out of my depth. The two of them chatted animatedly, taking very little notice of me, and I felt awkward and uncomfortable as I ate my way through the rich menu, washing it down with great swallows of wine. By the end of the main course I had begun to feel distinctly queasy, and excusing myself, made my slow, dizzy way to the ladies room. Ten minutes later I returned to the table feeling better, older and wiser. Needless to say, they had barely noticed my absence. That was the first of many dinners 'à trois' and L'Escargot became one of our favourite haunts. And once I had learned to avoid the pitfalls of over-ordering and careless imbibing, I felt quite the happy sophisticate.

Having worked at the Players, you were secure in the knowledge that when jobs elsewhere were thin on the ground you would always be welcomed back. My first weeks there extended into months, and continued intermittently over the years as my career see-sawed on its unpredictable way. I continued to search for obscure music hall songs and create funny, eccentric characters to perform them, but my most popular creation was Popsy Wopsy. I performed her four or five times on *The Good Old Days*, and I almost always ended my one-woman shows with her 'by popular request'. A chorus girl of dubious talent, Popsy sang under the note and danced behind the beat. Usually an accompanist will follow the singer, but with Popsy there was nothing to follow, and more time was spent rehearsing them to allow her to get it wrong, than assisting her to get it right. She was choreographed (oh yes she was!) by a talented friend, Doreen Hermitage, and I simply did what she devised, but on the wrong beat. Leonard Sachs' *The Good Old Days*' splendidly alliterative chairman, introduced her as his 'niece' with an insinuating leer, and dispensed reassurance by blowing encouraging kisses.

When I performed her in cabaret at a Lord's Taverners charity dinner, a reluctant young Prince Charles was prevailed upon to join us on stage and sing the Players' finale, 'Dear Old Pals'. A photograph in the next day's press shows me, in full Popsy gear, hooked onto the crook of one of the bemused Prince's arms, while a lustily singing Anita Harris in black tie and tails hangs onto his other arm. Bernard Cribbins in a battered top hat is beside me, but you'd be hard pushed to recognise the figure standing next to Anita. Wearing full pantomime prince regalia, a fetching blond wig and the shortest of tunics, and revealing a pair of legs that would shame any principal boy, is Hugh Laurie!

Without the grounding I received at the Players, I doubt I would have had the confidence or ability to perform my own one-woman shows in the years to come.

CHAPTER 12

I avoided questioning Harry about Avis and waited for him to make his own decision as to when he would tell her about us. It wasn't easy. Then one night as he walked me from the Players to Charing Cross station, he told me almost casually that the following morning he would be moving in with his friend Ian, and he thought we should start looking for a flat. He didn't mention Avis and I preferred not to ask, but I felt a surge of mixed emotions, relief and elation, as well as guilt and a heartfelt sympathy for the woman he was leaving.

Over the next few days we scoured the property adverts in local papers for accommodation within our … well, within Harry's price range, preferably in south-west London, and at last, after a depressing week, we found a cheap furnished flat at the top of a sadly neglected terraced house in Oakley Street, Chelsea. The landlady, an elderly, untidy woman with large breasts and a wide smile, shepherded us up three flights of stairs with carved wooden banisters, paused for breath, pointed to a steep, narrow set of steps, and led us up to a small square landing. A small table supported a small, twin-plated electric hob, under which lurked a small oven, and beside it sat a small, insignificant fridge.

"This," she announced, "is the rather small kitchen."

Another short flight to the right of this rather small kitchen took us (singly) up to the bathroom with its old tub supported on four clawed feet, a toilet, and a washbasin doubling as a sink. Somehow it had miraculously been accommodated under the sloping attic roof with its weathered dormer window. The rest of the flat comprised a modest sitting room with surprisingly large sash windows that overlooked the street, and a small back bedroom furnished with two single beds and a large wardrobe, leaving no space for anything more. Although it was in need of more than a little renovation, the rent was inarguably reasonable, and two days later we moved in. We unpacked our scant belongings, pushed the beds together and began to 'live in sin', for this was the fifties, when such flouting of convention was considered either shameful or intrepid.

Above: Number 74. Eda on the verandah holding me,
Brian and Sanna standing in front of 'my wall'

Right: The fairy dance that won me a diploma aged five

Aged nine, holding Kewpie

Eda and Harold's wedding picture

A.P. and Emily (Grampa and Granny)

Granny in her Women's
Auxilliary uniform with Uncle
Geoff in his Irish Regiment
uniform.

Above: Me with the family and 'flu on my batmitzvah

Left: With Tucker, feeding the pigeons in Trafalgar Square.

My father Harold as King Gama in PRINCESS IDA

Right: Harry H., 1963

Above: Harry with Eda on the verandah of number 74 on his way home from filming in Kenya

Right: With Oliver Reed in the Granada series IT'S DARK OUTSIDE

Left: THE FROSTREPORT
team: (clockwise)
Ronnie Corbett, John Cleese,
Ronnie Barker, Julie Felix,
David Frost, me.

Below: In bed with the
two Ronnies
(THE FROST REPORT)

Above: With Kenneth Horne
(HORNE A'PLENTY, 1968)

Right: With Michael Hordern
(SOME WILL SOME WON'T, 1968)

My portrait of Sir Michael
Hordern in The Garrick Club

With Bernard Cribbins in the
ABC series CRIBBINS, 1970

THE GHOSTS OF MOTLEY HALL,
1977. Me, Nicholas le Prevost,
Freddie Jones, Arthur English, and
Sean Flanagan

Mistress Quickly, RSC production of THE
MERRY WIVES OF WONDSOR, 1985

Left:
The 'OKLAHOMA
hat'. THE LATE
SHEILA STEAFEL
(1st one woman
show, 1981,
Edinburgh Festival)

Below: Harpo Marx
(A DAY IN
HOLLYWOOD A
NIGHT IN THE
UKRAINE, 1979)

Aged two with my father's shoe.
(Programme cover of the ill-fated
STEAFEL VARIATIONS)

Cabaret at a LORD'S TAVERNERS charity ball.
Bernard Cribbins, self, Prince Charles, Anita Harris,
and Hugh (The Legs) Laurie!

A visit to Johannesburg, 1990

I had written to my mother and told Aunt Eileen that I had found myself another more suitable bedsitter, and as they had become used to my shifting digs quite regularly it raised no questions. However, it wasn't long, before Eileen phoned to announce that she thought she ought to see my new premises and report her findings to my mother.

"I'll pop in tomorrow first thing," she said with finality.

At the time Harry was filming, and the following morning once he'd left I pushed the two beds apart, made one up, hiding the second pillow in the wardrobe, and covered the other with a blanket, trying to make it look unused. Aunt Eileen would, I hoped, refrain from opening any drawers and cupboards, but just in case I hid Harry's bathroom paraphernalia and other masculine bits and pieces in a carrier bag on his side of the wardrobe, then pushed over the few clothes he had hanging there and covered them with a sheet. If by any unfortunate chance she did discover them, I had my reply ready.

"Oh, those!" I would say. "They were left by the landlady. She's promised to move them. Hope she does, they're really in the way!"

Aunt Eileen was not the most reliable nor the most patient of drivers. On one occassion she had reversed out of her driveway so fast she had smacked smartly into a neighbour's car parked opposite, and because of the steep camber of the road the vehicle had keeled over onto its side. There it lay, rocking gently, as Eileen tucked a hasty note of apology under the windscreen wiper and continued on her reckless way. On the morning of her planned visit, she had spent an hour-and-a-half wending her haphazard way from Hendon to Chelsea, and by the time she arrived she was flustered and fed up and in no mood to linger. Having negotiated the Everest of the stairs, she accepted the proffered mug of tea, glanced cursorily around the premises and, expressing the hope that I would be happy in my new surroundings, hurried away, leaving the tea untouched except for a token smudge of lipstick on the rim.

Harry was earning quite well, and made it clear that unless I wanted to there was no need for me to look for a part-time job. For the moment that was fine by me; I loved 'playing house' and Harry was content. We had no social life to speak of because Harry was reluctant for me to socialise with his male friends, although I do remember being taken to a party in Notting Hill

Gate where a group of struggling, unknown actors had formed a sort of 'clan'. Amongst them were Sean Connery, Milo O'Shea, and Ian McShane. During the evening Harry didn't let me out of his sight.

"It's not you I don't trust," he told me, "it's them!"

I still had an agent, but my career, such as it was, seemed to be on hold. Nevertheless, I was confident that something would eventually turn up, and I was certain that I could persuade Harry to accept my future as an actress.

From time to time I was offered another opportunity to perform in a bill at the Players, and as before, Harry would pick me up. When he couldn't, having promised I wouldn't be seduced into accepting a drink from an over-friendly member of the audience - or fellow actor, come to that - I would take the tube back to Sloane Square and hurry home.

One evening, as I was leaving the theatre, Cynthia, who ran the box office, handed me a note. "Clement Freud left this for you," she told me.

He wrote that he had enjoyed my act, and invited me to go and see him at his newly formed club/restaurant above the Royal Court Theatre, leaving me his secretary's phone number. When I got back I showed the note to Harry.

"Isn't it great?" I said excitedly. "I'll give him a ring tomorrow."

Harry was not pleased.

"What does he mean, 'act'? I mean, what does he expect you to do? After all, you're not a cabaret artiste, are you? You don't exactly have an act, do you?"

Truth to tell, I was uncertain myself. I had no idea what I could possibly do in a club apart from being some sort of hostess. Nevertheless, the famed Clement Freud had summoned me, and who was I to refuse?

Not wanting to crush my good spirits, Harry agreed to my going to meet him.

"But I'm coming with you," he added firmly. "Okay?"

A quick phone call arranged an appointment, and the following Friday afternoon at four o'clock found a nervous and excited me, accompanied by a profoundly sceptical and disgruntled Harry, mounting the stairs to Clement Freud's new and exclusive club premises. I pushed open a pair of swing doors, and followed by Harry, entered a dimly lit, low-ceilinged supper room. Mr Freud was seated at one of the lamp-lit tables, and as we entered he rose and came swiftly towards us. Instead of the greeting I had expected, he walked straight past me, and putting a firm hand on Harry's chest, pushed him backwards and out through the swing doors.

"You can't come in here like that," he said. "You're not wearing a tie!"

I should have left then and there, but of course I didn't. Harry should have thumped him then and there, but he was either too taken aback or he didn't want to ruin my chances. But it was clear from the brief, awkward conversation that followed as I sat opposite Clement Freud, that whatever plans he'd had in mind for me had soured, and we parted icily. I found Harry pacing the pavement outside the theatre, seething with rage.

"Well?" he managed, with admirable self-control.

"It didn't work out. He asked a few questions but eventually told me I wasn't experienced enough."

Harry was triumphant.

"I knew it!" he said. "I warned you. It wasn't a job he had in mind. He fancies you! You know what would've happened if I hadn't gone with you, don't you?"

"Nothing would've happened!" I protested. "I can look after myself ..."

But Harry wasn't listening.

"Sheila, the world is full of blokes like him who think actresses are easy lays. Now do you understand why I don't want you to go into show business?"

Many years later I met Clement Freud at a charity event. By then Harry and I were divorced, and, for want of anything else to say, I asked if he remembered the afternoon when he had thrown the now national treasure Harry H. Corbett out of his club.

"Of course I remember," he said, in his inimitably supercilious way. "He wasn't wearing a tie."

CHAPTER 13

We lived in Oakley Street for about six months. While Harry was busy rehearsing or filming, I would spend the days cleaning, shopping and preparing our evening meal, and considering the limitations of our 'small' kitchen I managed to produce some reasonably tasty fare. When time lay heavy I'd sit and sketch or paint, and each early evening I would heave open one of the heavy sash windows, lean out as far as I could, and watch for Harry as he turned the corner from the King's Road into Oakley Street.

One morning, as he prepared to leave, Harry said, "Do you know what I'd really fancy for dinner tonight? Steak tartare."

"How do you make it?" I asked, never having heard of it.

"No idea! I had it in a restaurant once with Joan and Gerry, and it was great. Look it up." And he was gone.

I headed for a bookshop in the King's Road and, after some searching in the cookery section, found the recipe and surreptitiously copied down the ingredients. Raw beef? I couldn't believe it, but there it was. I headed for the butcher's.

"I'd like a pound of your best fillet steak," I announced.

He smiled his approval and placed a lump of meat on his carving board.

How thick?" he asked.

Oh, it doesn't really matter. I want you to mince it."

The butcher looked at me in disbelief.

"This is our finest fillet steak and you want me to ... mince it?" He could barely bring himself to say the words.

"Yes," I said hesitantly, beginning to doubt the dastardly deed myself. Sensing this, the butcher quickly replaced the fillet under the glass counter and reached for a dish of meat that was already minced.

"No, this is what you want!" he said, as though he was humouring a child. "First-rate, quality mince, lovely stuff! This'll do you!"

"No it won't," I countered, sounding exactly like the child he'd taken me for.

This is ridiculous, I thought.

154

Pulling myself up to my full five foot three-and-a-half, I drew on my Webber Douglas training, breathed deeply from my diaphragm, and said in what I hoped was a deep, calm and authoritative voice, "Thank you for your advice, but I'll take a pound of the fillet, please. Minced," adding unnecessarily, "if you wouldn't mind." A risky request to a man with a meat cleaver in his hand.

Back at the flat I laid out all my purchases on the table: a pound of alarmingly expensive minced steak, two eggs, one onion, a bunch of parsley, a jar of capers, a tin of anchovies, a bottle of Worcestershire sauce and, from my store cupboard, a bottle of olive oil. According to the recipe, nothing was to be cooked; everything was simply chopped and laid out on a plate in separate piles, with mustard, salt and pepper to hand so that "the diner can prepare his steak to his own taste". That afternoon I prepared everything as instructed, laid it all out on the small all-purpose table, now covered with a clean white cloth, and surveyed the result with scepticism. Surely this couldn't be the dish Harry craved? The ingredients on display looked exactly what they were: a meal waiting to be cooked. On impulse, I scooped everything into a large bowl, gave it a thorough mixing, then poured the oil into a frying pan and waited to serve my lord and master with the most expensive hamburgers he was ever likely to consume. Still in the first flush of love, Harry forgave me and said they were quite delicious, although his enthusiasm had a somewhat hollow ring.

By this time Bernard and Eileen had moved out of Hendon and purchased a large, elegant, converted stable in Hampstead. Every Friday evening, at the designated time of 6 p.m., Bernard would arrive from his office in Nottingham, where, during the week, he dispensed orders of inferior lace products. His weekend routine was planned, executed like an army manoeuvre, and never varied. Having greeted his wife with a civil, "Hello, I'm back," he would relieve the car of its stack of parcels: items either Eileen had requested during the week by phone, or comestible treats that he had purchased (she had a very sweet tooth) to win her favour. A quick, predictable snack, an early night in his own small room, and then the liberating joy of his Saturday programme: a manicure, a shave and hair trim in a smart hotel in Marble Arch, followed by a light lunch in the snack bar and an hour or so in the lounge watching football

(Eileen would countenance no television set or unsightly aerial on the roof of her converted stable). Then back to Hampstead to change into a sober suit and escort Eileen to The Cosmos, the only local restaurant they favoured. They always ordered the same dishes: Eileen, Vienna schnitzel; Bernard, the chicken (without the bacon, please). If his order happened to arrive with the recalcitrant bacon on it, he would wave it back to the kitchen, where I assume the waiter, unimpressed by the dietary laws imposed by Judaism, flipped the offending rasher off and returned the plate to the now conscience-free Bernard.

Having asked if I could bring a friend that I wanted them to meet, I introduced Harry to Eileen and Bernard at one of her ritual Sunday lunches. She seemed impressed by him, not only because he was at his most charming, but because she had never met what she called a 'real' actor before, and he answered her naïve questioning with serious consideration. Bernard, on the other hand, ignored us all, folding himself away on the sitting room sofa in a cocoon of Sunday papers.

I had written to my parents, telling them about Harry and our plans to marry, and although they received a glowing report from Eileen their response was much as I had predicted: they were disappointed by my alliance with a non-Jew. No one in either of my parents' families, she wrote, had ever married 'out', and although in the Jewish religion the bloodline is carried on through the mother (which meant any children would be Jewish by birth) it seemed a hard pill for them to swallow. My mother suggested I return to Johannesburg to discuss matters, hoping, I suppose, to talk me out of the proposed marriage, but when I showed the letter to Harry he smiled broadly and gave me a hug.

"It's not a problem," he said. "I'll convert."

"You mean, you'll become Jewish?"

"I think that's what conversion means," he said wryly.

"But it takes … I don't know how long, and you'd have to study with a rabbi and take some sort of exam and eventually have some sort of … bar mitzvah, I suppose."

"Well, it doesn't sound too painful, particularly as there's one essential that's already been done. Good thing I was born in a country with a hot climate!"

I was delighted and relieved, but not altogether surprised at the ease with which Harry agreed to convert. I had sensed that my being Jewish was part of his attraction to me. He seemed to identify with Jews, and he even looked Jewish himself. I remember going with him into a Jewish restaurant in Golders Green. The waiter handed him a menu, and then set about explaining the dishes to me!

Harry's proffered conversion somewhat pacified my parents. They were relieved that he had so readily agreed to adopt the Jewish faith, but were not overjoyed, particularly my father, who accepted my glowing description of Harry and my confidence in our prospects for the future with a certain amount of mistrust. It was arranged that Harry would attend the required sessions of instruction with the rabbi of a Liberal synagogue in St John's Wood, while I travelled back to South Africa to persuade my parents that Harry would be an ideal son-in-law.

I found it difficult being back at number 74 with its uncomfortable memories, and sleeping in the selfsame room, the bedding now faded, startled awake each morning at six when the sudden bright sunshine blared in making it impossible to stay in bed. The house had shrunk, the furniture seemed tasteless and ugly, and the glorious Steinway upright piano's dignified ebony satin finish, had mutated into a mock mahogany-grained glossy veneer; I could have wept.

Two weeks later as I was packing in preparation for returning to London, my mother came into my bedroom holding something behind her back and told me she had a surprise for me.

"I saw this in Sadie's shop," she said, "and I thought it would make a lovely wedding dress for you!"

Sadie, a friend of my mother's, owned a dress shop in the centre of town. She was short and dumpy, but what she lacked in stature she made up for with her stylish couture. Always immaculately coiffed and made up, she was never seen in the same outfit twice, and my mother, convinced that Sadie wore her own stock which she later replaced on the rails, took to inspecting the collars of any garment she was offered for the telltale signs of prior wear. From time to time my mother had sent me the odd (and sometimes very odd!) garment from Sadie's that she thought would suit me. Now she held up a simple, oyster-coloured, sleeveless chiffon frock with a hint of gold where the light caught it.

"What do you think?"

She waited for my enthusiastic response, but I was nonplussed. Although I hadn't given it much thought, this certainly wasn't like anything I might have anticipated wearing for the occasion.

I hesitated, before saying the most obvious thing I could think of.

"But it's short!"

"Very fashionable. You'll look lovely in it. Come try it on."

It seemed churlish to refuse. I looked at myself in the wardrobe mirror. The discreet party dress fitted perfectly and yes, it looked fine, but nothing about it said this is a special dress for a special day. My mother's whole being was willing me to like it.

"Thanks, mom, it looks lovely. It'll do fine," I lied.

My father, who disliked and avoided family get-togethers, had declined to attend our wedding, while my mother, as a matter of reluctant expediency, arranged to stay with Eileen and Bernard. She had never liked or felt comfortable with Eileen, ever since the occasion when, without thinking, she had thrown a sweet paper out of the window of Eileen's car. Eileen had braked with a severe jolt and threatened to send my mother off to search out the offending wrapper. Mortified, but never one to assert herself, my mother held her tongue.

She watched the wedding plans develop with a more and more jaundiced eye, finding herself pushed into the background and made to feel less and less like the mother of the bride. She did, however, manage one minor triumph. One day, as we three sat together in the lounge, Eileen explained to my mother how careful she had been to make me aware of the value of money and the virtues of saving. With a flourish she produced the abominated earthenware moneybox (with no visible means of access) that had appeared each week when she doled out my allowance, insisting I slot in a reluctant half-crown piece.

Nursing it in her lap, she announced, "I told her these savings would come in handy when she really needed them."

It seemed becoming a bride met the requirements.

"Now," she went on, "she can open a nice little post office account of her own."

What followed was a revelation, not only to me but also, judging from her stunned silence, to Aunt Eileen. I had never before heard my mother, usually so self-efacing, speak with such force.

"That money was meant for her keep. Good God, Sheila was old enough to look after herself and certainly old enough to manage her own affairs. Now she's about to become a married woman and you have the gall to treat her as though she were a child, and what is even more galling, especially to me, YOUR child! A post office account?" My mother turned to me. "What would you like to do with the money?"

I took a deep breath and looked from one to the other.

"I'd like," I said, "to buy a really good set of dictionaries."

"They're yours. Now go and find something we can use to break this thing open," she instructed, "and bring some newspaper."

A moment later I returned clutching a hammer I had found in a scullery drawer and an old copy of *The Jewish Chronicle*. My mother spread the newspaper in the empty hearth and placed the moneybox on it.

"Go ahead," she said, and sat back in her chair. The two women watched as I tightened my grip on the hammer and brought it down with a satisfying crack, shattering the hated orb into shards that rocked gently amongst the salvaged silver coins.

CHAPTER 14

And so it was that, after living together for just over a year, Harry H. Corbett (newly converted) and I were married in a synagogue in St John's Wood. Harry had Ian McNaughton as his best man, both sporting ill-fitting Mafia-like fedora hats, purchased cheaply for this one-off Jewish occasion. I wore the cocktail dress under a short oyster satin coat made for me by my father's dressmaker sister, Dulcie, and a matching pillbox hat with the merest suggestion of a veil completed the outfit. Having organised the affair from start to finish, Aunt Eileen had booked a large room in Burgh House in Hampstead for a sit-down salmon lunch, which Bernard seemed happy to finance, and it was he who walked me down the aisle.

We had no honeymoon; Harry was working, and anyway we had no money to spare. He had found a flat for us on the third floor of a Victorian house in Arkwright Road in Hampstead. The front windows overlooked an expensive boys' school, while the back afforded a fine view over London towards the city, and on a clear day you could just make out the dome of St Paul's. We had spent a few weeks before the wedding redecorating, Harry, with some of relief, giving me a free hand. The curtains that had been left behind I dyed blue, and using a bucketful of navy dye and a scrubbing brush, attempted to change the colour of the faded pink fitted bedroom carpet, which ended up a patchy purple. We went to a furniture auction and bought a battered chaise longue and two elderly armchairs which I eventually re-covered, and a few rolls of wallpaper and several tins of emulsion later we finally had our own place.

It is possible that neither Harry nor I thought of marriage as a long-term commitment to be cherished and built on, but rather as the continuation of a passionate affair. I was a very young twenty-three; Harry was ten years my senior and almost as unworldly. When I think back to those first days together, the excitement of love at first sight, the adventure of getting to know one another and the career possibilities, I can scarcely believe the muddle we progressively made of our relationship. We were absolutely right for each other, and we were, both of

160

us, thoroughly immature. In hindsight perhaps we loved one another too much, constantly testing our marriage with jealousies and misunderstandings. I thought Harry so attractive, so magnetic, that women were bound to throw themselves at him, and how could he resist? And, judging by his overprotective attitude towards me, it seems he thought I was fair game for the opposite sex and that I would succumb. This mutual lack of trust gnawed at the foundations of our union, and had it not engendered such pain and anguish it might have been laughable.

At first, marriage was a game confined to the four walls of our flat; a simple continuation of our life together in Oakley Street. Harry gave me a slightly more substantial housekeeping allowance, and, as before, I enjoyed cooking and trying out new and adventurous recipes. However, one day, he decided I was overspending on food.

"I'll take over the cooking," he told me. "I'll show you how to save money and still have good meals."

I spent the next day pottering and cleaning, waiting for the hunter to return with his offering. At six o'clock he walked in carrying a bag of vegetables and a loaf of bread.

"Good nourishing stuff," he told me as he stirred the chopped onion, carrot and potatoes in our largest saucepan filled with water, adding a pinch of salt and a shake of pepper. "This should give us at least three meals."

A hungry hour later he lifted the saucepan lid and we sniffed its contents.

What do you think?" he asked uncertainly.

"Try it," I suggested.

He stirred, lifted the spoon to his lips, blew on its contents and sipped.

We tipped Harry's offering into the gutter on the way to the local takeaway, and the next day he handed me back the purse strings.

As we sat and watched a rather passionate love scene on the television one evening, I asked Harry if he'd ever seen a blue movie.

"Yes. Why?"

"Just curious. I mean, what are they like?"

"Would you like to see one?" he asked with a laugh.

Feeling a trifle embarrassed, I nodded.

161

"Okay," he said. "We'll need a home projector and a screen. Your Uncle Bernard has one, hasn't he?"

He had, and with the excuse of showing a friend's holiday films I picked them up the next day. That evening Harry arrived carrying a round, flat tin and a bottle of wine. In those days one small glass was all I needed to lose my inhibitions, so it was clear that this was to be a night to remember. After dinner and a few glasses, Harry set up the equipment, closed the curtains, and soon we were sitting on a pile of cushions in front of the small screen. The film began. It was puzzling and we watched bemused. It was only in the final moments of the short reel when the man walked out of the room backwards we realised we had watched it in reverse. There was no point in rewinding, the moment had gone and we laughed too much. But there was still the rest of the wine.

I had always wanted to drive and Harry agreed to pay for a course of lessons. He was able to drive, but found it a disagreeable and nerve-wracking experience. Much later on when he was known celebrity, he bought himself an Alfa Romeo, but returned it within a fortnight, preferring from then on to be driven. I passed after only six lessons and bought a glorious old Lanchester in fine condition for only fifty pounds, and happily took on the role of chauffeur as well as housewife.

Harry had a habit of leaving things he had no further use for - used towels, shirts, coffee cups and so on - all over the flat, and I would tidy up after him with nothing more than an indulgent click of the tongue. It never crossed my mind to ask for his help with domestic chores, and in the evenings after dinner I would stand at the kitchen sink, elbow deep in soap suds, as he watched television from the depth of his comfy second-hand armchair, from which he would call, "Are you okay?" And I would cheerfully chirrup back, "I'm fine." I can recall only one major hiccup when, being intrinsically tidy (shades of my distaff side), I threw away a pile of what I assumed was waste paper lying on the hall table. They were, in fact, Harry's carefully collected monthly receipts due to be sent to his accountant the following day, and he was upset and furious. It was the first time he had seriously lost his temper with me, and I spent that evening, torch in rubber-gloved hand, sobbing miserably as I tried to retrieve the stained, soggy bills from the murky, mucky depths of the dustbin.

Harry's resolve to keep his home life entirely separate from his work meant that I was only peripherally aware of exactly what he was doing. I never mentioned the interviews my agent sent me for, which didn't much matter as they mostly came to nothing. When I did eventually get a one-line part in a television play, I was torn between excitement and trepidation. How would Harry react? It was becoming clear that I would have to pursue my career without his interest or cooperation. At best, I would have to manipulate each step of the way, at worst, it might become an outright battle.

"I suppose it'll be alright," he said when I told him, adding predictably, "as long as you still find time to do the shopping and cooking. And you must promise to come straight home after rehearsals ... no going to the pub with the other actors. And I don't want to hear what about you do each day."

And that's how it was. Once the television play had been and gone, I tried to settle back into the role of housewife, but in spite of us both trying to resume normal service, a rift was developing between us. Try as I might, I couldn't overcome the feeling of resentment at having been given time off to indulge my acting whim.

Soon after, I was called to a general audition for a play called *Milk and Honey*, written by Peter King. It was virtually a four-hander, starring Margaret Lockwood and Derek Farr, with the usual schedule of touring for a few weeks before going into London's West End. I read for the role of the scatty girlfriend of a suave man-about-town, played by Patrick Cargill, and much to my amazement I got the part. Harry was less than pleased, particularly as we were to tour for five weeks, but he said little.

The production meeting was held in a West End church hall, where the play was read and the technicalities were discussed. Derek Farr lived up to his name and appeared rather distant, whereas Maggie Lockwood, beautiful and funny, was charming and approachable. When something amused her she would throw her head back and surprise everyone the company with an unexpectedly loud, coarse, donkey-like bray! As for Patrick Cargill, he disdainfully ignored me - something to which I would become accustomed. Our director, the appropriately named George Sharp, was a narrow-shouldered, narrow-nosed man with a sharp tongue. I have learned over the years that, for whatever reason, many directors pick on one member of the cast, usually a youngster, who becomes their whipping boy. Perhaps Mr Sharp felt somewhat daunted by the two luminaries he had to handle as well as having to deal with the acerbic wit of Mr Cargill, but, whatever his brief, he chose me as his scapegoat, humiliating me throughout the run and making my life a misery.

It began on the first day of rehearsal when he was blocking the moves. Early in the first act, my character, Delia, had to run down a staircase, marked on the floor by wide strips of tape, shouting the deathless line, "Wudgy wudgy wee!" before throwing herself into Patrick Cargill's arms. Script in hand, I trod carefully along the lines on the floor, wudgy wudgy wee-ed, and, making a small, token jump, stood next to Patrick. Mr Sharp groaned.

"Oh no, dear, that won't do. Try it again."

I tried it again with a little more energy, and giving a slightly higher jump towards my fellow actor. With a heavy sigh, the director looked around the rehearsal room.

"I hope we haven't made a big casting error here," he said to the assembly. Then he turned to me. "For God's sake, let's see some commitment!"

Blushing with humiliation, I put down my script and, taking a deep breath, shrieked, "Wudgy wudgy wee!" and hopped kangaroo-like on the floor markings, heading for Patrick, and throwing myself at him so hard we both toppled over onto the floor. I was mortified! Then I heard Margaret Lockwood's extraordinary laugh. It triggered my own panicky amusement, and giggling almost hysterically I scrambled to my feet.

"Oh God, I'm so sorry!" I panted, turning to face the now upright Mr Cargill.

He said nothing, but the venomous look he shot me as he brushed the dust from his immaculate suit spoke volumes.

Things got predictably worse through the rehearsal period. Sharp's tongue grew sharper, and I couldn't wait for the performances to begin so that I would be free of his tyranny. It wasn't, however, to be. Once on tour he often turned up to see the show, and would leave notes at the stage door criticising my performance and making suggestions for improvement. If we did happen to cross paths outside any of the theatres, he would avoid making eye contact with me. To make matters worse, Patrick Cargill was hardly an ideal partner a beginner like me.

On stage he would ad-lib lines or change moves, often mistiming feed lines and killing what were sure-fire laughs. The surprisingly good notices I received did little to make up for the fact that I was having a miserable time. More than that, when Harry and I spoke on the phone I couldn't confide in him, fearing it would be grist to his anti-career mill.

It soon became clear that the play was doomed to failure, and to cheer myself up I drew a large calendar, charting the days of performances we had left. Oh, the feeling of pleasure when each night after the curtain came down, I crossed the current day off! Finally the last night arrived, and it was over. I shredded my home-made calendar and, as I shovelled the pieces into the waste bin, there was a knock on my dressing room door. It was Mr Sharp.

"Well, goodbye, my dear, and good luck," he said. "We might even work together again, who knows?"

Me. I knew.

CHAPTER 15

I had often joked that if heated hair rollers and the contraceptive pill had been invented earlier, our marriage might have stood a better chance. As it was, most nights, as I did as a schoolgirl, I went to bed wearing an uncomfortable row of metal curlers meant to coax my straight hair into glamorous curls. It was hardly an incentive for romance and was a pointless price to pay, since the next day the kinks would hold for an hour or so and then relax into their natural state. As for contraception, it never occurred to me that Harry should take on this responsibility, and as the usual form used by women at the time was that most unpleasant of devices, the Dutch cap, that was what I used. I loathed the time-consuming nightly ritual when, after a long day, I had to spend time struggling to put the rubbery, slippery, nasty object in place. More and more often I couldn't face the tiresome routine and, fearful of falling pregnant, refused Harry's advances, much to his understandable anger and frustration. From time to time, when guilt or my own sexuality overcame me, I performed those bathroom gymnastics, but what should have been love-making was too often a duty and a chore.

Early on in our relationship, Harry had said that one day he wanted a son, giving me his views on what would be expected from me as the mother of his offspring. Once I had settled down and done with acting, I would devote myself entirely to the child's care and upbringing, while he, being a man, would never involve himself in its physical care, such as changing nappies, feeding and so on. Nor would he be seen doing anything as emasculating as pushing a pram or toting a child carrier. My own preferred plan, I told him, was to wait until I had an established career before I considered having a child, and, although the subject was never broached again, it was there - the elephant in the room.

Joan Littlewood was Harry's mentor and close friend. She lived in a large house in Blackheath with her young partner and co-director of Theatre Workshop, Gerry Raffles. One evening Harry came home and drew a sheaf of music out of his briefcase

- songs from the 1914-1918 war. He was excited by the idea that they could form the basis of a musical, and the following Sunday I drove him over to Blackheath where he put his concept to Joan. She said she thought it might have possibilities.

Joan and Gerry owned a small motor boat that could, at a pinch, sleep four. One weekend they invited Harry to join them on the water and, if he wanted to, he could bring me along. I was much in awe of them, of the boat and, in fact, of the whole set-up, and being thoroughly out of my depth I kept as low a profile as I could. That evening, as we all sat on deck moored in Cowes, Joan prodding at a pot of stew bubbling over a Primus stove, Harry began to discuss our marriage as though I wasn't there.

"And," he said, concluding his list of dissatisfactions, "she won't agree to have a baby."

Joan looked at him in disbelief and then laughed heartily.

"For God's sake, Harry," she said, once the fit of coughing provoked by the burst of laughter had subsided, "don't take any notice of her, just get her pregnant. It can't be that difficult!'"

Truth to tell, I wasn't at all sure I wanted a child. Both my parents had had an ill-concealed aversion to children, were awkward in their presence and were unable or unwilling to communicate with them. Sensing this, our friends felt uncomfortable when they visited, and we preferred spending time with them in their own homes. We were never treated as youngsters, my brother and I, but rather as adults in embryo. So engrossed were they in their own animosities, my parents seemed oblivious to the fact that they were emotionally suffocating their children. Often in heated moments my mother would remark sharply that she couldn't wait for us to grow up, and at a surprisingly early age my brother voiced his determination never to have children of his own. As for me, I have always been a little fearful of these small aliens who appear to expect something from me that I am unable to deliver. It leaves me feeling guilty and inadequate, the more so because deep down I harbour an irrational fear of the actual act of giving birth, seeming a physical expectation too far. It doesn't take rocket science to realise that this response to children was mine by my parents' example, so deeply ingrained that I despaired that if did I have a family of my own, I might well become the unresponsive and inadequate mother of unhappy children.

It would, though, be churlish not to acknowledge, and be ever grateful for, the creative and artistic talents I inherited from the two extraordinary individuals who begot me. However, nothing comes without a price, and along with those creative gifts, it seems I inherited family traits that were negative and destructive, and that contributed towards the ruination of a flourishing career. Nature or nurture? Or do I really carry an anti-achievement mechanism within me? If I doubted this self-scrutiny, it was confirmed when I visited my father's spinster sister Dulcie in her small house in Manchester. Sharing a pot of tea, we discussed what she called 'Our Family Flaw'.

"We always thought we knew best, never listened to reason, and were a thoroughly arrogant lot." She contemplated me with a beady eye. "Well, at this rate it looks as though you won't be having any children and neither will your brother Brian. And a jolly good job, too!"

Meanwhile, Harry's career soared. He was working constantly either in TV, film or theatre, sometimes getting up at six in the morning to be taken to a studio, filming all day, and then being driven to the West End to appear in a play that evening. Foolishly he was swallowing 'uppers' to see him through the day and sleeping pills when he got back at night, but actors are only too aware of the transience of work, and when it's there they grab it.

Alun Owen, one of Harry's friends, was an up-and-coming Welsh playwright whose reputation was growing fast. Harry had an idea to update the story of *Beauty and the Beast* into a modern version. Alun agreed it had great potential as a television play, and it was arranged that he would write a few scenes at a time, and then send them to Harry for his input and approval. All went swimmingly until the two men fell out over quite another matter; Harry was to direct Owen's play *Progress to the Park* at the Theatre Royal in Stratford East, but after a week or so Joan Littlewood took over. The written scenes stopped coming and the matter was never mentioned. It must have been a year or so later when, glancing through the listings in the *TV Times*, I saw *The Rose Affair* by Alun Owen scheduled to be shown that week.

"How could he, Harry?" I fumed. "You've got to do something about it!"

But Harry didn't seem bothered.

"It's his problem, not mine," he said stoically. "He'll have to live with himself."

The Rose Affair went on to win a TV award as Best Play.

CHAPTER 16

Once again I was waiting for a call from my agent. Harry was still his chauvinistic self, insisting that any and every domestic chore was mine, and any request for cooperation was refused on the grounds of emasculation. Small irritations like his reluctance to put things back where they belonged, became major vexations, as did his habit of removing his shirt and singlet together every night so that on washdays I had to untangle and pull them apart. There were other minor provocations that assumed ridiculously major proportions, and I began to regard the weekly housekeeping money as a salary I had earned.

Harry's insecurities made him possessive and jealous of any friendships I had, even friends who were gay, and we had no mutual friends. When he brought fellow actors back to the flat I would stay in the background, providing drinks and snacks when requested. We seldom went out in the evenings, and dining at seven, then television and then bed became routine. Now and again Harry would invite a chum or two to join us for an evening meal, and having cleared it away I would retire to the bedroom, leaving them to their whiskey and their shanties. I nagged him into buying me a second-hand upright, and once the delivery men had wrestled the elderly piano up the stairs, I passed the time of day recalling pieces I had learned as a child, and waited and waited and waited for the phone to ring with a call from my agent.

Yet, in spite of all this, when Harry was out or away, at night I would stand in the darkened sitting room looking over the distant London lights, tears spilling down my cheeks, lonely, and longing for him to be home. My days in the ever more isolating flat were spent missing him, impatient for his return. Then, in the late the afternoon, I would hear his footsteps on the stairs, his key in the lock, and for no accountable reason my mood would turn. The man I loved and lived for became a figure of oppression, and my greeting would be cold and unwelcoming. I knew my behaviour was irrational and destructive, but it was like a recurring bout of malaria, a perniciousness I couldn't control, a pattern I couldn't break.

Our future together was crumbling, the chasm between us was growing ever wider, and I was helpless; there seemed to be nothing I could do about it.

They say that girls often 'marry their fathers', and in many ways Harry did strongly resemble mine. They were similar in stature and generated the same dynamic energy, but, more than that, they both adhered to their own intransigent opinions and theories. Too intimidated to confront him with her frustrations, my mother had set about punishing my father for aborting her career and subjugating her to his selfish demands, and when I began to realise that I was mirroring my mother's behaviour towards my father, it came as a shocking revelation. Here was another precept that I had learned by example: marriage was a tactical game of war.

It took several days, but eventually I plucked up the courage to try to explain, as much to myself as to Harry, why my behaviour was so erratic, why I blew hot one minute and cold the next. He arrived that evening with a small parcel tucked under his arm and dismissed my enquiry with a casual wave of the hand. I followed him into the sitting room.

"Harry, I have to talk to you."

He had thrown himself into his armchair and was examining the wrapping on his package.

"Oh yes? What about?" he asked, still concentrating on the task in hand.

"About us, Harry. About me. About me and the way I've been behaving. It's difficult for me to …"

I was speaking quickly, determined not to break down, but Harry interrupted.

"Before you go on, just give me a minute."

He got up and, parcel in hand, he headed for the bedroom, patting my shoulder as he passed.

"Won't be a sec," he said.

I sat down on one of the upright dining chairs, feeling much like a patient in a doctor's waiting room. Well, at least I'd made an inroad on this particular can of worms. A few minutes later he called me into the bedroom and we sat together on the side of the bed. He put an arm around my shoulder.

"Now," he said sympathetically, "tell me what this is all about."

Tearfully, I told him how my attitude to his arrival each evening belied how much I missed him all day, how I couldn't

171

wait for his return, and how the sudden switch into the dark, ugly mood that had tainted our evenings seemed out of my control. He was unusually attentive, prompting me to go on if I faltered, and when I'd done I waited for his commiseration, his understanding and, I hoped, his forgiveness. He bent down and pulled a small, new, shiny tape recorder from under the bed.

"I recorded that!" he crowed triumphantly.

Running to the bathroom, I locked myself in to weep out my humiliation and rage while Harry tried to persuade me out with sympathy and apologies. Finally admitting his lack of sensitivity, it appeared that he had, however distractedly, listened to my outpourings, and after talking together well into the night it was agreed that I should seek help.

The first psychiatrist I consulted was recommended by my indulgent GP. He turned out to be a pleasant, mild-mannered man in his early forties, and having listened to me recounting the details of my problems, decided, surprisingly, that the fault lay with Harry, and suggested that Harry come with me to the next session. Unsurprisingly, Harry was adamant that he wouldn't attend, and it was only my tearful appeals that eventually persuaded him. When we arrived, however, it was clear that he had no intention of cooperating. He sat morosely in the chair beside mine, a notebook in one hand, a pen in the other, ready to take notes on what I had to say, while steadfastly refusing to acknowledge, when asked, that he had any issues of his own. The consultant's attempts at professional cajoling were fruitless, and after a wasted hour, as I followed Harry out, the nice man smiled weakly and shrugged. There was little point in going back.

The next analyst I turned to for help had been suggested to Harry by a fellow actor, whose wife had been 'making life difficult'. On the appointed day I parked my car in a convenient cul-de-sac in St John's Wood opposite the modern block where he consulted. He took my coat, gestured me towards a long leather couch, and told me he was a Freudian.

"I work with dreams," he continued. "From now on you will keep pen and paper at your bedside, and the instant you wake up at any time you will write down your dreams. Lie down."

I lay down.

"Try to relax and free your mind."

I tried to relax and free my mind.

He sat in a chair behind me and said nothing. I said nothing and waited. I wondered whether I was supposed to say something or stay silent, and decided to stick with the latter; after all, he was in charge. The silence stretched and my attention began to wander. I looked in detail at the flocked paper on the wall ahead of me, pale grey it was, with little curlicues of silver. Expensive, I decided. Finally he spoke.

"What are you thinking?" His voice was friendly, reassuring.

"I was thinking," I said, "that if the decorator who put up your wallpaper had just pushed that drop - that one there, to the left," - I pointed – "if he had pushed it up just a couple of centimetres it would have matched in perfectly."

His response was unexpected.

"You've taken against me already, haven't you?" he asked.

I sat up and looked at him in surprise.

"No, I haven't ..." I began.

He leaned forward. "That wallpaper is a substitute," he said. "You've made a judgement. You've decided I'm flawed, that I have imperfections!"

"Not at all. I mean, I've hardly ... I don't know you!" I babbled.

"But you're quick to judge, aren't you? Aren't you?" he repeated.

"Not that I'm aware of."

"Well now you ARE aware!" He sat back, suddenly calm. "Excellent!" he said. "We're getting somewhere." He checked the Rolex on his wrist. "Time's up. Same time next week?"

As I left I couldn't decide whether I was going to return or not. After all, I couldn't keep changing psychoanalysts. As I approached my car I saw that someone had let down all four tyres and left a note on my windscreen.

"Don't park here again," it said. So that was that, the decision had been made for me.

Next I thought I'd try group therapy.

The first interview with the assessor, Lauren, seemed to go well, and as I left, in answer to her parting shot, "See you on Tuesday," I replied with a jolly laugh, "Not if I see you first!"

On Tuesday Lauren, sitting in prime position in the semicircle of six of us, introduced me.

"Sheila," she said, "has some sort of issue with me, and before we continue with our get-together I think it would be helpful to clear the air. Don't you, Sheila?"

Unsure of what she meant but wanting to please her, I thought it wise to concur.

"Definitely," I nodded.

Lauren nodded, then looked at me through narrowed eyes.

"Why did you come here today?" she asked.

"Because ... because when I saw you last ... er ..."

"Friday," she prompted.

"Friday, you agreed ..."

"We."

"Sorry?"

"WE agreed."

"Oh, yes. Sorry. WE agreed that joining this ... this ..."

"Group."

"Group, would be ... helpful."

Lauren nodded.

"Helpful," she repeated, and then paused. "Then why," she continued, weighting each word, "did you turn on me as you left?"

"What?"

"You said you would avoid me if you saw me!"

"No, I ..." Then I remembered. I laughed with relief. "Oh. No, you don't understand ..."

"Don't you tell me what I do and don't understand! Understanding is my job! I am a very understanding person! Ask anyone here!"

She glanced swiftly around the group, who nodded and muttered their support, casting poisonous looks in my direction. Lauren held up a commanding hand.

"No," she said, with a slight, martyred smile, "let me deal with this." Turning to me, she asked, "Do you understand the hurt you've caused me?"

Of course I did.

"And are you sorry?"

Of course I was sorry.

"Then we will say no more about it. And from now on I'm sure we'll see eye to eye."

It took a physical effort to refrain from answering, "Not if I see you first."

Finally, it was decided that I should consult Jonathan Miller's father, an eminent psychotherapist with a fine reputation. His

174

rooms were in an impressive, rather daunting red brick Victorian building near Harley Street. The darkened hallway smelt musty, and the iron-trellised lift groaned as it winched itself up to the second floor. The carpeted corridor deadened my footsteps as I headed for the brass-plated door. Obeying the instruction to PRESS the button, a muffled ring sounded. After a while the door was opened by an elderly woman, who led me down a passageway and left me at an open study door. And there, behind a heavy mahogany desk, sat the great man himself. He made a half-hearted attempt to rise, then thought better of it and waved me towards the chair opposite.

What followed was a pleasant half-hour or so spent with this big-framed, avuncular, if somewhat world-weary man with a shock of white hair, who listened to my woes with sympathetic nods and made me feel that, at last, here was someone who might give the answer to some of my problems. His hands were crippled with arthritis, and as our chat drew to an end he grappled, crab-like, with the drawer of his desk, opened it and, struggling the lid off a bottle of pills, pushed a few into his mouth. After a minute or so he spoke.

"Well," he said, "you're an actress, so I'd like your professional opinion."

"MY opinion?" I was taken aback.

"Yes. You see," he said, leaning back and contemplating the ceiling, "my son Jonathan is a qualified doctor, but he seems keen on becoming part of the world of entertainment. What do you think?"

"Well ..." - I hesitated, feeling distinctly ill at ease - "I know him ... well, no, I don't exactly know him, but I know his work, and he's brilliant at everything he does, and ..." I stopped, at a loss, and in an attempt to hide my embarrassment I delved into my handbag, pretending to search for something.

"That," the great man observed, "is a very large handbag."

"Yes, it is," I agreed.

It was truly very large. Made of soft beige suede, it had a handle that could be shouldered or casually swung from the hand, where it just skimmed the pavement.

"And what's in it?"

I hesitated. "Er ... not much."

"What exactly?"

"Well ..." - I fumbled through the sparse contents – "there's a

175

comb, and my wallet, a packet of tissues, my car key, the door keys, oh, and a pen." I smiled weakly. "That's it."

"That's it," he repeated.

"Yes," I almost whispered, "that's it."

"Do you realise," he said slowly, "that your handbag represents your womb? And yours ..." - he paused – "yours is very large. And very empty."

As the ancient lift delivered me to the ground floor, I was closer to tears than to any solution to the muddle I was in. But of one thing I was certain: nothing was going to change my mind. I was going pursue a career, a successful one, and one that would make Harry proud to be married to me ... or not.

CHAPTER 17

After three years our marriage was showing even more signs of strain; when we did spend time together we seemed to quarrel about trivia. Harry would knock back tots of whiskey and console himself by singing the sea shanties he loved so well, while I, full of self-pity, painted my feelings out in a series of gloomy daubs.

One day my agent called to say that I was to meet and read for Lindsay Anderson, with a view to taking over the part of Barbara from Ann Beach in the West End production of *Billy Liar*, with Tom Courtenay in the title role. I got the part and, much to my surprise, on the opening night Harry sent me a dozen red roses, though he refused to see my performance.

Apart from the joy of being in a play in the West End with Tom Courtenay, two things stick in my mind. One is that I had to eat oranges throughout my scene with Billy and, because I dug my thumbs into the fruit to peel them, after a while the acid made them ache and my nails were softening. I mentioned it to the stage manager and, thereafter, each night she would carefully cut the offending peel off in one piece and tuck the fruit back inside, and I would fake it. The other memory is that every night during Tom's long monologue in the second act Mona Washbourne, who played Billy's mother, summoned the entire cast to congregate in her large dressing room for a small drink and an obligatory chat. Mona was Queen and refusals were out of the question,

By now I had sold my lovely old Lanchester to a couple of American students (an inordinately stupid transaction that I still deeply regret), in favour of, God help me, a shiny little Mini Cooper. Harry would usually meet me at the stage door after the performance to make sure I drove straight home, and one evening, as I started the car with him beside me, I suggested we visit Peter Cook's newly opened club, The Establishment, in Soho, rather than go straight home. He wouldn't hear of it; it was too late, it was not his scene, and it would be full of 'luvvies'. I dug my heels in.

"Well, I'm going!"

As I stopped at the next corner he opened the passenger door, leapt out and stormed off in a rage.

I sat at a table in the club, chatting and drinking wine with Dudley Moore between sets with his trio, and after a while we were joined by Patrick McGoohan, who, to my relief, didn't recognise me. It was about one-thirty in the morning when I mounted the stairs and tried to turn the key as quietly as I could, but the door to our flat wouldn't budge. It was bolted and I was locked out. I tried some gentle knocking, only too aware of the other tenants in the building. No response. Defeated, I curled up in the bend of the stairs, hoping that Harry would relent. Eventually, however, stiff and cold and exasperated, I returned to my car, huddled for warmth in my inadequate coat. I slept fitfully and was woken at dawn by a tapping on the windscreen. Harry waved as he climbed into the early morning pick-up car on his way to the studios.

When the run at the Cambridge ended, the play transferred to the Golders Green Hippodrome. By this time I was acutely unhappy and I suppose it must have shown on stage. After a matinee one Thursday my dressing room phone rang and the stage doorman told me someone wanted to see me.

"Who is it?" I asked, in no mood for a social call.

"His name is Murray, and he says you need to see him."

It was an odd thing to say, which perhaps is why I agreed to allow this unknown to come to my dressing room. He was short, wiry and fox-like with narrow green eyes, and he spoke with a soft Canadian accent.

"I was in this afternoon," he said, "and I felt that you're deeply troubled. I would like to help you, if I can."

He stayed for an hour. I can't recall exactly what was said, but I do know that after a while I felt unburdened and calmer. As he left, I asked him where his sensitivity came from.

"I'm a Rosicrucian," he said.

I regretted not asking how I could contact him, and on my way out, on the off-chance, I asked the doorman if anything had been left for me.

"That gentleman left this," he said, handing me a note, "but he said not to give it to you unless you asked, otherwise tear it up."

We met up from time to time and, although I found many of his ideas and beliefs hard to accept, he said one thing in particular that helped me through what was a dark and bleak time.

"If you don't throw the ball back, there's no game."

It helped me to stay in control of my emotions during exchanges between Harry and me that otherwise would have erupted into hurtful and damaging rows.

CHAPTER 18

Steptoe and Son began as a one-off television play, 'The Offer', by Ray Galton and Alan Simpson. It had been commissioned by the BBC as part of a series of short plays written by them under the title *Comedy Playhouse*, but although it appeared in a comedy slot it broke the mould, focusing on inter-generational conflict. It was decided to cast straight actors in the parts of Harold and his father Albert in order to add gritty realism to the mix. Harry was cast as Harold, a thirty-something son filled with social aspirations and pretensions, and Wilfrid Brambell as his father Albert, a 'dirty old man' set in his grimy and grasping ways. It was the beginning of a hugely successful series, which was to run from 1962 to '66, when TV was still black and white, and then in colour from 1970 to '75. It was also the start of a relationship between the two that was to curdle over the years and lead to a hostility that, certainly in Harry's case, blighted his life. By the time it was in its second year, Harry would complain bitterly about having to feed Wilfrid helpful hints with his lines during the show, either because he hadn't learned them, or because, battling with alcoholism, he couldn't remember them. He felt he was carrying Wilfrid at the expense of his own performance, and the acrimony between the two fictional characters became fact. By the end of the series, the two men detested each other and were barely on speaking terms.

Brambell was an Irish actor who had earned a reputation for playing old men even when he was only in his forties. I never met him, but I am told that in real life he was nothing like his Steptoe persona, but rather dapper and well spoken. A homosexual at a time when it was almost impossible for public figures to be openly gay, he had a difficult private life, and at one point was arrested and charged with 'cottaging'. It seems that he was an obdurate man with few friends, and when he died of cancer at the age of seventy-two his funeral was attended by only a handful of mourners.

Steptoe was the beginning of a new direction for Harry's career, but it created a huge dilemma. On the one hand he basked in the recognition and adulation, enjoying the entrée that stardom gave him into disparate parts of society, from villains like the Krays to members of the establishment like Harold Wilson. On the other, although he brought great dramatic pathos to the part of Harold and created a character that hit a nerve with the public, he felt that he had betrayed himself by abandoning his career as an actor of repute. When he told me he had been offered the title role in the film *The Bargee*, a character virtually the same as Harold, I suggested he turn it down, and instead pursue the possibility of joining the newly formed National Theatre Company, but by then he was thoroughly immersed in the *Steptoe* series, past, present and future, and enjoying the benefits that were coming his way.

If we had been mature and taken charge of our lives, Harry's mounting success could have secured our future; as it was, it compounded our problems. His social life became part of his career, and I was excluded from everything except the domestic routine. I knew I wasn't pretty or glamorous and I found it hard to believe that the love I felt for Harry could be reciprocated. I never felt that we were a couple; I never heard him say 'we' or 'us', it was always the singular, 'me' and 'you'. When I asked him to take me with him on his evening outings his reply was always the same, "I won't be able to keep an eye on you, and I don't want other men chatting you up."

Eventually, I nagged him into submission, and he agreed to take me to some reception or other at the Kensington Palace Hotel. As we were about to leave, I stood at the sitting room door wearing a low-cut, bottle green dress and waited for his approval.

"I can't take you out wearing that!" he blustered. "You're all arse and tits!"

"Well, I'm not changing!" I barked, and flounced into the sitting room.

Harry left, slamming the door behind him, and I stomped into the bedroom, flung open the wardrobe doors and pulled the garments out, throwing them onto the floor in a heap. None of them would pass Harry's Scrutiny of Approval! I fetched a large pair of scissors from my sewing box and, sitting on the bedroom floor, set about furiously cutting the pile of clothes beside me into pieces. When he returned in the early hours of the morning, Harry found me lying on the bed in bra and panties, with an empty wine bottle beside me. I waved at the pile of shredded fabric with its strips of bottle green.

"Jus' buy me a sack, Harry," I slurred, "but for Chris'sake take me out, even 'f it's jus' the once!"

He took me out the following week to Danny La Rue's West End nightclub, not wearing a sack, but a dress I had bought making sure that it conformed to Harry's code of modesty. His welcome by the doorman and the maître d' made it clear that he was a regular, and we were shown to his 'usual' table on the edge of the small, circular dance floor. As we sat down, a middle-aged man approached us.

"I hope you don't mind, Mr Corbett," he said politely. "I just wanted to tell you ..."

Before he could finish, Harry cut in with a quiet ferocity.

"I am not here on show, I am out for an evening with my wife. Why don't you sod off?!"

I prickled with embarrassment as I watched the poor fellow slink away. Harry regained his cool and the evening went pleasantly enough, until during the cabaret Danny and the rest of the cast acknowledged his presence with personal jokes and references. I felt as though I'd intruded into private territory, and, I suppose to his credit, Harry did show signs of discomfort. Not nearly as much, though, as when we were leaving and the hat-check girl called out, "No teddy bear tonight, Harry?" It was the only time I saw Harry blush.

Harry and Wilfred were invited to perform a sketch in the Royal Variety Show, and at the last minute Harry presented me with two tickets. I rushed into the West End, bought a pair of silver cufflinks, persuaded an engraver to do a priority job and cut a single 'H' into each one, and left them at the stage door with a good luck card. That night a girlfriend and I sat in the stalls of the London Palladium, watching the glitz and glamour, and at last *Steptoe and Son* was announced. To my astonishment, about halfway through the sketch Harry turned to Wilfrid and, flashing his shirt cuffs asked, "D'you like my new cuffs, then? Pretty smart, eh?" and then continued with the dialogue. I was thrilled and flattered, but, more than that, I couldn't believe his confidence in ad-libbing a line in front of a VIP audience that meant nothing to anyone but me and wasn't even funny!

Harry was approached by the publicity agent, Freddie Ross, who offered to 'look after him'. Freddie had developed and nurtured other celebrity careers, including Tony Hancock's, and Harry accepted with alacrity. Freddie assured me that she was relieving me of the burdens that his newly acquired renown would bring. She organised his publicity, his social commitments and even his personal appearance, shopping for his wardrobe. When he was late coming home, it was Freddie who phoned from wherever they were. Usually I could hear music and chatter in the background, but she would tell me not to worry and that she was keeping an eye on him, on one occasion adding, "Anyway, the women he fancies always look like you," which was, of course, a great comfort. Harry was spending not only his working hours but also his leisure time surrounded by interesting and attractive females, and I was only too aware that there was another characteristic he shared with my father: they both loved women. As far as I was aware, my father had simply been an incorrigible flirt, whereas I was fairly certain that Harry would find the temptations on offer impossible to resist.

The raise in my housekeeping allowance went towards opening an account in the drinks department of a local store. Whiskey became my comfort and my palliative, helping me to sleep, instead of lying awake in the early hours listening out for the arrival of a taxi. Now and again Harry came home unexpectedly earlier than usual, waking me up to join him in a takeaway he'd bought on the way home. I'd lie in bed half asleep, Harry in his overcoat lying on top of the covers, both of us munching, both quiet, both for the moment content, but these occasions were few and far between. More often than not, through my drugged sleep I would be aware of him slipping into bed, trying not to disturb me. In the mornings, when I sorted out his clothes, I would often find telltale marks of lipstick on the collars of his shirts. I said nothing, afraid that if I confronted him he might choose to call it a day and leave me; after all, I wasn't the sort of wife he wanted. He took a trip to Rome for a few days, saying that he had an interview for a film, but later I was reliably informed that he had taken a pretty actress, who had appeared with him in an episode of *Steptoe*, to an Italian seaside resort. Still I said nothing. From time to time our silent acrimony erupted into ugly verbal clashes, and I remember taking myself to see a West End production of Edward Albee's *Who's Afraid of Virginia Woolf* and drawing a strong parallel between our marriage and the fractured relationship on stage.

Harry won a Best Actor award at the end of 1962 for his performance in *Steptoe*. He was filming in West Africa and wasn't going to be able to accept the prize himself, so he suggested that I attend the function in his place. It was a grand affair: a dinner at the Dorchester Hotel followed by the awards ceremony. I had been placed at a table of BBC dignitaries and I couldn't have been more out of my depth. I'd had an outfit specially made for the occasion by William Rothery, a splendid dressmaker and close gay friend of mine. Although I may have looked the stylish, sophisticated actress-wife of a star, that was as far as it went. Never a great conversationalist, I found it almost impossible to join in the banter around the table. I picked at the elaborate food on my plate and wished myself anywhere but there. They had seated me next to Tom Sloane, then Head of Light Entertainment, and once the dishes had been cleared and the awards were about to be presented he leaned over to me and said in a low voice, "If Harry had been here I'm sure he would have mentioned Wilfrid Brambell in his thank you speech, don't you?" And he winked. I was panic-stricken! I hadn't considered that I would be expected to make any sort of comment, except perhaps a hasty 'thank you' into the microphone. If I'd been told I had to make some sort of speech I would never have agreed to attend, or would have asked someone to write something appropriate and learned it by heart. But to ad-lib even a short sentence at such a grand affair was beyond my capacity.

Harry's award was announced. I made my way to the platform, was handed the heavy metal trophy, and muttering a quick 'thank you' at whoever it was who gave it to me, returned quickly to my empty chair. Tom Sloane patted my hand patronisingly.

"I understand," he said.

No, you don't, you really don't! I wanted to say. But had I been able to explain my inadequacy to him, I would probably have been able to make the short acknowledgement he had suggested.

Although his working relationship with Brambell was irksome and onerous, between times Harry was fitting in other jobs that he enjoyed. Our marriage trundled on, but it wasn't working for either of us and we were growing further and further apart. We had more searing rows, and I would throw a few belongings into my car and spend the night with friends, only to return to a bitter Harry, convinced that I had stayed with some lover. I would cry, we would make up and all would be well until the next spat.

Then I got my first featured role in television, a small part in a dramatisation of *Kipps*, which involved a short spell in Manchester. I was on the train when I remembered I hadn't removed the contraceptive cap from the night before, and, knowing only too well what he would deduce, I called Harry as soon as I got off the train. Before I could speak he told me he had found the empty container in our bathroom, and accused me of taking it with me deliberately! Nothing I could say would convince him otherwise and, angry and upset, I slammed the phone down. I had a room booked in a pub close to the Granada studios, as had several other members of the cast. That evening, still smarting, I comforted myself with too many glasses of wine, and when an actor I knew coaxed me into bed, having already been accused and found guilty, I decided I had nothing to lose. A few days after my return to London, my cleaner told me agitatedly that arriving early one morning she had heard a woman in the bedroom with Harry, and a little later heard him hurrying her out. What could I say? It was as though we were being manipulated like puppets in some nightmarish Grand Guignol, with no control over our destinies.

I was feeling at my lowest when a letter arrived postmarked New York. It was from Tucker, my dear, gay friend from my time at Webber Douglas, and, he ended as he always did, with a casual invitation to visit him sometime in New York. It couldn't have been more opportune. Harry was only too aware of the precariousness of our future together. He knew of my long-term friendship with Tucker and, feeling somewhat reassured by the fact that Tucker was gay, he agreed, that a few weeks apart would give us both a sense of perspective. I wrote by return and accepted Tucker's kind offer.

CHAPTER 19

Once he'd returned home to the States, Tucker and I had corresponded regularly, but as time went by the letters inevitably became sporadic. I knew that he and Dan had initially worked as actors, both appearing successfully on and off Broadway, but first Dan, and then he, too, had switched to directing television and theatre. Tucker had booked me into a cheap hotel not far from his apartment on Riverside Drive. The room-with-shower on the sixth floor was the size of a ship's cabin and had a narrow window that overlooked a yard full of garbage bins. During the day Tucker was directing and editing programmes, so I would walk around the city sightseeing, and I came to like New York more and more. Most evenings I would meet him at his apartment and he would cook, impressing me with his pasta-making as he ground out worms of home-made spaghetti, or surprising me with the range of delicious dishes that he could conjure up in his cupboard of a kitchen. All this excellent fare we washed down with good, cheap Californian wine. We went to the movies, caught a few off Broadway shows and went to museums and free exhibitions. Filled with nostalgia, one Sunday we took the Staten Island ferry, and Tucker recited *Recuerdo*, the Edna St Vincent Millais poem I had grown to love in those long ago bedsit days.

Then, shortly after I arrived, Tucker opened his apartment door wearing a black eye patch.

"Don't be shocked!" he said reassuringly, "I should have mentioned it before. You remember in London I told you about the trouble I was having with one of my eyes? Well, it got worse and after a while I had to have it removed. But it's okay," he added hastily. "You wouldn't have noticed because I usually wear a glass eye in the socket. But, to tell you the truth, it's not all that comfortable, so when I'm home ..." and he tapped the patch.

I hugged him hard. "Oh, Tuck, I wish you'd told me before."

"No point. No need. And you needn't worry. You'll never see me without one or the other, the eye or the patch. No one ever has, no one ever will, not even my mother. It looks ... repulsive!"

As we ate our evening meal, I tried to avoid looking at his eye patch and made every effort to be my usual casual self, but I was aware that our friendship had shifted gear slightly. After dinner we lay together on his small sofa bed watching TV, Tucker with his arm around me, my head leaning against his shoulder, and as I looked up at him I noticed that the patch had slipped upwards, and I could see the hollow eye socket. It wasn't anything unpleasant or shocking; in fact, it looked nothing special.

"Tuck."

"Mmmm?"

"Why don't you take that patch off?" I said, as casually as I could. "I mean, it can't be comfortable, and you can't go on wearing it all the time I'm here."

I could feel his arm shift, but he stayed where he was.

"I can't take it off," he said. "I told you, there's a hole in my face where an eye used to be and it looks awful!"

"Oh, come on, it can't be that bad!" I cajoled. "Risk it. Let me take it off. I promise to tell you if I think it's awful and you can put it back. Okay?"

I reached up and slowly lifted the patch off his forehead. Tucker watched me intently, waiting for my reaction of horror and disgust, but with a slight shake of the head I looked back at him blankly. He pulled open the empty socket with two fingers, expecting me to recoil.

"So?" I responded dismissively.

He sobbed for a long while and I held him close. Then, unsurprisingly and quite naturally, we made love, and afterwards Tucker said, "Wow! I had no idea ...," and we laughed because we both knew exactly what he meant.

The next day I moved out of my hotel and into his apartment, and although that was the only time we made love it had freed and deepened our friendship. Tucker was gay; that would never change, nor would I have wanted it to. I loved him thoroughly, but the love I had for him was quite different to the passion that tied me to Harry.

One weekend Tucker took me on a visit to his hometown in Watertiwn, Connecticut. The house in which he was brought up was an old colonial-style building with pillars at the front and a veranda with a faded floral swing seat. In true movie style we sat on it together, Tucker and I, not sipping mint juleps but

187

knocking back G&Ts, and his parents were delighted that their son had at last found a girlfriend.

Like all good Americans, Tucker had been seeing a psychotherapist twice a week for several years. One day, just before I left, he told me that he was going to cancel his session.

"I just feel so good about myself!"

He made the phone call, and as he listened to her response I saw his confidence drain away. Shaken, he put down the receiver.

"I have to go back," he told me. "She's pretty angry. She says she'll be the one who decides when I'm ready to leave. I guess she's right."

It maddened me, and made me wonder who needed who the most. Still, Tucker was his own man, and I was leaving New York feeling calmer and more settled, although still uncertain about my future with Harry.

CHAPTER 20

We struggled on with our marriage, but it was clearly disintegrating. Harry had earned a reputation as a womaniser, and I discovered that he was having affairs. It came as no surprise and I couldn't really blame him; after all, living with me had been no bed of roses. I once found a small passport photograph in his briefcase of a well-known actress (who, ironically, DID look rather like me), and his lame excuse was that she had asked his opinion as to whether she should use it for *Spotlight*, the actors' directory. A passport photo? I didn't think so! I was unhappy and insecure, and wanting to be comforted I convinced myself that what happened in private concerned only those involved with no harm done. It soon became a mutual deception, with both of us floundering between liaisons. Harry clumsily tried to hide his misdemeanours, while I concealed mine so deftly that he never suspected.

At last, and not before time, we agreed on a trial separation. I moved out and found another flat a ridiculously short block away. Harry agreed to pay the rent, convinced that this was just a hiccup in our lives and it wouldn't be long before I returned to the fold. The intention had been that this period apart would give us time to reflect on whether we wanted a future together or apart. As ever with us, it was a naïve concept, and we would often spend nights together, either at my new flat or in Arkwright Road.

One afternoon he turned up at the flat saying we needed to talk. He followed me into the kitchen as I set about making coffee.

"I want you to come back," he said bluntly.

He sounded desperate. More than that, he looked a mess; his clothes were rumpled and he needed a haircut. A wave of deep affection flooded through me; he looked like a bewildered, lost kid.

All right, I decided, if he says he loves me, I'll go back.

"Why, Harry?" I asked. "Why do you want me back?"

I waited for him to tell me how much he loved me and that he couldn't live without me.

What he actually said was, "The flat's a tip, there are no clean shirts, and I haven't had a decent meal since you left."

If pride had allowed, Harry would probably have told me what I needed to hear, and were it not for my own pig-headedness I would have let myself see beyond the mundane (if valid) reasons he gave. Instead, our two pairs of stubborn heels stayed firmly dug in.

Work was coming in. I was getting good parts in prestigious productions and scooping up flattering notices which led to even more opportunities. One of the straight roles I played was a villainous lesbian in a four-part detective series, *It's Dark Outside*, and one of my fellow actors was the young, but not yet notoriously famous, Oliver Reed. We recorded it in Manchester, and each Friday the cast would leave for London, reassembling the following Monday. One weekend, as I was leaving the studios, I discovered Ollie in the car park. He was in a rage.

"My damn car won't start!" he blustered. "And I haven't got time to wait for the AA. Are you driving back to London?"

I was.

"I don't suppose I could cadge a lift off you, could I?"

He could.

Roadworks made the journey slower than usual, and it was nearly midnight by the time we reached my flat. He tried several taxi firms but there were either no cars or long delays.

"Why don't you stay?" I suggested. "Then you can book a cab to pick you up early tomorrow morning."

"I don't see why not," he said, yawning.

I could have made up the bed in my cupboard-sized spare room, but it was late, the bed was piled high with ironing and other odds and ends, and we were both tired. Sharing a bed didn't seem to bother him, and as we both lay there I wondered if he would make a move, or if I should make a move, or if, indeed, there was a move to be made. By the time I had talked myself into putting out a tentative hand, Oliver was gently snoring. Ah well, I said to myself, at least I can honestly say I've been to bed with Oliver Reed.

Harry and I spoke often on the phone, but the possibility of a divorce was never mentioned. Then, during one of our conversations, he made the absurd suggestion that we go on a 'divorce honeymoon'. I was taken aback.

"Does that mean you want a divorce?"

"Not necessarily," was his response. "Let's just go away together and see how things work out."

We spent ten days in Portugal determinedly living in the present, ignoring the past, and never discussing the future. It was good and we were happy, with only one hiccup of my own making. Remembering the holiday I had taken in Barcelona all those years ago with my Spanish-obsessed fellow student Alida, I persuaded Harry to attend a local bullfight, assuring him that he would find it as exciting and exhilarating as I had. With some misgivings he agreed to accompany me, but as we watched the young heifers being herded in he swiftly turned and left.

When I caught up with him he said, "Did you see their eyes?"

Yes, I had, and I felt ashamed.

On our return, as we stood queuing for a taxi at Heathrow, Harry dropped his bombshell.

"Your flat or mine?" he quipped, or so I thought.

We had just spent the most serene and companionable time together, and, thinking he was lightening the moment with a little banter, I countered with, "It depends. Your career or mine?"

I realised too late the implication of what I had said. The look on his face spoke volumes.

"I think it's time we called it a day, Sheila, don't you?"

"But it's been the most wonderful ten days ..."

"Yes, it has!" he agreed. "And that's exactly why we should stop now on a high, before we start to mess up again."

We were at the head of the queue and an available cab approached.

"I'll get the next one," he said, pushing my case into my hand.

I dropped it and stood my ground.

"No, Harry, at least ..."

"All right, you get the next one. You're on your own!"

And, grabbing his bag, he leapt into the ticking cab and slammed the door behind him. The queue behind pushed past me as I stood, numb, watching the car disappear into the line of traffic.

CHAPTER 21

Theo was different from anyone I had ever known. I met him at my first lesson with a new singing teacher, where he was filling in, accompanying her pupils on the piano. We hit it off instantly, and later that afternoon we went for a coffee in a nearby restaurant and discovered that we had much in common, including our mutually foundering marriages. Theo was rather on the podgy side, his face round, his eyes slightly bulging, his lips full and sensuous, and there was something offbeat and dangerous about him that I found attractive. We got to know one another very well very quickly, and I soon discovered that he was a brilliant musician with a quirky sense of humour and was quick to judge - as I later found out to my cost. I loved listening to him improvising jazz on the mini piano I had bought.

"If ever we fall out," I told him, "just sit down and play and I'll admit defeat!"

We spent more and more time together, and after six weeks or so he moved in with me.

Often I'd go to gigs with him, sitting on small stages trying to look inconspicuous behind the drummer and bass player, the music pulsing through my body. One day Theo, along with several other musicians, was invited to be part of the backing group for a hugely popular American singing star who had been booked to appear on the TV show *Sunday Night at the London Palladium*. There was a party afterwards at the Westbury Hotel and Theo met me in the foyer. The star's suite was noisy, full of musicians and hangers-on, almost all of them male, and almost all of them high on something or other. The host was nowhere to be seen, and after settling me into a comfortable chair with a glass of wine in my hand, Theo disappeared. After a while, the shouting and laughter and throbbing beat of the high-volume music began, to get me down and I considered searching Theo out, but trying to find him seemed too daunting a task, so I stayed where I was.

I noticed two pretty young girls sitting on the sofa opposite me. One was being nuzzled by a member of the group, and I watched with some alarm as he groped under her miniskirt. To my shocked surprise, she leaned back submissively, and after a moment or two he pulled her to her feet and led her off to what I supposed would be the bedroom, followed by several interested onlookers. Another young man, somewhat the worse for wear, collapsed into the newly vacated space and threw his arm around the other girl's shoulder. She seemed nervous, but when he whispered in her ear and waved his free arm in the direction the other couple had taken, she giggled, smiled at him flirtatiously and nodded. The man heaved himself to his feet and headed off in search, I supposed, of his next fix, and I went over to her and sat down.

"Hi, I'm Sheila," I said, hoping I sounded casual. "I'm here with the pianist, Theo. Who are you with?"

"Oh, I'm not here with anyone in particular," she said brightly. "Me and my friend are being paid to be here."

"Really?" The penny dropped. "Paid to do what?"

"Well … you know …"

"Is this something you do often?" I asked her.

"No!" she said quickly. "Actually, I'm working as an assistant stage manager at the Royal Court Theatre, but … well, the extra money will come in handy, and I thought it would be fun."

"And is it?"

"Not really." She looked achingly vulnerable.

"You really shouldn't be doing this, you know," I told her firmly. "It's demeaning, and apart from anything else, it's dangerous. I think you should forget the money and go home, don't you?"

Just as she was about to speak, the young man reappeared and stood in front of us, swaying slightly.

"Ready, hen?"

After a moment's hesitation she said, "Sheila says I shouldn't."

The young man looked at me with sudden interest.

"Is that right?"

"Yes, that's right," I said, beginning to realise that I might have got myself into something I couldn't handle.

By now the girl had stood up and was edging away from the sofa, heading, I hoped, for the door.

"Hey, you guys, how about this?!" The young man spoke loudly in a broad Scottish brogue, slurring his words. "This here is Sheila, and she's decided that sexy young lady over there should not perform the services for which she's been hired ... and for which, I may add, she would, indeed, be handsomely remurin ... renuman ..., - he finally got there - "remunerated ... by the generosity of our talented host and benefactor!"

There were cheers, most of the young men in the room were, by now, taking notice, and he turned to me with a broad, ugly grin.

"Right then, dear lady," he drawled, "since you seem to have taken the high moral ground on behalf of a younger member of your sex, it would seem only fair that you offer your own, and from the looks of you, possibly professional services on her behalf." He faced the crowded room. "Don't you agree?"

Another cheer went up. He grabbed my arm and I tussled with him, trying to twist out of his grasp, but he yanked me out of my seat and began pulling me towards the bedroom.

"Theo!" I yelled.

With enormous relief I saw him making his way towards us, pushing people aside. He stopped a few feet away, his smile bland, his pale blue eyes icy. Slipping his hands deep into his pockets, he rocked gently on his feet, then clicked his tongue disapprovingly.

"Hey, man," he said, his voice quiet and steady, "that's my woman."

The release was immediate, the apology profuse, and the onlookers moved away muttering. I felt humiliated rather than grateful, and was furious with him for leaving me alone in such volatile company. I was about to demand what the hell he'd been doing all that time when I had a sense of apprehension, and reasoned that it would be wiser to let that particular sleeping dog lie.

CHAPTER 22

As far as my career was concerned I was getting noticed, and although I knew that he was uncomfortable in the role, I often sought Harry's advice. I was cast in a revue at the Lyric Theatre in Hammersmith. The cast was talented, but as rehearsals progressed it became clear that much of the material just wasn't funny enough. Before we opened there were previews, and I asked Harry to come and give his opinion, not only of the show, but of my performance. Reluctantly he came, seeing me on stage for probably the first time. However, he refused a seat, preferring to stand at the back of the stalls in the sparsely filled auditorium, and he left in the interval. A scribbled note at the stage door read, "You could walk away with the show." I didn't know what he meant, nor, if I did, how to set about doing it!

The press slammed it. Bad notices, even my own, have always made kick my heels in the air with wicked glee, and *Punch* came up with one that was deliciously derisory:

"There are good revues and there are bad revues but there are also revues so dire and deplorable, containing sketches of such brain-rotting ineptitude, that only Duty, Stern Daughter of the Voice of God, drags a critic back after half time to take more punishment. ... Some of the jokes are so feeble and antique that medieval jesters would have had their tongues torn out for daring to utter them. ... The evening's most amusing feature was the small squat goblin of a St Trinian's Britannia, and she was painted on the curtain."

I managed to dodge the brick bats.

"There was a brief glimpse of blue sky among some heavy clouds. Sheila Steafel, a South African girl who, by controlled underplaying, by tiny improvisations, and by always giving more to her lines than they, in all conscience, ever deserved, suggested a talent that one day might be allowed to emerge."

Theo and I were getting on well and settling into a routine. I wasn't in love with him, and Harry was constantly on my mind, but the sense of relief at being able to discuss things and speak my mind, made up for the very real sense of guilt and the nagging doubt as to whether I had made the right choice.

One evening, to my astonishment, Harry arrived at my flat with two 'heavies' - stocky, well-built men whom I had never seen before, wearing ill-fitting suits. They followed him as he pushed me aside and stormed into the sitting room, demanding to see Theo.

"Where is he? Where's this b****** lover of yours?"

Theo was in the kitchen, carefully rolling a joint.

"In there." I pointed.

Harry gestured at the two men to stay where they were and strode into the kitchen, slamming the door behind him. To my astonishment, the muffled exchange that followed was verbal rather than physical, Harry barking out his hurt, and Theo level and soft-spoken. Harry's henchmen looked uncomfortable and somewhat sheepish, relieved, perhaps, that their services were, so far at least, not required. The kitchen door opened and Harry came up to me, his expression hard and set. He lifted his hand, and I braced myself for the expected blow, but his palm was turned upwards.

"Give me your wedding ring."

The pain was sharper than any blow he might have delivered. I twisted it slowly off my finger and handed it to him. Then, with Harry leading the way, they left. As one of the 'heavies' passed me, he muttered a low, "Sorry."

I went back to the kitchen. I felt weak, I felt sick. I leaned against the door.

"Well?" I asked pointlessly.

Theo licked the edge of the spliff with care, then looked at me and smiled.

"You know," he said, "I've always wanted to meet him. He's a lot shorter than I imagined."

We were beginning to share a social life, and on this particular night Theo had invited a couple of his musician friends to join us for dinner. The casserole was in the oven, the table set, and Theo sat improvising at the piano when the phone rang. I went into the bedroom to answer it.

"Who is it?" Theo called.

"It's Derek," I replied, closing the door to muffle the sound of the music.

Derek was an actor I had worked with on a TV production earlier in the year, and he'd been pursuing me ever since. This seemed a good opportunity to explain that, although I liked him as a friend, I now had a live-in lover and was no longer 'available'. Halfway through our conversation the piano playing stopped, but I thought nothing of it. When I opened the bedroom door I found Theo standing in the hallway with his jacket on, holding his small suitcase of belongings.

"I don't want to have to deal with other men who want to sleep with you," he said flatly. "I'm going back to my wife."

And he was gone.

This couldn't be happening! I felt a gaping hole in the pit of my stomach, my mouth was dry and the sound of crashing waves filled my ears. Panic gripped me and all I could think of was Harry. I had to see him, to be with him. I knew he had been filming in Shepperton and was staying in a nearby hotel. I turned off the oven, flung on a coat and, without thinking, set off in my car to find him. I drove recklessly down dark country lanes, getting lost and reversing out in a panic. Distraught, I frantically searched the ill-lit area around the studios, but could find nothing resembling a hotel. At last I came across a pub and, neither knowing nor caring how dishevelled I looked, ordered a large brandy from the curious barmaid and asked if she knew of a hotel nearby where actors stayed when they were filming.

"No, dear, no hotels," she replied, "but we do put actors up here."

"Is Harry H. Corbett staying with you?" I asked, trying to keep my emotions under control.

"Yes, but he's not here at the moment, dear. I believe he's spending the night back in London."

I sat outside the Arkwright Road flat trying to pull myself together. It was midnight, and I was torn between Harry's anger and my own desperation. I had to see him, to be close to him, even for just a minute. It was no use; I couldn't hold down the panic that overwhelmed me. I walked quickly up the front steps, rang the bell and waited. After a long while Harry, bleary-eyed, opened the door a few inches.

"It's you! What's the matter?" He seemed put out rather than concerned or angry.

"Theo's gone. He walked out on me this evening and I thought ... I wanted ..."

I didn't know what I thought or what I wanted, nor did I know what I expected from this man who had every right to send me packing.

"Wait here," he said not unkindly, and leaving the door ajar he mounted the stairs. In an attempt to keep out of the cold, I edged into the hall, and as he reached the top flight I heard Harry hush a woman's voice. Suddenly aware of the ludicrous situation I had put myself in, I was overwhelmed with an urge to turn and run, run away from ... myself. Who else? But this was a scenario of my own making, and I would have to play it out to its bitter end. I stepped back into the cold of the night, and a few long minutes later Harry was back. Through the gap in the door he handed me a half full bottle of whiskey.

"Go home," he said. "Get some sleep."

I instructed a solicitor, and the wheels of divorce ground slowly into action. I had to be assessed, not by one but two psychiatrists, to verify I had suffered some sort of mental anguish during our marriage. I was required to write an essay of sorts, noting all the occasions where cruelty, mental or physical, could be cited. It was embarrassing and humiliating, made even more so by the solicitor's advice to exaggerate whenever I could if I wanted the divorce to go through.

In spite of all this, I couldn't let go. Harry stopped taking my calls, and when I did manage to speak to him he was cold and distant. I began writing to him instead, long self-indulgent letters of love and regret and self-recrimination, aware that after the initial few he would more than likely throw them away unread. I still hoped blindly for some sort of reconciliation, but at last, drained and defeated, I had to accept that it was over, the damage was irrevocable, and it was time to move on.

CHAPTER 23

Many of the productions I was in were filmed on location away from London, and from time to time, in the evenings after a few too many glasses, I would console myself in the arms of some or other compliant partner, proving unwittingly Harry's expressed opinion of the morality of actresses. Occasionally, I would become infatuated, convincing myself that my love was requited, but more often than not these encounters were brief and ended painfully.

I was once again in Manchester, this time playing a distinctly eccentric role in a series called *The Liars*. Chrissie is the backward daughter of a puritan Victorian family, who falls head over heels in love with a foppish lout (played by the splendid Freddie Jones), who arrives riding a bicycle. Her unrequited love turns her senses and she soon believes herself to be a bicycle, proceeds to stuff herself full of food and, uttering the unforgettable words, "I am a happy little bicycle!" dies of overeating with a beatific smile on her face. My performance was noted as "grotesque, funny, and pathetic", a fair description of the market I was to corner in years to come! After the recording, as I was leaving the studios ready to drive back to London, the commissionaire called me over.

"Congratulations, miss!"

I was a little perplexed at his unexpected enthusiasm.

"Thanks. Did you watch it, then?" I asked.

He frowned, and then his face cleared.

"No, no, it's your divorce! Just read it in the paper, it's come through. Didn't you know?" And he waved the copy lying on his desk.

I was left short of breath, as though I had been kicked in the stomach. I'd had no forewarning to prepare myself for this body blow, no idea that Harry had been to court. As before, a selfish, illogical sense of panic gripped me, swamping any sense or reason. I had to speak to Harry. With that one thought in my head, I dashed to my car and drove fast towards the motorway. I had to talk to him, to hear him, to be reassured that he was still there even though he was free of me. Catching sight of a phone box at the side of the road, I pulled over sharply. I dialled his number but the line was engaged, so I climbed back into the car and continued onto the motorway. I drove frantically into the first service station and called his number again, and this time Harry answered. It must have been an impossible call to deal with as I sobbed out my garbled, self-indulgent, adolescent misery. But he listened, and he tried to soothe me. He told me that in spite of the divorce we would always be close, and no, I wasn't to feel bad about those letters I'd sent, he understood. And he told me to drive carefully.

Before he put the receiver down for the last time I made a final request.

"Will you do something for me, Harry?"

"What's that?"

"Will you give me back my wedding ring?"

I could hear him breathing.

"I'm sorry, I can't," he said at last. "I threw it away."

No Harry, you didn't. We both did.

* * *

It was 1982. I was driving through Oxford Circus into Regent Street with, as always, Radio 4 playing, when at the end of the headlines the newsreader announced, "The actor Harry H. Corbett ..." and I knew what was coming. I drew over to the side of the busy road, sitting still and shocked as cars passed by and pedestrians hustled on their way. Apart from the welling grief, to my bewilderment I felt a sense of release; no more aching possibilities, no more wishing, no more longing. Now it was final, Harry was gone. He was only fifty-eight.

His agent phoned to tell me that he'd had an earlier heart attack but refused a bypass, and he died of a second massive attack. His wife requested that I didn't attend his funeral, and in return she wouldn't attend his memorial service. And so, in the actors' church in Covent Garden, I said my goodbyes, wearing the flat, black flamenco hat he had bought me on our 'divorce honeymoon' in Portugal. And I regretted that there was no lone piper to play him out as he had once requested, but perhaps I was the only person he had mentioned it to.

I still dream of Harry, I dream of him often, but now I no longer wake in tears.

PART 3:
SWINGS AND
ROUNDABOUTS

THE FROST REPORT

"How d'you fancy drowning in petrol?"

I was in the Arts Theatre Club coffee bar, lingering once again over a tepid cup of coffee and hoping to catch any mention of likely jobs that were going, when the improbable question was posed. A friend who had recently become a floor manager at the BBC was, he told me, working on Michael Bentine's comedy sketch series *It's a Square World*.

"They're looking for an actress to sit in the sidecar of a motorbike and ... well, drown in petrol. It's to go under the titles, so it's probable no one will even know it's you. Why not get in touch with the office? You can say I suggested you."

Well, why not? Nothing to lose and a fee to gain. A few days later I was sitting in the sidecar of a motorcycle in a petrol station, dressed in a dowdy coat and headscarf, waiting for the camera to roll. The sketch was about a biker who drives into a forecourt with his wife in the sidecar and pulls up at a pump. The big, blonde, busty attendant comes over to serve him and inserts the nozzle of the pump into the tank. Then, while the husband chats her up, the sidecar slowly fills up with petrol and the wife (me) drowns. The effect was achieved by having a double glass panel inserted on the sidecar window and, as the water filled the gap between the two sheets, all I had to do was keep an eye on the level and expire accordingly.

Jimmy Gilbert was about to direct *The Frost Report* for the BBC. He happened to see the sketch. And surprisingly, cast me as the female member of the team, which comprised John Cleese, Ronnie Barker and Ronnie Corbett, thus kick-starting my career in comedy. From time to time other prime comedy actors would join us, notably Nicky Henson, and each week the folk singer Julie Felix filled the music slot. The show was fronted by the ubiquitous David Frost, and each week explored a different topic (Politics, Medicine, Class, and so on). Antony Jay (who later co-wrote *Yes Minister* with Jonathan Lynn) would put together a scholarly piece about the chosen subject, and the writers would meet up with David and Jimmy for a discussion, then go away to write the sketches and David's links. When viewed from today's perspective, the list of writers is awesome: Terry Jones, Michael Palin, Eric Idle and Graham Chapman, who prefaced the *Monty Python* series, and Michael Wale, Neil Shand, Marty Feldman, David Nobbs, Peter Tinniswood, Peter

Vincent, Keith Waterhouse and Willis Hall, John Antrobus and John Law (who wrote the definitive 'Three Classes' sketch), and Barry Cryer and Dick Vosburgh, both of whom became close friends. And I feel privileged to have known and worked with them all.

The Frost Report became a huge success, a 'must see'. We rehearsed each week in a church hall just off Baker Street. David was always late, and because proceedings couldn't start without him, everyone else got into the habit of arriving late too. Before work began there was the obligatory game of football, part of the rehearsal ritual, and at last we would gather in an upstairs room. Jimmy sat at the head of the long table to read the sketches that had been sent in and decide which were the strongest and most apposite. One of the secretaries would often put the tagline of the joke at the top of the page as its title, and, as Jimmy always read the title out first, he defused the joke and the sketch didn't get the laugh it deserved. When we realised that our beloved director was choosing material based on our response, and that good sketches were falling by the wayside, we made a point of laughing heartily in spite of the resulting damp squib. We rehearsed for the next few days, finally performing the show in front of an audience in the BBC Shepherd's Bush theatre. It went out live, which was, to say the least, an adrenalin-pumping experience!

These were pre-feminist days when there were few women comedy writers around and there were none on our show. I was mostly written in as a female feed for the male actors, who had the bulk of the material, but now and then I had the opportunity to perform characters that I could really get my teeth into. One was playing John Cleese's mother, treating her adult son as though he were still a naughty schoolboy; another was as John's secretary, who, when he removed her glasses ("Why, Miss Jones, you're beautiful!"), responded, "I'll never wear them again," and, missing the door, walked out and fell over the balcony. I also played the nurse to Cleese's dentist, when Ronnie B., the comatose patient in the chair, dreamt he was pursuing the nurse through fields, haystacks and ditches, followed by the irate dentist. When he came round they were all three dishevelled and covered in mud and straw.

I was beginning to be recognised in public, and unlike some celebrities I never minded it; after all, it's not only flattering but also part of the job. One evening after the show had gone out, my agent and his partner took me out to dinner at a very chic Chelsea restaurant, popular not only with the gay community but also with members of the 'hooray' crowd. I knew that I was looking glamorous. I still had my TV make-up on, false eyelashes included, my hair was cropped fashionably short, and I wore a little black number with shoestring straps. At the time I drank whiskey as an aperitif, and I smoked rather chic (I thought) long brown cigarettes called More. My two hosts had, for the moment, left me on my own, and as I sat sipping and smoking I noticed a table nearby with five or six people talking animatedly and glancing at me from time to time. I knew they were talking about me, and, trying to look nonchalant, I took another sip from the glass tumbler and flicked non-existent ash from my cigarette. Suddenly, from across the room a woman's cut-glass voice yodelled, "Well, I think it's a man!"

Frost Over England won the Golden Rose of Montreux for the BBC in April 1967, and David and Jimmy Gilbert went over to France to collect the award. At the ceremony David made the acceptance speech, and although we actors were thrilled and proud, we felt our own contributions towards the programme's success hadn't been acknowledged. When we got together to start rehearsing the next series, Ronnie Barker handed out a parchment diploma to each of the cast. It was headed 'ROSE D'OR de MONTREUX' and was inscribed at the bottom 'présenté à ...' with our individual names written in script. But that wasn't all. In true and brilliantly wicked fashion he had written the following 'news report'.

THE GOLDEN ROSE MYSTERY

Last night police were still investigating the mysterious circumstances in which the 'GOLDEN ROSE OF MONTREUX' was carried off last month. Although international operator David Frost is known to be directly connected with the incident involving Europe's most prized possession, people in the know are beginning to suspect that there were at least four other men involved, and possibly two women (according to some reports).

Although there has been no mention in the press of these undercover men, it is now believed that they may have played quite a large part in the affair. Late last night the police still had not found the answers to these questions:

1. Who was the mysterious stranger in dark glasses who arrived with Frost at Montreux on the day the Rose was snatched? (The fingerprints on the solid gold handles were not those of Frost). Could this man have played any part in the organisation of the events that led up to the grab?

2. Why has no one been able to trace the three men and two women who, disguised as tourists, mingled with the crowds at London Airport, and who organised the get-away cars, right under the very noses of pressmen and photographers?

These questions will have to be answered soon, otherwise Frost will have to carry the can for something he did not do on his own. Unless, of course, he volunteers the names of his henchmen to the authorities. Knowing Frostie, I don't think he will.

To his credit, David took it in good part.

The winning Montreux programme was shown widely and I received several fan letters from abroad, including a most charming one written on a page torn out of an account book:

First I would like to greeting hello!

In the beginning of my letter I present myself. My name is Bouguena Azzedine aged 30 years old my job is a check in the University Free from all obligations I lived in a typicall town was situated in the east of Algeria Batno. It is my own country.

Miss Steafel I would like to tell you about my request? I intend or proposed you a project. I produce Films with its title The woman it's life.

On the life it's woman often that I would like to tell you something about my Production of this Film. I introduction of this Film started by horror and finished by a natural life but the Object of this Film explain and known that the woman really is life. The detail are: jail-sex the courts and the mafio cultivation and the domain of political, the conclusion is the natural life and the normal. this Film I think that possible be real in these life.

Hey Miss Steafel? I hope you understand what I would like from these letter if there is a complication Please tell me if you accepted my project I'll send it to you.

In the end I am writing to hearing from you soon Truly yours.

I turned him down as gently as I could.

At the end of the *Frost Report* series David threw a celebratory party for everyone concerned. David's parties were, and I believe still are, spectacular affairs, and happily I attended a few. The first I attended was held in his house in Knightsbridge where, for his guests' amusement and further self-knowledge, he had hired a graphologist, a phrenologist and a fortune-teller. I avoided all three, as my writing is appalling (I am left-handed but was forced at school to write with my right), my hair looked good and I wasn't having anyone mess it up (well, not that early in the evening!) and I preferred contemplating the contents of a wine glass than the depths of a crystal ball. The next was an Xmas party, and late in the evening David's guests were herded into his large sitting room. John Cleese appeared dressed as Santa, carrying a large sack over his shoulder. With a "Merry Xmas, ho ho ho!" he threw its contents - small royal-purple boxes from the Bond Street jewellers Asprey's, each holding a small treasure - for anyone to catch. The box I caught contained a slim silver swizzle stick that opened up to resemble the skeleton of a miniature umbrella. It is a gift I still cherish, but it remains unused, since without the bubbles, champagne, my favourite tipple, is like elastic without the snap.

At another time David took over the whole of Battersea Funfair. From rides, games, competitions and prizes to candyfloss and fish and chips, everything was available and free - a childhood dream come true! As ever, he had invited an illustrious crowd, and I remember Judy Garland arriving on the arm of John Bay. There was an odd sense of unreality that night, because although there must have been two hundred or more people they were thinly scattered over the vast space, and with only two or three couples at a time white-knuckling their way around the helter-skelter or joyfully bashing into each other's in dodgem cars, the shrieks of laughter and delight sounded eerily thin.

However, the party I remember with some misgivings took place at the end of the *Frost Report* series. David took over the White City stadium as a 'thank you' to all those who had contributed to its success. The actors were told to wear sports clothes and running shoes so that we could join in the fun, and although I had some qualms about it (sport, for me, has never been fun) I duly complied. The final programme had just gone out live, and by the time everyone concerned - actors, make-up girls, stage managers et al. - had tidied up and changed out of their studio gear, we were all the last to arrive at the venue. The huge tiered restaurant overlooking the arc-lit stadium was crammed and noisy with celebrities, critics and BBC high-ups, all in their best bibs and tuckers. There were betting slips at each of the guests' places, the happy punters were eagerly marking their choices, and I was nonplussed to find our names, as well as those of a few celebrities, entered for various races. I had just sat down when I heard my name called over the sound system; it seemed that I was due to run a three-legged race partnered by the poet, lyricist and fellow South African, Herbie Kretzmer. I trotted down to the grounds, found my partner, we tied our legs together, got set and were off. It didn't take long before we'd twisted ourselves into an irredeemable knot, so we gave up, kissed and commiserated, and, considering I had now sung for my supper, I headed back to the table. As I reached it the call came again, this time for the sack race. Glumly I stomped back to the track, heaved myself into an over-large, itchy hessian sack smelling of farm and after struggling with the task of mobility, fell over, remaining defiantly prone until the winning cheers told me that the race, and my evening, were over.

Once *The Frost Report* finished it was clear that everyone involved would go on to bigger and better things. For Cleese and some of the writers it was, amongst other things, *Monty Python*, and for the two Ronnies it was exactly that. And for me? When I look over my press cuttings for 1966, I am amazed at the impact I made. Articles and interviews appeared with headlines like 'THE ONE THEY'RE CALLING FUNNY GIRL 1966', 'SHE'S THE FUNNY GIRL OF TV', 'THE FUNNY GIRL WITH A TOUCH OF PAGLIACCI' (!), and embarrassingly, 'FACE THAT HELPS LAUNCH 1,000 QUIPS'. My agent and I were invited to lunch by Billy Cotton Jnr, then the Head of BBC Light Entertainment, and he asked me what I would like to do in the future. I told him I'd like my own comedy series.

"Who would you like to write it?"

I named two of the *Frost* writers, a team that I thought would be ideal. The following week my agent called me to say that they had agreed to the project, a slot for a pilot programme had been booked for the following August, and we would all meet up at the end of June - which we did, in Billy Cotton's office. After the hellos we sat looking at each other expectantly.

"Well now, where's the script?" asked Mr Cotton.

"Script?" The writers were nonplussed. "We haven't written anything yet."

It was too late to make the deadline, and that was that.

At the time an article had appeared in the *Daily Express* asking: "Why has British television always been so reluctant to build series around women comics? Perhaps it's because, good though our top comedy writers may be, they are all men, and they simply don't understand how to turn out material for the girls."

At any rate it was too late. The slot disappeared into the vast BBC ether, along with another of my golden opportunities.

DANCING FOR HENRY MILLER

It's not often that one gets a call from one's agent with a request to catch a hasty plane to Paris to meet a film director. Come to think of it, it's not often one gets a call from one's agent. However, on this particular day my agent did indeed call to say that an American director, Joe Strick, was casting the movie version of Henry Miller's *Tropic of Cancer* and wanted me to fly over to Paris to audition for him. Now, having sneaked that particular brown paper covered book off my parents' shelves when I was in my teens, I knew that Miller was one of the first writers whose so-called 'pornographic works' had been printed, with *Tropic of Cancer* eventually achieving the status of a masterpiece. It's an autobiographical work concerning the sexual experiences of a young man who finds himself stranded in Paris, and the part the director had me in mind for was one of Miller's ex mistresses. In the book she is portrayed as a married woman with aspirations of becoming a concert pianist, but I had no idea the film company, had decided that it would be more filmic if the character was an aspiring ballerina, whose whim her rich husband indulges by building her a dance studio in their large country mansion.

I was sceptical about my chances but didn't mind too much; just being invited to take the trip to Paris was exciting enough. I was met at Orly airport by Joe Strick's secretary, Sally, and was limousine-ed to one of those large, elegant apartment houses in a wide tree-lined boulevard. Joe turned out to be a big, kindly American, and not at all as daunting as I had expected. He explained over a cup of coffee that the character was to be 'foreign', but he didn't mind from where exactly, and as I do a pretty convincing 'general foreign' that was no problem. Then he asked if I could dance.

"Dance how?" I asked.

"Well, at a bar."

"Oh, I can do that!" I answered, imagining that one of the scenes was probably set in a club of some sort, and that the character, perhaps a little the worse for wear, finds the tempo of the background music irresistible.

"Would you mind showing me?" he asked. "Why not use the back of that chair to hold onto?"

Oops, I thought, she's obviously drunker than I'd imagined.

Hanging onto the proffered chair, I began to gyrate as provocatively as I could, with a shimmy here and a hip swivel there. Joe Strick watched me in amazement, then threw back his head and guffawed.

"Great, kid, but that's not quite it! What I meant was dancing at a barre. B-A-R-R-E. Barre, as in ballet. You know?"

"Ah," I managed, feeling extremely foolish.

Now, it just so happens that I had been to ballet classes from a very early age; I even have a snapshot of myself, obnoxiously cute, posing in a sagging tarlatan tutu. However, in spite of my enthusiasm, I didn't stand a chance as a ballerina because I was born 'turned in' rather than 'out'. My knees stay stubbornly facing front, my legs refuse to swing any higher than a coffee table and, to my everlasting regret, I cannot do the splits. Whilst never exactly improving, I persisted with dance classes on and off through the years, acquiring just enough technique to get away with looking as if I knew what I was doing.

Joe watched me with interest as I readjusted my body (as well as my head), turned my feet outwards as far as I could and, holding onto the chair back, began to plié, my free arm circling (I hoped) elegantly.

"That's just fine," said Joe, putting a gratifying end to my demonstration. Then he added, "Can you do it en pointe?"

En pointe! I froze. I had once tried to learn to dance en pointe and failed miserably. Whenever I managed to get myself onto my toes I would find it impossible to straighten my buckling knees, and I staggered around looking like an inebriated frog.

"How long have I got before you start shooting the scenes?" I asked, trying to sound casual, my mind racing.

"Ten days," came the reply.

It never ceases to amaze me what actors will do or say to get jobs.

"Ten days," I echoed, my voice sounding a little higher than usual, "Fine. That's about all I'll need to brush up on my technique."

I assumed the interview was over. It wasn't.

"How do you feel about wearing just a tutu and pointe shoes?"

I wasn't absolutely certain what he meant. At least, I hoped I wasn't absolutely certain what he meant.

"A tutu and shoes and ...?" I hesitated.

"No top. Bare boobs," he said bluntly. "The scene is a sequence where Henry dreams about you dancing topless. How do you feel about it?"

I'd never been asked to expose any part of my anatomy to the public before, but, although I felt a certain reluctance, this was a 'legitimate' film being made by a well-known director for a large company and based on a classic.

"No problem!" I said. Lying.

At that moment the true measure of what I had taken on hit me. Not so much the bosom baring, although that did nag at the back of my mind, but the fact that I had only ten days to get to grips with that most unnatural and painful terpsichorean feat.

"Would you mind if I phone the Dance Centre in Covent Garden to arrange a few private lessons? It might be a good idea if I didn't waste any time and started tomorrow."

Sally found the number and I fixed a lesson for the following morning with Arlene Phillips who was one of the dance instructors. Then I asked whether there was somewhere in Paris where we could buy pointe shoes "to save time tomorrow", and again she obliged, looking through the phone book and finding an address.

"Come on," she said, picking up her coat, "we'll drop in on the way to the airport."

The small boutique stood in a narrow, cobbled arcade, and together we climbed the dark staircase lined with photographs of dancers in various poses and signed with messages of gratitude and affection. At the top was a heavily embossed glass door, and pushing it open we found ourselves in a dimly lit, carpeted salon, down the centre of which stood a regimented row of elegant, gold, crimson-cushioned chairs. Out of the gloom a gaunt, ageless woman appeared and approached silently.

"Oui?"

She tilted her head to one side like a curious bird. Sally's French was way ahead of mine, so I left her to do the explaining, and seeing a display case nearby, wandered over to inspect its contents. There, artistically laid out, were boxes of powder, coloured sticks of make-up and the most unlikely sets of eyelashes, while at the far end I noticed a collection of small triangular beards. How sweet! Perhaps they're for dwarves or midgets, I thought. How very accommodating! Sally called me back and the assistant waved me towards one of the chairs. Then she sat on a low stool in front of me, put my unshod foot onto what looked like a Japanese growth restrainer and adjusted it to my size.

"Moment," she said, and left us to await her return.

"You see that cabinet over there?" I whispered to Sally. "It's got a collection of the cutest little beards on display. Go and look!"

Sally went over, then came back smiling hugely.

"You are naive!" she said. "Those are merkins. Strippers and dancers wear them if they've shaved their pubes for work and want to look normal at …well, other times!"

This trip was proving educational.

The assistant returned, balancing a pile of boxes in her arms. She took a small square of green plastic and spread it carefully on the floor in front of me. Opening a box, she reverently took out a satin shiny pink shoe with its toe end squarely chopped off.

Having eased my foot into it, she stood up and said with unexpected authority, "Levez!"

I stood up as instructed and put the blunted end of my shod foot onto the plastic square, reluctant to do much more.

"Levez! Levez," she repeated with some irritation, demonstrating with her hands that I was to rise up, like Lazarus, onto my toes. I looked helplessly at Sally.

"Alors," the assistant said with a shrug, then with an imperious "Madame!" she waved Sally to the other side of me. They each grabbed hold of an elbow and hoisted me up.

"Put me down, put me down!" I shrieked, as the unexpected pain of the full weight on my toes shot through me. I dropped back into the chair.

More dialogue passed between them and at last a compromise

seemed to be reached. I sat there without protest while my feet were shoved in and out of various sizes of aptly named 'pumps', until it was agreed which size was suitable for me. I left the shop with my purchase feeling distinctly disheartened, but as I climbed aboard the plane my spirits lifted. After all, I was going to be filming in Paris, and I was clutching the most chic of French packages, inside of which nestled my very own pair of genuine ballerina's pink satin pointe shoes.

That night back in London, Sally phoned to say that she would be sending a cassette of the music I was to dance to, and she asked me to get my ballet coach to devise a short sequence for me to perform. I put the phone down with foreboding. There was no time to lose, so I decided that I would start getting used to wearing the shoes that very evening. My mother, who was visiting me at the time, sewed on the ribbons that had been supplied, both of us guessing where, exactly, they should go. I was about to slip the shoes on when I remembered seeing dancers first wrap their toes in some sort of padding. All I had was cotton wool but it seemed adequate, so I padded up, pulled the shoes on, and tied the ribbons around my ankles. The moment of truth had come. Gritting my teeth, I tried to get up onto my toes. Useless. I tried again and still couldn't manage it. Then I had a brainwave. I had some ironing to do. Surely the support of the ironing board would be just what I needed, not only to keep me up on my toes, but also to help me straighten my knees. Thus it was that, despite the pain, for almost an hour that evening I ironed my weekly wash while standing en pointe with only partially buckled knees. When I removed the shoes I found that the heat and pressure of my sweating feet had compressed the cotton wool into stone-hard pads, and, peeling them painfully away, I discovered that my toes were raw and red and bleeding. I knew I was in trouble.

At the dance centre Arlene took one horrified look at my feet. She couldn't believe my stupidity.

"You've blown it! It's unlikely you'd have made it in ten days anyway, but now, no chance! You'll have to wait for your toes to heal. What you're supposed to do," she said, "is harden the skin of your feet by soaking them in surgical spirit. And when EVENTUALLY you put on your pointe shoes you wrap your toes in animal wool, which has some spring in it. Animal wool, definitely not cotton wool!"

"Look Arlene," I said, gripping her shoulders, "There's no question about this, I've GOT to do it! It's a wonderful opportunity. Besides," I wheedled, "it's only a very short sequence. Come on, we can do it."

She looked at me, then at my raw feet.

"We both," she said wryly, "must be crazy."

The first task was to abandon the Paris purchase and buy a pair of pointe shoes two sizes larger, a couple of boxes of animal wool, several bottles of surgical spirit and a quantity of plasters. Then we were all set to go. I discovered that pointe dancing is not, as I thought, performed on the ends of the toes, but on the 'knuckles', as it were. You more or less throw yourself onto them. As for straightening my knees, it took many painful hours and much determination to achieve. Yet, despite the eye-watering dousing of raw toes in surgical spirit, and the stiffness and cramp of muscles I had no idea I owned, somehow I managed, and by the time I got to Paris ten days later I had a simple but effective routine that I could perform passably well … and very, very sore feet.

I had been booked into a small hotel in the centre of Paris, and the filming was done just outside the city in Malmaison, an impressive, rundown old mansion built by Napoleon for Josephine. Early each morning a car would pick me up, along with the French actor playing my husband, and drive us to the location, returning to the hotel late that same evening. This meant that, disappointingly, I saw very little of the city itself. Nonetheless, I enjoyed my days at the location hugely, watching the other scenes being shot, getting to know the rest of the unit, and wandering around the rambling house and overgrown gardens. Henry Miller was being played by a fine actor of considerable reputation, Rip Torn the Second, his father having been Rip Torn before him. My character was involved in two scenes: the first, a dinner with my husband and Henry, during which he flirted outrageously with me whenever my husband's attention was greedily fixed on his dinner plate; the second, the dreaded dream sequence.

Filming in France was very different from filming in England; the system was much more relaxed. We would start shooting in the morning at nine-thirty or so, break for lunch around two o'clock, and go on late into the evening, until it was decided that enough footage was 'in the can'; unless, of course, they were shooting outside, in which case the light dictated the schedule.

Lunches at Malmaison were the most fun. The location caterers would put trestle tables out on the vast front lawn, cover them with gleaming white linen cloths, and set out plates of cold meats, sausages and cheeses, huge bowls of salads and fruit, long loaves of crusty bread and large unlabelled bottles of the local wine. Actors and crew would sit on long benches, eating, drinking and chatting in the warm September sunshine, and from time to time Henry Miller himself would join us. He was well into his eighties, and would arrive in a large car, dressed in an immaculate white suit and panama hat. He loved the idea that there were three actresses on hand playing three of his erstwhile mistresses.

One day, as he sat with us at lunch, a glass of wine in one hand, a cigarette in the other, he turned to the director and said, "Tell me Joe, who's playing the Afro Asian girl in the movie?"

Joe Strick looked puzzled.

"What Afro-Asian girl, Henry?" he queried.

"Oh come on, Joe," said Henry, with some irritation. "You know, the Afro Asian girl who used to recite the bible while I was f***ing her."

"But Henry," said Joe, confused, "there is no Afro-Asian girl in *Tropic of Cancer*."

Henry looked devastated.

"Goddamit!" he said, with a regretful shake of the head, "did I forget to write about her?"

They had adapted a few of the smaller upstairs rooms into the make-up and wardrobe departments, as well as a couple of dressing rooms, while the filming itself was done in some of the larger rooms downstairs, redecorated as needs dictated. One scene was set in a brothel, and a long room with an ornate ceiling had been metamorphosed into a sleazy salon furnished with over stuffed sofas and worn chaises longues. A dozen or so extras cast as prostitutes were to lounge provocatively in various states of déshabillé, and, assuming that they would be less embarrassed to appear partially nude than bona fide actresses, Joe and his assistant Sally had cast a number of local dancers and strippers. Once the dialogue between Rip, as Henry and the Madame of the establishment had been rehearsed and the moves plotted, the extras, still discreetly covered by a variety of shawls and dressing gowns, were given their places and told

214

what was required of them.

"Right ladies," the first assistant called, "let's have those wraps off!"

And off they came, one by one. As they stood exposed, Joe stared in disbelief. They were shaved, every one of them - not a pubic hair to be seen! This was out of period, so they were unusable and would all have to be paid off and released. An expensive day's shooting was lost. Joe sat dejectedly in a faded armchair while Sally delivered a short speech in French explaining the situation to the astonished cast. As the women got up, the murmur of disappointment grew, and, re-wrapping, they reluctantly left the set ... all but one. Since the announcement a young woman had been sitting quietly in a corner with her handbag open beside her, and as the room cleared she made her way over to where Sally and Joe were discussing this unexpected setback.

"Pardon, monsieur," she said urgently, clutching her gown tightly around her and tugging at Joe's sleeve.

Joe wasn't in the mood for any sort of interruption and he turned round with some irritation.

"What is it?"

She launched into a flow of French, which he clearly didn't understand, so he turned to Sally, gesturing for her to deal with the matter. The woman repeated her speech even more animatedly and then threw her open gown. In lieu of the missing pubic hair was a triangle of careful squiggles drawn in with a dark brown eyebrow pencil. I never knew if they recalled her when they re-shot the scene, but had it been up to me I would have left her as she was, and given her a special feature.

"My first scene, the dinner à trois, took two days to shoot and seemed to go well. At the end of the second day Joe beamed at me.

"Tomorrow," he said, "is your big day. Ready for it?"

"Ready? Absolutely!"

Well, I was as ready as I would ever be; I had spent as much time as I could throwing myself onto my toe knuckles in those squared-off shoes, practising my routine. Early the next morning the car delivered me to Malmaison and I was shown the set. They had converted the conservatory at the back of the house into a dance studio, and the full-length windows running the length of the conservatory had been curtained off to enable

215

the lighting man to get the effect he wanted. Joe called me over to him.

"Would you like us to close the set so that only the people directly concerned with shooting the scene are allowed in? It might make it easier for you."

"Yes, I'd appreciate that," I said, and meant it.

Claire, the young French girl who had been designated as my dresser during the filming, was waiting for me upstairs. In spite of my poor French and her even poorer attempts at English, we had become quite friendly over the few days we had been working together, and on the small bed she had laid out a pair of pink panties, and a stiff pink tutu - hardly what could be called a costume!

"You have wiz you ze shoes, oui?"

I had with me the shoes, oui. I took them out of their plastic bag, along with the animal wool, the surgical spirit and my collection of plasters. Then, with a sigh of resignation, I stripped off and pulled on the skimpy ballet gear. As she reached for the shoes I stopped her.

"Not yet," I said. "Not just yet."

Wrapping a shawl around my naked upper torso, I followed Claire down the corridor to see the make-up man - or rather, for him to see me. He was a pleasant faced man, probably in his fifties, small, rotund, and balding. We stood and eyed each other.

"Alors," he said brightly, "first, ze face."

Somewhat relieved, I sat in the swivel chair at the dressing table, covered with pots and puffs, bottles and brushes. He worked in silence, frowning with concentration, and when he had done, he motioned me to look into the brightly lit mirror. I saw a pale face with dramatic eyes, my hair scraped back into a pleat. The effect boosted my confidence; at least I looked like a ballerina. It was now inescapably time for 'le body make-up'. I stood in front of the little Frenchman, trying to appear nonchalant, and removed the shawl. He kept his eyes down, busily unscrewing the lids off several wide, flat compacts of pancake, sorting out various sponges and then dunking them into a large bowl of water and squeezing them out. I waited, chilly. Eventually, he raised his eyes and, taking a step back, surveyed my boobs critically through half-closed lids.

"Ah, pauvre petite!" he said sympathetically. "You have ze

216

gooseberries!"

I was somewhat put out. My breasts weren't large, but they certainly didn't warrant that sort of comment!

Seeing the look on my face, he laughed.

"You are cold, I can see!" And he rubbed his arms to demonstrate what he meant.

"Oh, goosebumps!"

"Goosebumps," he repeated, and we laughed; the ice had been broken and I managed to relax a little.

Taking a large, damp spongeful, he began briskly busying himself with my upper torso. He worked quickly, his tongue protruding slightly from the corner of his mouth. With the tip of his little finger, he delicately lifted up one breast and patted underneath it with the sponge, and then repeated the manoeuvre with the other, all the while whistling tunelessly between his teeth. This man, I thought, has class!

On the set Claire appeared at my side with the shoes plus all their paraphernalia and I prepared my feet for action. The soundman started the tape, the music began, and with it one of the longest days of my life. It was one thing to dance a routine, but quite another to dance a routine to be filmed. First I performed it to show Joe what I was going to do. Next I did it and re did it for the cameraman, and then I had to redo bits of it for the lighting technician. When the camera finally turned I did it in full, in long bits, in short bits, and eventually in bits out of sequence. The embarrassment of bouncing boobs was quickly superseded by the torment of tortured toes. Only a skeleton crew watched me suffering, and I vaguely wondered what the rest of the technicians were doing with themselves. I found out during a short break while the lights were being refocused. In need of a breath of fresh air, I strolled round to the back of the house where the conservatory windows had been curtained off, and found a dozen or so of the crew on their knees, bottoms uppermost. I couldn't have cared less; by that time my concentration was strictly below my waist rather than above it.

At lunchtime Claire found me sitting in my dressing room, my aching feet propped up on a chair in front of me. I stared at them miserably.

"You will take them off, the shoes?" she asked solicitously.

"Don't touch them!" I yelped. "I'll never get them back on again!"

217

By teatime I was beyond caring, felt no pain and could have gone on indefinitely. Claire was more anxious than ever, as she stood watching me pirouette and sweat and endure, her face contorted in sympathy with each painful move. At last the shoot was over, the day was done, and the scene was, as they say, in the can. Exhausted and leaning on Claire, I just about managed the stairs to my dressing room, and as she gently peeled off the shoes I sank back and thought: I did it, I bloody did it! And that was no exaggeration, because somewhere in a cupboard in my loft, wrapped in a faded but unmistakably chic French packet, lies a pair of pink satin pointe shoes, with bloodstains to prove it.

The film eventually came out, and the general view was that it was neither particularly good nor particularly bad. It seems that the producers ran out of money, and so midway through the quality deteriorates. As for me, when I saw it in a cine centre near Trafalgar Square at its London release I loved it, and was thrilled to have been in it. Joe had included a lingering shot of Henry Miller - nothing to do with the plot, just the whim of a director with foresight and sensitivity. And now and again I remind myself, with pride tempered with more than a little disbelief, that I once danced for Henry Miller.

Looking through my cuttings, I found just one review of the film written by a Colin Hardcastle. It is less than flattering:

There are a few cheap laughs from references to faeces and syphilis, a two-second shot of Henry Miller himself, and the sound of children singing Frère Jacques in the background, presumably for atmosphere. The combination of pretentious philosophising and pornography, which retains a tenuous hold on the reader of the book, totally fails to make any visual impact.

And of the actors he wrote:

Rip Torn ... seems to change character almost every scene, and of the women who treat us to a view of their pubes, only Sheila Steafel is convincing as a person.

READY WHEN YOU ARE, MR DeMILLE

The film was originally called *Melody,* but later for some reason it was renamed S.W.A.L.K. In time it became a cult movie, and it was one of the first films produced by David (now Lord) Puttnam, and directed by Waris Hussein. The story and screenplay were by Alan Parker and the director of photography was Peter Suschitzky - not a bad line-up! I played the dotty, gushing mother of Daniel (played by Mark Lester of *Oliver* fame), Jack Wild (ditto) played his mate Ornshaw, and Roy Kinnear (sorely missed) played Melody's (Tracy Hyde) father and Kate Williams her mother. It is a tale of love in a comprehensive school, and according to the *Evening Standard,* "The story may sound glutinously silly, but it is done lightly and effectively."

We filmed during holiday time in a school in Hammersmith, a vast Victorian building, adapting the rooms to the script's needs, and, apart from a day when I had some sort of gastric bug and lay groaning between shots, a happy time was had by all. One pivotal scene involved a dinner party, and Waris decided to shoot it from the point of view of the children at the table, making the loud, mindless adult chatter, combined with the shovelling of food into mouths, seem gross. We spent two days eating a concoction that looked like lasagne but was mostly scrambled egg, while the camera filmed us from every angle in long shot, medium shot and close-up. There were close-ups of mouths chewing and talking, of forks going up to mouths and down again, in fact of every permutation they could think of. It became impossible to swallow the stuff, so buckets were placed off set, and after each shot one or other of us would leave the table to spit out the now almost nauseating mouthfuls.

During the filming I was offered a cameo role involving only a single day's shooting, and, generously, the *Melody* schedule was rearranged so that I could have the day off. The film was *Percy,* which starred Hywel Bennett and featured Britt Ekland, Julia Foster and Denholm Elliott. The film is about a man who, after a nasty accident with a chandelier, is given a penis transplant, and he goes in search of the donor, equipped with a list of deaths in the hospital where he was re-tooled. I was to play a rabbi's wife, and a chauffeur-driven car picked me up bright and early, sweeping me off to Pinewood to film in a proper professional studio for the very first time. My costume had been fitted during the previous week, and once dressed and made up I was shown onto the set and introduced to the director, Ralph Thomas, and to Hywel Bennett. The scene took place in 'my' drawing room, and through it I was to serve Hywel tea from an elegant china service and offer him a biscuit, which he was to take and eat. That bothered him.

"I'm on this very strict diet," he explained, "and I put on weight very easily."

The producer was insistent that he should eat something, and after a long discussion a biscuit lookalike was devised by the canteen, made mainly, as far as I can recall, of hard-boiled egg.

"And I'm only going to nibble at it," said the star.

We rehearsed the scene, and Hywel pretended to eat the 'biscuit', promising a genuine nibble on the take. The warning bell rang to alert everyone that we were about to shoot.

"Quiet, everyone! Mark it!"

"Scene seventeen, take one!"

"And ... action!"

The camera turned, and, with Hywel sitting on a sofa opposite me, I began to speak my lines. When at the given point I offered him the plate of biscuits, he took the fake one, and I watched him nibble reluctantly at a corner. The last two days of stuffing lasagne down our gullets flashed across my mind and I dried, the lines wiped out of my head. I was transfixed by the anomaly of yesterday's force-feeding and today's whimsical indulgence.

"Okay, let's go again."

Again the bell, the sudden hush, the tension, and again my sense of disbelief kicked in. We began the dialogue, but anticipation of the biscuit nibble to come wiped everything out of my head once more, and I sat staring blankly at my fellow actor, who was beginning to show the teensiest sign of irritation.

Before we started yet again, the director called out something encouraging like, "Don't worry, dear, let's try again."

And try again I did. But I was beginning to panic, and as my nerves got the better of me the teacup I handed to Hywel rattled noisily in the saucer. I was living through 'The Actors' Nightmare'!

"Cut! Take five, everyone."

The crew melted away, Hywel stomped off to his dressing room, and Ralph Thomas came over to me as I sat, miserable and mortified, on the abandoned set. Putting a sympathetic arm around my shoulder, he walked me round the darkened studio, quietly trying to boost my confidence. Somehow I got through the scene, but I've seen the film and, although those elusive lines are certainly there, there's little else to commend my performance.

I wasn't one of those fortunates whom 'the camera loves'; my looks didn't conform, and consequently I never had much opportunity to hone the art of screen acting. I did stand briefly and thrillingly next to Kirk Douglas as Woman in Lift in *To Catch a Spy*, sat next to Tom Courtenay in *Otley*, lay on the side of a swimming pool beside Dick Emery, and got to move around as a fairly mad scientist in *Bloodbath at the House of Death*, a film that starred Kenny Everett. Oddly, two of the smallest parts I played in the sixties gave me the most recognition, because the films themselves became cult movies. One was *Daleks' Invasion Earth*, in which I played Young Woman, and the other was *Quatermass and the Pit* as Young Reporter, wearing a memorable red beret.

In 1974 I was in what can only be described as a 'powder blue' movie, directed by Bob Kellett, an innovative and enterprising film director and a friend of long standing. It was produced by Wilbur Stark, father of Koo, and was entitled *All I Want is You … and You … and You*, and the only critical comment I found is from *Cinema Today*:

> *The mind boggles. A slapstick sex farce, this is a bizarre amalgam of intellectual fringe theatre frolic and a tit and bum show for football supporters on a spree.*

The story is set in a country house group therapy clinic run by a Dr Brack. Unknown to the guests, the doctor has a supposedly paralysed wife Wilma (me), who is given to stabbing people. An advertising agency due to choose a new vice president has booked in a group of contenders. During a session of 'touch therapy', a figure resembling Harpo, but actually Wilma (shades of things to come!) enters and tries to stab a few of them, but, disguised as Groucho, Dr Brack intervenes. (Are you with me so far?) Various couples mix and mingle, mostly in the nude and sometimes in a swimming pool. Our director assured the cast that the 'blue' bits would be discreetly handled, and any naughty bits were as distantly vague as the storyline. I do, however, vividly remember the fine old country house used as the filming location. Wilma's bedroom was set in the conservatory, which had an enormous tree growing out of its centre, the branches curving against the high glass-domed ceiling. I lay 'paralysed' in a large four-poster bed, and to prove to a guest that my legs were numb and useless Dr Brack had to stick a knife into one of them. I knelt with both my legs tucked under me, while two stabable polystyrene limbs were laid out in front. My only contribution to the 'blue' element of the film was when, dressed as Harpo, my coat fell open briefly to expose one breast before I clamped my top hat over it. We never got to see the final cut. It appears that Mr Stark tucked the rushes under his arm and disappeared, and it was only finding the review that made me aware it had been finished and distributed.

The Frost Report had given me celebrity status, and I was invited to take part in several game shows, which I accepted but probably should have turned down. I couldn't hack it, I was useless at being a jolly, outgoing member of a panel, and I found it grindingly uncomfortable. Why did I do them? Good exposure, my agent said, and it was a fair fee for doing very little. The only quiz programme I appeared in several times and greatly enjoyed was *Call My Bluff*, always on Arthur Marshall's team and constantly teasing Frank Muir. The only other panel show I managed to have fun on was *Juke Box Jury*, in which we had to give our opinions on current pop records.

A few days before this particular programme was aired I was interviewed by the producer of a film entitled *Monsieur Lecoq*. It was to be filmed in France and to star Zero Mostel playing himself, not only as an adult but also as a baby (presumably in a Very Large Pram!) The role on offer was the dual one, Zero's wife and also his mother, but disappointingly, my agent called to say that I hadn't got the part. The day after *Juke Box Jury* went out she phoned to tell me that the producer had changed his mind. It seems he had been watching TV with his kids, seen me in the programme, and decided I was right for the part after all. The cast included John Le Mesurier, Julie Newmar and Akim Tamiroff, as well as Ronnie Corbett, with Seth Holt directing. I was flown to Van Gogh's famed Arles, where we began shooting.

Zero was larger than life, charming and abrasively witty. Along with Seth and the producers, he and his wife were staying at the Auberge De Noves, a small, unpretentious hotel on the outskirts of the town that boasted a three Michelin star restaurant. One evening, as a treat, a few of us were invited to join them for dinner. It is the only time I have sat in a dining room that was silent except for the discreet clatter of cutlery on plates and sighs of ecstatic gastronomic pleasure.

We usually ate in a local restaurant where the fare was good but plain. One evening I ordered sea snails, the speciality of the house.

"Are you sure?" asked the owner's wife uncertainly.

"I love escargot," I told her in slow English, to make myself thoroughly understood. "I eat them in London, so of course I am 'bien sûr'."

On the plate she brought to my table were three snails, large, grey and steaming; there was no attempt to disguise them in any sort of sauce. They sat there, upright and defiant, the size of billiard balls and just as unappetising. All eyes in the room were on me. Bravely picking up my fork, I tried to spear one, but it refused to give. Abandoning the fork, I shovelled it onto a handy spoon and with some effort put it into my mouth and chewed … and chewed … and chewed some more. It was no use. With thumb and forefinger I extracted it as delicately as I could, and acknowledged the round of applause from the locals.

We had been filming for about ten days when issues between Zero and the production company, Columbia, overtook the project, and a decision was made to shelve it. We were packed off home, and what would have been a fillip to my career turned into a flop.

SOME WILL

In 1970 I was cast in a film entitled *Some Will, Some Won't*. It was a remake of the 1951 film *Laughter in Paradise*, which starred Alastair Sim, Eleanor Summerfield, Joyce Grenfell and George Cole. Our version had an equally glittering cast, comprising Ronnie Corbett, Thora Hird, James Robertson Justice, Dennis Price and, again, Eleanor Summerfield, who this time played the Joyce Grenfell part while I played hers, and Michael Hordern replaced Alastair Sim. The only review I could find of our version stated, "This is a very bad remake with all the subtlety left out and some crude slapstick put in!" Seeing it I have to agree, but at the time there were two huge pluses for me: firstly, it was my first sizeable film role and I relished it; and secondly, I got to know Michael Hordern.

I played Michael's secretary, and although I was overawed to be working with an actor of his stature he was unpretentious and easy to get on with. We seemed to 'click', and it wasn't long before we were spending time together off the set, doing crosswords and exchanging opinions on this and that. Once the filming was done we would meet regularly for dinner, and it seemed a perfectly natural consolidation of our mutual affection when our friendship became an affair. From time to time we would send one another short missives with odd bits of gossip. He had recorded the stories of Paddington Bear, and he sent me the following delightful note, dated May 1979:

Lunched with the Queen, P.P. and 7 others at the Palace today. If I wasn't a Royalist before, which I was, I surely am now. I fell for the lady. Gone the grumpy-faced creature beloved by the cartoonists, protocol out of the way she's almost a comedienne. Light on her feet, funny stories (imitations and all!) And a fan of Paddington!

Over time our affair lost its passion, turning instead into a deep and lasting friendship. He was well known as a keen fisherman, and I often found a freshly caught trout wrapped in newspaper outside the door of my flat, left in the early morning on his way home from his country cottage. When his wife Eve died Michael was devastated, and, hopelessly undomesticated, he wasn't coping with the practical side of everyday living. When I visited him in his country cottage I was surprised at how scruffy the place had become and duly organised decorators to move in and renovate the rooms, while I made fresh sets of curtains. His fridge was in a very sorry state, and when I forced the freezer compartment open, found it solid with ice. There was nothing for it but to hack at it, and when at last I had tunnelled my way in, I found a solitary bag of ancient frozen peas. I put buckets and newspapers in place to catch the melting ice and instructed Michael to wait for the thaw. He phoned the next morning to complain that there was a faint hissing coming from the dripping appliance. "Dump it outside immediately," I urged, "and buy another before you asphyxiate!"

The Garrick Club had requested that Michael provide them with a portrait of himself, and when he mentioned it to me I asked if he would consider letting me try painting him myself. He agreed, and I was delighted. However, I was also wary, and asked that we keep it to ourselves for the moment, because I was never absolutely certain that my paintings would turn out well. He sat for me four or five times and we agreed that the final result was worth offering to the committee. They liked it, but requested that I "paint in the rest of the cardigan"! (As is my wont, I had left the lower part roughed in). Michael sat once more in his M&S cardi and I put in the details, button for button. The amended canvas was offered up, and a week later Michael sent me the following postcard received from 'Nunc' Wilcox (who, he assured me, was on every committee and virtually ran the Garrick!)

Michael,
Your portrait was greeted with great pleasure. She really has "got" you and in doing so has enabled you to give us a picture which we shall value enormously. Congratulate her for me.
Many thanks
Nunc.

And now, hanging in that illustrious club alongside the Reynolds's and Gainsborough's, an elaborately framed portrait of Sir Michael Hordern can be found, and on it a brass plaque engraved with both our names. What more could a girl ask for? Although the Garrick's stringent rules stipulate that no women are allowed into the bar where the portrait initially hung, I was smuggled in to sneak a look while Sir Michael and the barman kept a lookout.

Towards the end, when Michael was really poorly, I went to see him in The Clinic. The nurse called me aside.

"Can you persuade him to eat? He's refusing his dinners."

I sat at his bedside and asked him what the problem was.

Taking my hand, he said, "Sheila dear, I simply can't have dinner at 6 o'clock in the evening, it's uncivilised!"

They agreed to change his mealtime to 8 o'clock.

Our relationship lasted for twenty-four years, and although he was twenty or so years my senior we were never particularly conscious of the difference in our ages. Michael Hordern, Sir, was a lovely man, and I miss him still.

HAMBURG WITH RELISH

There was a time when being seen in a television commercial was considered the bottom line, a sign of financial desperation. How things have changed! Nowadays actors watch with envy as celebrities endorse products they wouldn't consider having anywhere near their supermarket trolleys. As for voice-overs, there seems to be a closed circle of elite performers who dominate them. The repeat fees can be highly remunerative, and unlike the visual side it is possible for the same voice to advertise several different products at the same time. It is a skill, and any actor who can knock exactly two-and-a-half seconds off a 'take', or 'lip synch' speech exactly to picture, let alone fit more words than you'd think possible into the shortest time AND make sense of it, is bound to be worth his or her weight in Gold Blend. Miriam Margolyes is not only brilliant at this job, but is also extremely honest and blunt when it comes to dealing with people. I was once in a recording session with her when she expressed her honest and less than flattering opinion of the script to the panel of advertising executives. I was shocked, and as we left the studio I told her I thought that she was asking for trouble, and if she didn't curb her openness she would ruin her chances of work. She ignored my advice, became a major voice-over star and built herself an enviable movie career in Hollywood, while I stayed firmly earthbound.

Ages ago I was in a TV advert for Hovis. It was the only visual I ever did in this country and was, I think, the first commercial that Alan Parker directed, winning him an award. As far as I recall, an ordinary, timid 'he' sat on a park bench with an equally ordinary, timid 'me', and I offered him a choice of two exotic teas out of two separate thermos flasks to accompany our Hovis sandwiches. Later I did do a promotional film, *Grounds for Suspicion*, when the cafetière was new and about to percolate into our lives. Amongst the cast were Penelope Keith, who played my sister, Aubrey Woods, Fred Emney and Glyn Houston. Not bad for a short coffee sales pitch.

Another promotional film I did was for NatWest, alongside Kenneth Williams. I hadn't worked with him before and was really looking forward to it, but it turned out to be a deep disillusion. We filmed in a tiny studio in Battersea. Kenneth was dressed as Dracula, complete with fangs et al., and I played his sidekick in a long black gown and long black wig. The technicians, all youngsters, struggled with the unwieldy set of large tombstones in the restricted space, while Kenneth, bored and fed up, complained bitterly about the set, his costume and the tedium of waiting. There were more problems with the lighting, and as Kenneth's temper grew shorter his tongue became viperish. He had us all twitching with nerves and the atmosphere was static with agitation. Eventually he cornered me and proceeded to discuss in detail and at length the ineptitudes of the script and the crew. I thought it wisest to agree, and when we were called back onto the set I squeezed his arm.

"If we ignore them it might get us out of here quicker!"

My hint seemed to work, although the climate in the studio, as well as my opinion of him, never quite recovered.

Casting for most visual commercials begins with an audition, and because they are looking for a particular type you can bet your tube fare that each time you're going to bump into the same group of contemporaries. You walk into reception and join the hopeful row of women of a similar age, complaining about their agents, the script they've just been handed and the time they've been waiting, and assuring each other that they'd rather not take the job even if they were offered it. One by one they're called in, you wish them luck and don't mean it, and then it's your turn and the real embarrassment begins. The clients, a few advertising agency hotshots, plus the film director and casting director, sit at one end the large bare room behind a table covered with half full trays of tempting sandwiches (actors are always hungry) and used coffee cups. To one side stands a bored young man with a video camera poised on a tripod. Cue humiliation. Some of the actions you're asked to perform are often cringe-making, but the money factor looms large, so you grit your teeth and, hating yourself for doing it, do it. I have munched my way through a packet of inedible biscuits while registering their yummy-ness, and shown embarrassed surprise (or was it surprised embarrassment?) as two other actors discussed my (hopefully) imagined body odour, and I have been asked to promote an orange drink while crossing the studio as a very ancient granny who explodes. It was an impossible task, and as I left I remarked what a pity it was that flatulence was involuntary. Another observation that lost me a job was when I was asked to lick my way suggestively around an ice lolly. After a minute or so I stopped and said, "This can't be right, it's getting smaller!"

Sometimes, if you're lucky, a small bonus will appear in the shape of a commercial to be shot abroad for a foreign market. This means that no one seeing it will know who you are, you'll earn a nice little fee, all expenses paid, and you'll see a new and exciting city. Not true, of course; all you'll see is a dim impression as your pickup car speeds to the location at six o'clock in the morning, and a bleary-eyed view as you're driven back to your hotel at some unearthly hour of the night.

The foreign commercial I auditioned for was to be shot in Germany. Instead of the usual clutch of executives in the casting studio, there was just one frantic woman plus the statutory bored camera operator.

"Now darling," she twittered, "I've just spoken to Hamburg on a rather dodgy line. They want you to rumba or samba or something, so I rushed out and bought this tape. I'll play it and you dance round with ... come in, whoever's next!"

A large-bosomed actress hesitated at the door.

"Right, you keep your back towards the camera," she instructed, "and you," - she tugged me into position – "just dance in a sort of South American way and flirt with the camera."

I gyrated in what I thought would pass as a sort of samba and ogled.

"Lovely, darling," she crowed. "Now tell them something about yourself."

"My name is Sheila Steafel," I simpered shamelessly. "I've never seen Hamburg and I'd love to, and I know Hamburg would love to see me."

"I liked very much your amusing video," said the bearded, balding German director. "You say you should have the job, I give you the job."

It was three days later and I was in Hamburg advertising a building society, though how the script related to it was hard to tell. An elderly waiter with a tray full of glasses crosses a busy dance floor just as the band leader announces, "Ladies' Choice," whereupon a stream of hysterical and presumably sex-starved women frantically pursue him, and coat-tails flying (wired horizontally, how else?) he escapes through a fire exit. I can only surmise that the message somehow referred to 'interest'! Three of us had been imported from the UK: myself, an elderly, gentle actor with a Charlie Chaplin moustache who was to play the waiter, and a rather brash dancer who did the samba with tremendous verve and featured a splendidly raucous laugh. When at one point she was asked by the director to give him a different reaction, she beamed, "Sorry, dear, I've only got the one!"

We were filming in a nightclub called the Cafe Keese in the red-light district, and in spite of its location it was considered not only respectable but also quite chic. Its name was up in neon amongst the flashing signs promoting Erotisex, Peep Shows and Sex Messe, which translates as Sex Markets, although the English reading sounds more accurate to me. In the UK, film extras have their own union and rules, whereas in Germany they can use anyone to hand, so, for several nights before the filming, cards had been placed on the tables in the club inviting anyone who fancied it to come along in their own finery and earn a few Deutschmarks to fill in the background, sitting at tables, smoking, drinking and chatting. Around thirty or so men and women arrived at some unearthly hour of the morning to be herded into a narrow corridor where, bumping rumps, they struggled into their evening wear. Once in costume, they were commandeered by the production assistant who stood on a table and barked his instructions in German through a megaphone throughout the day. One particular exhortation was delivered so often and with such ferocity that I felt compelled to ask a nearby technician what exactly he was saying.

"He says that above all they must enjoy themselves."

The filming ran on for its scheduled two days, making very few demands on what talent we had, and time lay heavy. One or two extras acknowledged we three Brits with a nod but kept their distance, until, towards the end of the last afternoon, a woman in her thirties diffidently approached me.

"Excuse please, what is your real job?"

"I'm an actress," I told her.

"Why you do this, then?"

"Well," I said, seeing no reason to lie, "for the money. What do you do?"

She turned to a woman nearby and, putting an arm around her shoulder, said, "We are, how you say, oars."

I looked quizzical.

"Oars!" she repeated. "We making money from sleeping with

229

men."

"Oh, whores!"

"Jah, oars!" And we all had a jolly good laugh. "You know Hamburg?" she asked.

"No," I said. "First time and, well, no time."

"On the other side of the road just here is very special shop. You should see this before you go. It is called The Condomerie!"

"The ... Condomerie?" I wasn't sure I had heard right.

"Jah! All sizes, all colours, all flavours: banana, strawberry, chocolate! Even some with pickles sticking on them!"

"She means 'tickles'," her friend corrected.

When the tea break came I made the hazardous crossing over the Reeperbahn and stood outside Das Condomerie. There they were, pegged out on lines, rows and rows of rather chic little hats for pixies. Some were fiercely triangular, some artistically curved, others with extraordinary twists, and several sporting appendages with intriguing characteristics. More confused than enlightened, I crossed back over the street.

It was our final day, the last shot was shot, the director called out the German equivalent of "Cut and print!" and the assistant director yelled what I supposed was "You can stop enjoying yourselves now!" Wrestling my way through the clamour of shouting of technicians and runners dismantling equipment, I reached Herr-Who-Had-Hired-Me and held out my hand.

"Thank you so much for giving me this job," I said, smiling as winningly as I could and hoping for future castings. "It's been a wonderful experience!"

It was clear he wanted to get on with directorial things, but I held onto his hand.

"Tell me, why do you go to the trouble of getting British actors over here for your commercials instead of using your own German actors?"

He looked at me, probably for the first time.

"You British actors are so much more disciplined, so much more creative," he said, "and so much cheaper!"

THE OTHER HALF

Robin Midgeley, who ran the Phoenix Theatre in Leicester in the seventies, invited me to be in the first production of Alan Ayckbourn's *How the Other Half Loves*, opposite the fine comedy actor and a friend of long standing, Hugh Paddick. Rehearsals were tremendous fun, although Robin did find the two of us quite a handful, and we opened for the short run to gales of laughter and appreciative applause. After the show the stage manager announced over the tannoy that we were called for notes the following afternoon. We sat onstage while Robin delivered the notes he had made during the show, along with some observations from the playwright himself. Each time he came to a note for me he said, "Sheila, lovey, I'll talk to you about that later." And he said it so often, that I began to feel uneasy. When the session was over and we were left alone Robin seemed equally ill at ease.

"Sheila, lovey sweetie," he said - his usual approach when he had something difficult to say, "it's probably my fault. I should have stopped you earlier, but ..." He paused.

"But what?" I asked, holding back the rising panic.

"Well," he said carefully, "Alan says you're too funny."

I stared at him. "Too funny?"

"Yes," he said, warming to his task. "You see, he says - and I agree - that he has written a black comedy, and he wants the laughs to come from the situation and the characters, not from the ... er ..."

"The actor?"

Robin nodded. "Exactly."

"But I thought that was what I was doing!" I said, thoroughly confused. "I mean, I don't know how to do it any differently."

"Why don't you try tonight not going for the laughs? Okay, sweetie baby?"

"Okay."

I sort of understood what Alan meant, but I wasn't sure how to do it. The only thing I could think of to avoid getting laughs was to mistime the funny lines deliberately, so that night that's what I tried to do. It was an interesting exercise and not at all easy, but I managed to kill most of my laughs, and by the interval, instead of an endearingly hopeless housewife, my character had transmuted into an irritatingly useless slattern, and the audience clearly disliked me. A distraught Hugh came to my dressing room.

"Stop it!" he begged. "The play is limping, it's lopsided and I can't carry it!"

So I stopped, and in the second half we were back on course. However, unsurprisingly and regretfully, I have never worked with Alan again.

I stayed on at the Phoenix for the next production, *The Three Sisters*, directed by James Ferman, who later became the controversial director of the British Board of Censors. I played Olga, and Hayley Mills played the youngest sister, Irina. Hayley's twenty-first birthday happened to fall on the day of the dress rehearsal, and she celebrated by treating us all, cast and crew, to a sumptuous Fortnum's hamper. There's class for you! It was my first stage role in a classic, and my confidence received a huge boost when one of the notices said I had "the compassion and wistfulness to make the spinster Olga a memorable character." And not a single laugh!

How the Other Half Loves did go into the West End, with Robert Morley playing the part that Hugh had taken and, of course, without me. It had a long run there - long enough for Mr Morley to relax into it and have fun doing his own thing. I suspect that by then Alan Ayckbourn must have given up on it, which is why, two years after I played in it at the Phoenix Theatre in Leicester, I got to play it at the Lyric Theatre in Shaftsbury Avenue for nine eventful months.

Perhaps Robert and I hit it off because we had both been born on the same day (though not in the same year!), under the twin sign of Gemini. This meant there were four of us in our friendship, and therefore always someone to agree with. He was a delight, not only to work with, but also to be with, a splendid, larger than life character with a zest for life and a love of his fellow man. In order to keep himself from being bored through the run, Robert would think up different amusements. For example, at the end of act one the six characters had to sit round a dinner table eating a two-course meal. The food would be prepared for each performance by the stage management, always the same, and the most expedient. Robert hit on the idea of a competition, challenging each member of the backstage crew to produce two courses costing a small, limited amount, which he would pay. Each night a notebook and pencil were placed at each place setting, and when the interval curtain fell we gave marks for the meal we had just eaten. The results were surprisingly good, and at the end of each week the winner was given a bottle of wine, provided, of course, by our generous star.

On stage Robert Morley was fearless, and one of his delights was ad-libbing. He was given a new dressing gown to replace his old one, and that night on his first entrance he walked straight down to the footlights, turned himself around, and asked the audience, "What do you think of my new gown? Not bad, eh?"

At one point in the play my character visited Robert, and to reinforce the illusion that I had left my baby offstage 'in the hallway' I carried a large bag with me with several toys and other baby things visible, while the lower part was bulked up with crumpled newspaper. One evening, just as we were getting into the scene, with me on the sofa and Robert sitting in a large armchair, outside, he suddenly asked, "What have you got in that bag?"

I was thrown for a moment, but swiftly recovered and said, "Baby things. For the baby."

"Show me," said Robert. I hesitated, but realised that I would have to play along, so I pulled out a scruffy teddy bear and held it up.

"Nice," said my co-star. "Name?"

"Bear," I said.

"Very imaginative. What else?"

I pulled out a rag doll and a one-eared rabbit, waved them at him, and was about to put them back when he asked, "And what else? I can see there's more in there."

All I had left was newspaper. I tried to glare him down, but he wasn't having it. "What?"

Reluctantly, I pulled out a handful of the screwed-up print.

"What's that for then?" he asked. And for some reason my muse smiled on me.

"Cheaper than nappies," I said, and I got an appreciative laugh from the audience, who by now seemed to know what was going on.

While we were playing this game of Hold The Play, Robert had been fiddling with the telephone on the side table next to him, and had inadvertently unscrewed the earpiece. He was now holding one half of the receiver in each hand, and looking at them with some puzzlement. The rest of the act demanded that the telephone was in working order, and Robert's attempt to reunite the two parts was failing miserably.

"Let me help you," I suggested, and made to get up.

"Certainly not!" he said defensively. "Stay where you are! I'll do it!"

His podgy fingers were not ideal for fine coordination, but, frowning with concentration, he doggedly persisted, peering closely at the job in hand. There was nothing to do but wait, so the audience and I held our collective breath. At last the threads connected, the earpiece and receiver were reunited and Robert acknowledged the enthusiastic applause with a wave of the hand.

"Now, where were we?" he asked. I had absolutely no recollection of where exactly we had abandoned the script.

"Won't be a minute," he said to his adoring public, and then, heaving himself out of his chair, he crossed to the prompt corner, had a muttered conversation with the poor ASM whose job it was to keep us on the straight and narrow, and came back beaming.

"Right, then," he said, and the play rolled on.

What Alan Ayckbourn would have made of it doesn't bear consideration!

When the run of the play finished in London we took it to the Alexandra Theatre in Toronto, and on my way back to London I stopped off in Los Angeles to see if I could further my career in the States. As ever, things didn't go to plan. My current lover, a misogynist who had me in his thrall, happened to be on a BBC assignment 'over the road' in Hawaii. He summoned me to join him and, slavishly submissive, I cancelled all interviews and hopped on a flight as bidden, thus tossing away any imminent opportunities to work America.

It was during the run at the Lyric that my friend Dan, from drama school days arrived in London and came to see the play. I asked for news of Tucker.

"Didn't you know?" he asked me in surprise. "He died about six months ago."

I was devastated. Since my trip to New York to visit him, the correspondence between Tucker and I had become sporadic. Then in one of his letters he mentioned that he was anxious because he had begun to stutter. "Don't be so silly," I'd replied. "You're just being your usual neurotic self. You'll be fine." It was, in fact, the first sign of a rare condition known as bulbar palsy, and it slowly took its devastating toll on his life.

Dan told me of Tucker's amazing strength and courage during the progression of his illness. He was determined to stay independent for as long as possible, having adjustments to his apartment made as his needs dictated. As his health deteriorated, he used the capabilities left to him to surmount his growing incapacities, and his specialists sent children with similar problems to visit him, to be reassured that in spite of their handicaps they had a future with possibilities. Eventually Tucker became too ill to manage on his own, and moved into the home of his brother Dick, his Dutch wife Amy and their three sons. By this time he was paralysed and couldn't speak but he was as sharp minded as ever, and Dick set about adapting his room with insight and sensitivity. So that Tucker remained in charge of his own privacy, Dick wired two lights, one red, one green, onto the outside of his bedroom door, which Tucker controlled with a pointer held between his teeth. Each evening at 'cocktail hour' he would, as ever, enjoy a gin and tonic, but now poured into his feeding tube. He typed notes and letters onto a pad with the pointer, and Dan told me that as he deteriorated he said that he had been in grief, first over his love life, and now over his 'life life'. It was the only time Dan ever remembered Tucker feeling sorry for himself.

The things that Tucker loved most in his life were the joys of speech and the pleasure of good food. The irony at the end of his life was that he could neither speak nor eat. He was only thirty-nine.

I wrote to his mother, and she sent me a notebook that he had filled with his favourite quotes and gleanings from literature and life. But more remarkable were copies of his correspondence with the late William F. Buckley, American writer, broadcaster, and intellectual of note. The initial letter sent to Buckley is missing, but what follows is a moving insight into the remarkable individual that Tucker was.

The letters begin on 5th August 1970, when Buckley thanks Tucker for his "eloquent letter" (which is missing) and asks, "Would you be free to lunch with me?"

This is Tucker's reply of 13th August 1970:

Lunch with you would be a joyful honor, even an honorable joy - take your pick, but – and this really saddens me - I must decline. About a year ago, just when things were beginning to look good, things began to look bad. I came down with a rare and ridiculous complaint known as bulbar palsy. This is a kind of neural paralysis which affects the medulla oblongata (an organ which I had hitherto had none but the pleasantest relations) and is progressive in nature.

Indeed it has progressed to a point where I am now, not to put too fine a point on it, completely mute. I am thereby landlocked in several hundred ways, and I am afraid lunch would be out of the question. But having your ear, I would hate to let it go.

By default the letter wasn't delivered until 23rd September, when Buckley wrote:

Dear Mr Ashworth
I finally received your letter. I am truly sad, and marvel at your ebullience under the circumstances. Of course, I would dearly love to hear from you - either directly, or for publication. Write, and tell me about yourself. Also, is there any hope to recover your voice?
Yours faithfully
Wm. F. Buckley Jr.

Tucker wrote again on 2nd October 1970, as follows:

Dear Mr Buckley
Before I unleash on you my ceaseless quotations, the spokesmen of my willing spirit, a word about my weak flesh. No, recovery chances are not good. Hope springs eternal, however, and on November 9th I am scheduled to enter the National Institute of Health in Bethesda, where even if I cannot be helped, the study of my case may prove useful, their pamphlet somewhat turgidly informs me, to "generations yet unborn". About this my general feeling is that of the Jewish lady who wanted to give the dead actor an enema: it can't hoit.
As to my mood, ebullience is not quite the word. Of course I do have my dark passages, blue funks, why-was-I-borns. But I know a trick or two. Trick One: when casting about for words appropriate to my distress, I pass by such listless effects as "damn!" and "shit!" and opt instead to go the whole hog:
Thou art a soul in bliss; but I am bound
Upon a wheel of fire, that mine own tears
Do scald like molten lead ....
The power and the glory of such lines (from Lear) being so dazzling, and their overstatement of my woe so delicious, that I am forthwith cheered. Isn't that, after all, the ultimate purpose of Tragedy - to cheer us up?

Buckley's reply of 15th October 1970 reads:

Dear Mr Ashworth
That was as exquisite a letter as I have ever received. Tell me, what
objection would you have to doing some book reviews, thereby
exhibiting that talent which is death to hide? It is simply not right to
husband to myself alone what you are writing.
My best
Wm. F. Buckley Jnr.

Tucker refused the offer, writing, "Alas, pigs can't fly." But he
did keep the door ajar

... not for pay, or even for attribution, but because I love writing,
and also because I would like to fulfil a long time ambition of mine
to publish something under the penname of Scollay Under.

Tucker left his body for research into the illness that brought
him down.

WORKING ON AIR

Radio is a favourite medium with most actors. There's no
learning of lines to be done, the working schedule is short and
concentrated, and one's personal appearance doesn't matter too
much, although I have noticed that casts of radio plays often do
resemble the characters they play. The reason why British radio
drama sounds so authentic is that, although it's recorded in
sound, we are given moves, entering and exiting through free-
standing doors, sitting at tables to eat and drink with
appropriate props, and so on - even cuddling under duvets,
though seated on adjacent chairs rather than in a bed. We walk
on different textured flooring and often wear appropriate
clothing so that the microphone will pick up the rustlings, for
instance, of long skirts and jewellery in period pieces.

Apart from recording radio series with Roy Hudd and David
Jason, plays on Radio 4 and The World Service, stories on
Woman's Hour and some pieces of my own writing on *Laughing
Aloud*, as well as three shows of my own called *Steafel with an 'S'*,
the most rewarding radio project I've been involved in was
written for me by Arnold Wesker. *Yardsale*, first as a stage play,
which later translated into a perfect piece of radio drama. To

quote John Wain of *The Listener*:

Anyone who heard Yardsale, the moving and truthful monodrama written for S.S. by Arnold Wesker, will have realised that, even amid the very high standards that prevail in radio acting generally, S.S. is outstanding.

Well, I could hardly be expected not to include that quote!

Years later, while I was with the RSC in Stratford-upon-Avon playing Mistress Quickly in *The Merry Wives of Windsor*, Arnold directed me in *Yardsale* in the annual 'Not the RSC' festival. It was the ideal place to try it out, as it only plays for forty minutes, too short for a full evening's entertainment. We talked of the possibility of a companion piece and decided it would have to have a contrasting character to play against the thirty-something American divorcee portrayed in *Yardsale*. I suggested an extremely old woman who walks agonisingly slowly from the wings, taking an age to get to the centre of the stage, and then says, "I didn't f***ing plan it this way!" "Fine," said Arnold, "but that would have to be the end of it!"

What he did write was *Betty Lemon*, a wonderful piece about an old crone in a wheelchair. Unfortunately, I never got to play the role, but Brenda Bruce did play her later in a run of both plays at the Lyric Hammersmith studio theatre.

Arnold adapted his controversial play *Shylock* brilliantly for radio, casting me as Shylock's sister. It is a reworking of Shakespeare's *The Merchant of Venice*, and although the core plot remains the same, the relationships and motivations are much different. Some consider this his finest play, although bizarrely it has never been produced on stage by a London management.

The third Wesker radio play I was fortunate enough to work in was *The Rocking Horse*. It gave me the opportunity to resurrect my long-lost South African accent for the first and only time in my career.

As most of us jobbing actors do, I have voiced cartoons, read books onto CD for the blind or for a crust, and dubbed films, once re-voicing Ursula Andress in *She*. I also had the bizarre experience of re-voicing the actress Julie Ege in *Up Pompeii*, in a love scene with Michael Hordern, with whom I was having an affair at the time!

Week Ending was a current affairs satirical sketch show on BBC

Radio 4, recorded on Friday mornings, transmitted on Friday evenings and repeated on Saturdays. I joined the programme in 1971 at the behest of the then producer, the late Geoffrey Perkins, and I stayed with it for the next seven years. I was the first female in the show; until I arrived, the team, comprising David Tate, David Jason and Bill Wallis, had played the women's parts themselves. I was good at character voices and accents, but I had never done vocal impressions, and although I found it challenging I didn't do too badly. Because we worked well together, the programme was fairly indestructible, and young BBC producers were given the opportunity to work on it as training in light entertainment. Comedy writers were encouraged to send material to the production office, which became a sort of 'nursery' for talent, and many went on to highly successful careers in radio and television, including the likes of Andy Hamilton, Guy Jenkin, Barry Pilton, Jimmy Mulville and Douglas Adams.

The producer I enjoyed working with most was Griff Rhys Jones, (oh yes, he was!) and the least, Jan Ravens, who was, incidentally, instrumental in getting me sacked. I admit, though, that I had it coming. While the series was running, I had gone through predictably bad relationships with lovers, all the stress relating to getting a mortgage and buying a house, a court case involving a builder, and all the chasing and organising of my one-woman show. I carried this shoal of issues with me into the studio each Friday, and when I wasn't recording I tried to sort them out using the studio telephone. (Once I'd left the programme, it was christened 'The Steafel Memorial Phone'!)

Because there were generally fewer women's parts to be recorded than men's, I would ask the producers if they would mind recording my bits first so that I could leave early, rather than waste time hanging around. Usually they complied, but Ms Ravens was having none of it. It was the first time that I'd been thwarted and, now I think about it, the first time that my position as 'the alpha female' had been challenged. I was not pleased, but how displeased Ms Ravens was became clear when Bill Wallis mentioned that his contract for the next session of recordings hadn't yet arrived, and neither had mine. Confident that I was irreplaceable, it never crossed my mind that anything might be amiss. Instead, I worried for Bill in case they were reconsidering his future. I asked to see Monica Sims, then Head of Radio Light Entertainment, and one early morning I sat opposite her at her vast desk, ready to do battle on his behalf. No, she assured me, Bill's contract was on its way ... but mine wasn't. I couldn't believe my indispensable ears! What were they going to do without me? What they did was replace me quickly and easily with the talented and much more amenable Sally Grace.

During my first stint in the programme, with the greatly missed Geoffrey Perkins as producer, I invited the cast, the crew and some other friends to a fireworks party at my house. At the end of the evening Geoffrey stayed, not just for the night but for almost a year. He was a good bit younger than I, although he didn't know by how much. On my birthday, with him beside me reading a newspaper while I was driving, he yelped in disbelief as he read out my age which was printed in the 'birthdays today' column. I tried to laugh it off, but failed! During the time he lived with me I 'persuaded' him to lose weight, cut his hair and even change the way he dressed. I expect I kyboshed any growing affection by treating him thoughtlessly, once being scathing about a Xmas present that had clearly taken a lot of thought but that I considered inappropriate. Why he stayed on I can only surmise, but I still have a card that he sent me which reads: "I like you just the way you are ... horrid!" So it was hardly surprising when he decided to go on a skiing holiday with some friends of his own age, one of whom he later married. As I waved goodbye I remember feeling more like his mother than his lover! Shortly after he returned he told me he had put a deposit on a flat and was leaving. I was more annoyed than upset, put out because he hadn't seen fit to discuss it with me or tell me, until it was a fait accompli.

One of Harry H's maxims was: "Be nice to those on the way up, because you never know who you're going to meet on the way down." If only I had learned to keep that precept in mind. Geoffrey was made BBC Television's Head of Comedy, and after a while I began to wonder whether there really were no longer any suitable parts for me in BBC comedy scripts, or whether I was paying the price for the time we'd spent together.

Geoffrey wasn't the first so-called 'toy boy' to move in with me. A while after my divorce I began an affair with W.B. who had just started a theatrical agency, but being highly motivated and ambitious he was clearly destined for bigger and better things.

He declined to pay anything towards the rent, offering instead to do a weekly supermarket shop that never quite materialised. How long he lived off me I have wiped from my memory, but I do remember being jealous, neurotic and unhappy during this period, displaying all the predictable symptoms of insecurity when age is an issue. Eventually he packed his bags and left for pastures new and richer pickings. Some years later, while shopping in West Hampstead, I caught sight of him seated at a table outside a chic patisserie. After the 'hellos' and 'how are yous' came the 'and what are you doing nows'. I was telling him that my career was flagging and things weren't particularly easy, when his mobile phone (at the time a real status symbol) rang. After he had clinched the call, he informed me that he was one of the producers of a highly successful long-running West End musical, which showed no signs of closing, and he was doing remarkably well out of it.

"That's great," I said. "I really must get to see it."

"You should buy a ticket," he replied. "You'll enjoy it."

Then, tucking his phone into his pocket, he sauntered off.

I caught a glimpse of him not long ago in a television news clip, a famous film star climbed out of her limousine at some glittering event, and W.B. emerged from it behind her.

NOT ALL ROSES

Let me tell you about the most miserable and unhappy job of my entire career. My agent sent me to meet a BBC director about a play scheduled to go out on the prestigious *Wednesday Play* slot. The play called for a heavy, plain actress to play the lead, a female journalist who drinks, swears, smokes cigars with the boys, dresses like a cross between a truck driver and a schoolmarm, and - wait for it - is a top fashion writer! I met the director in the bar of the Television Centre and he seemed disinterested and disgruntled. Having explained the character to me, he said he was fed up with trying to find the right actress, and if I thought I could do it I could have it. I should have realised then and there that I was being offered a poisoned chalice, but the prospect of a lead in this TV slot was irresistible. And so, knowing I was utterly wrong for the part, I accepted.

There followed meetings with the designer, fittings with the wardrobe department, and sessions with the make-up artist, until there was almost nothing left of me that wasn't being remodelled. They built me a large padded body, round shouldered, big breasted and broad hipped, and gave me a tousled, mud-coloured wig and a large pock-marked nose made of putty. I was given a sort of gumshield to tuck under my lower lip in order to push it forward, making speech awkward. The clothes were a mixture of 'his and hers', and, once dressed and made up, my energies were spent trying to move while keeping everything in place. Acting was not only out of the question but also the last thing on my mind.

I think it's worth outlining the plot. Fashion editor resigns and sets about finding a husband. She coughs her way into a boutique, transforms it from failure into success, and marries the owner, who is gay. He goes to bed with a teddy bear, she goes to bed with a South American shrunken head, and he is (unsurprisingly) terrified. I am unable to dredge up exactly how it ended, but the good news is that it DID end.

The fine cast (wasted) included Donald Churchill, Patsy Rowlands, and Peter Butterworth, who played the boutique owner. Rehearsals for me were mortifying. Whenever I began a scene, the director would turn his back on me, shaking his head and sighing audibly. When I'd finished he would return to directing the other actors. It was upsetting to say the least, and one night I phoned him at his home and pleaded with him to recast the role.

"Too late," was his curt reply.

There was one light moment during rehearsals when Peter Butterworth arrived late one morning.

"Sorry," he said breathlessly. "Tube trains are running slow, and just as I was about to dive out of the opening doors the man next to me said, 'I recognise you. Aren't you Peter ...? Well, not wanting to hang about I said, 'Butterworth' and dashed off. He caught me up at the barrier. 'There was no need for that!' he said angrily, 'I was only asking your name.' 'Yes, and I told you. Butterworth.' 'Oh, I'm terribly sorry,' he said apologetically, 'I thought you said 'Bugger off'."

It was the day of recording and I stood in the hanger-like BBC studio dressed in my full glory and barely able to move. We were shooting a fashion show that my character had organised, and the set was a large restaurant with elegantly dressed extras sitting at tables, while in a screened-off area stood rows and rows of dress rails crammed with garments. Via the diminutive, pushy female floor manager I was informed by Herr Director (who was in the production box overlooking the studio) that he wanted to film me through the clothes, and in order for the camera to see me I was to push the clothes to one side. Well actually it was to three sides, because he wanted to shoot three different angles in quick succession. Three different marks were taped onto three different parts of a rail full of clothes, and I was instructed through the floor manager's earphones as to what needed to go where, when, and in what order. It was, to say the least, confusing, the more so because Herr D. insisted that it should all happen in double-quick time. The coat thrown casually over my shoulders seemed determined to slip off, I had a cigar in my mouth as well as my 'lip-pusher', and I held a clipboard in one hand, leaving the other free to shove the clothes onto their marks.

"And ... cue!" cued the female dwarf, pointing a commanding digit in my direction.

I tried to hit what I thought was the first mark and failed.

"Sorry!"

"Let's go again. And ... cue!" The digit pointed once again.

Totally confused by now as to which was which, again I failed to hit the mark. The studio was deathly quiet. Sweating now, I tried again and failed. A murmur arose from the extras and "Oh, for Christ's sake!" blared over the tannoy from Herr D. The sound of fast footsteps rattled down the metal staircase and he strode angrily towards me.

"It can't be that bloody difficult!" he said, through clenched teeth. "One!" he thrust a clutch of clothes to one side. "Two!" Another thrust. "Three!" Then, leaning close, he hissed venomously, "Now, DO IT!"

The clatter of footsteps and the slam of a distant door, followed, and I stood in the deathly silence. I was breathing deeply, trying not to break down.

"And ... cue!"

And ... I flipped.

Yelling an obscenity, I threw the clipboard at the maddening girl with her commanding finger, headed blindly for the nearest door, threw it open ... and found myself facing a blank wall; the door leading nowhere was part of the set. It was a humiliation too far and there was no holding back the tears. I fought my way blindly to my dressing room and tried to pull myself together.

243

No one came to commiserate or to chide, and after a while a knock at the door summoned me back to work.

We only had that one day to record the piece and should have wrapped up by 10 p.m., but because of the delays and tricky shots through lobster claws and other such things that Herr Führer had devised, we were heavily into overtime. The final scene was supposed to be a deeply emotional encounter between Peter and myself, but because there was no time, it was chopped into small segments so that the cameras could reposition for each shot. Any dramatic intent went out of the window and Peter and I simply performed by numbers. At last, at very last, the hideous day was over. It was nearly midnight, the dressers and make-up artists had gone home, and the Television Centre was deserted. I pulled off the false make-up, threw the 'gumshield' into the bin, and with difficulty shrugged my way out of the unpleasant, sweaty padding. Crossing the empty, echoing foyer, I lifted a weary hand to the night duty officer at the desk and decided that, though comforting, my dogs were not quite the solace I craved. I drove instead to the house of an understanding friend, where, provided with a bottle of vodka and a comfortable sofa, I spent a grateful night of oblivion.

The reaction to the play can be summed up by a notice written by James Thomas in the *Daily Express*:

Miss Steafel is one of our few expert comedy actresses, and so little true humour is written for women that I felt sad indeed to see her wasted not merely on rubbish but upon something which was far more nasty than funny. Seldom has such a perky music track drowned out so much dialogue. Or were they so ashamed of it that they felt it was better to blot it out?

The only other misadventure I had with a television director was in an episode of a popular comedy series that starred a wonderful elderly actress. I was to play a postmistress, and at the first rehearsal when the read-through was done, the director said he hoped I wasn't going to use a funny voice or 'do' funny faces, because although this was a comedy series, he didn't want anything done just for laughs. Of course not, I agreed, wondering if during the read-through I had somehow sounded odd. Next he plotted the moves, and when it came to the post office scene I stood and waited, script in hand.

"You sit here," he told me, pointing at a chair, on which I duly sat. "You'll be behind the counter, and I'll come in quite close."

He held up both hands and made a square with his thumbs and forefingers through which he peered. Then as I read my lines, he slowly came towards me until we were almost nose to nose. He dropped his hands.

"I told you," he said, "we don't want any mugging. Just play it straight."

"But I haven't done anything except read the lines," I protested.

He wagged a finger mischievously at me. "Oh, I know you! Now come on, let's try again."

I was confused. What had I done? We had only begun setting the moves. I hadn't learned the lines, and truth to tell I had only a vague idea of how I was going to play the character. The director was back in his first position, fingers framing me as I tried to immobilise my face and speak at the same time. I sounded and looked as though I'd had a stroke. Once more he dropped his hands and gave a deep sigh.

"Tell you what," he said, with kindly tolerance, "why don't you go over there, sit down, have a good think, and I'll come back to you."

I went over there, sat down, and had a good think. Ten minutes later he came over to me.

"Well, have you had a think?"

"Yes, I have," I said. "I think you've just got time to recast this part." And I picked up my coat and left the rehearsal room.

As I was dialling my agent on the foyer phone, he emerged from the rehearsal room and, apologising, promised to 'leave me to get on with it' if I agreed to return. The rehearsals that followed ran peacefully enough, though in an atmosphere of eggshell treading. My scene came early in the show, and the recording in Birmingham in front of a live audience went well. Once I was cleared, I picked up my overnight bag, and was on the train back to London before the recording in the studio-ended. A few weeks later, to his credit, I received the following letter:

Dear Sheila
I have just edited your episode, and thought you'd like to know it

looks very good. Thanks for a first rate performance. I know we started the week a little at odds with each other but I was full of admiration at the end. Once again a very sincere thank you and I really do hope we work together again in the future.
Yours

THE WRONG DIRECTION

It seems only fair as I'm admitting to my own misdemeanours, that I spill the beans about a few directors who have behaved badly, not only towards me but also to other actors I worked with. My working relationship with one director began cordially enough, and I can't pinpoint exactly when it began to crumble; however, as rehearsing progressed and I watched him treating some actors with contempt and derision, I began to lose respect for him. During these rehearsals (which often felt like tutorials as he lectured us about syntax and structure), we were made to improvise scenes, and were even charged with writing out mini-biographies for the purposes of creating real, rounded characters. However, when the designs for the set and costumes arrived he did a U-turn. The empty box set looked like a cross between a Conran room and a cell in an eighteenth-century lunatic asylum. The actors playing lesser parts were freakishly made up so that their faces looked like vampire masks, and I was made to wear a bizarre marmalade wig with two horns of hair above the temples. My straight performance was completely upstaged by my comical hairdo.

As I've mentioned before, quite often a director will pick out a member of the company, usually a youngster, and use him or her as a 'whipping boy'. Our director was no different, but he chose to humiliate an elderly and experienced actor playing a servant. He taunted him constantly, and the more he did so, the more the old man would muff his lines. Each time he was made to look foolish the atmosphere in the rehearsal room curdled. The rest of the cast tried to joke their way through the upset and stress, only to be given a hearty ticking-off for not taking their work seriously. I never was good at hiding my feelings, and the director must have sensed my growing disapprobation.

The crunch came when the production office asked me to do a live TV interview with Terry Wogan to publicise the play. I agreed reluctantly, having recently appeared on *Wogan* and

246

thinking it too soon for a second interview. More than that, apart from praising the cast, I had little enthusiasm to impart. The interview meant going directly to the studio after rehearsal, and the television company offered to send a car to pick me up from home, take me and my bagged-up glamour outfit to the rehearsal room, and later ferry me to the studio. That particular day was the first full technical run when everyone involved - producers, designers, musicians, technicians - would watch the production through and take notes. This was scheduled to start at 2 o'clock sharp, and it was arranged that the car would pick me up at one. Of course it didn't turn up. At 1.30 I anxiously phoned the rehearsal room to explain that I was going to be late, but, as my character didn't appear until the second act, at least (I thought) I had some leeway. I was upset and angry by the time the car arrived shortly before 2.00, and as we crossed London, inevitably held up by the traffic, I almost wept with helpless frustration. The only comfort was the fact that they could run act one, and I might, by the skin of my teeth, arrive just in time for my entrance. At long last we got to the rehearsal rooms. Bag in hand, I leapt out of the car, raced up the stairs and pushed open the heavy door, to be greeted by a blast of hostility. Conversation froze as thirty or more people turned to glare at me with collective loathing. Then the director's voice broke the icy silence.

"Now we can start. Act one beginners, please."

It was war, and I'm not at all proud of the way I behaved during the following weeks. I complained bitterly about the tiny cupboard of a dressing room I'd been given, which was too small to house my costumes, so they hung outside in the corridor, while the company manager's large room was more often than not vacant, as he spent most of his time in the adjacent pub. Small irritations became insufferable. I wasn't happy and I showed it, making myself thoroughly unpopular with everyone. The director and I avoided one another, but I remember an altercation when, at a chance meeting, he commented dryly, "I just love difficult actresses," and I countered with, "And I love directors with no integrity." It is unsurprising that when the production company gave a Sunday garden party for all the actors in the several West End shows they had running at the time, I was the only person excluded. I was crushed and hurt but knew the damage had been done, and the chance of working for that particular company again was slim. Even worse, it was likely that other managements would be forewarned, and I had set foot on a very slippery slope.

When faced with directors who make work an unhappy or daunting experience, most actors tend to mutter darkly to one another in corners, sharing their miseries and grievances, but seldom confront the perpetrators because they hold the key to future employment. These few megalomaniacs strut their stuff in rehearsal rooms, draining confidence and creativity out of their victims with cruel observations and acid humour, and I have seen strong and talented actors reduced to confusion and tears.

It was my second term of employment with a prestigious theatre company, and I was both proud and delighted to have been cast in three plays during the season. One of the directors I was to work with had an impressive and far-ranging CV, and his productions were much praised, making him popular with managements. I had heard rumours, though, of his deep unpopularity with actors. There is a form of quick and cutting wit favoured by gays that can be amusing, and this director was a past master at it. During the first week of rehearsals I laughed at his neat observations, none of them too cruel, and decided that he and I would get along after all. However, it soon became clear that he had chosen a young, inexperienced actor as a whipping boy, and his tongue developed a razor edge. It became embarrassing to watch the humiliation that the lad was put through. Worse was to come when he humiliated one of his leading actors, whom I later found sitting, miserable and tearful, behind one of the rehearsal room screens, nursing his battered ego.

One morning we found a notice pinned to the rehearsal room door stating that no food or drink was to be taken inside, and when we DID go inside we were to sit and watch the production in progress. We were allowed no books, no distractions, and no movement. Instead of generating creativity, the atmosphere became one of tension. Fearful of any reprimands, actors tiptoed around to get to their places and with over-compensating smiles tried not to incur the megalomaniac's temper. As ever, I showed my feelings, and although it became clear that the antipathy was mutual, it resulted in only one or two minor spats. Until, that is, at the end of a long day, when I finally lost my temper.

A friend had taken one of my dogs to a vet in Cambridge for emergency treatment, and I was anxious to get back to him. The rehearsal was due to finish and it was clear that we weren't going to get to my entrance, so with some trepidation I asked if I could leave. With a look of thunder, the director spat out a vilification, not just of me but the entire cast. We were all summarily dismissed and, enraged, I tore off my heavy rehearsal skirt and threw it at him, shouting out some lame insult meant to wound. The skirt fell short of its mark, as did my verbal abuse, but thereafter we kept our wary distances.

After the show on the opening night I changed out of my costume as quickly as I could, hoping to avoid the embarrassment of his obligatory visit backstage, but as I fled down the corridor I saw him coming towards me, surrounded by acolytes. Here was my chance to tell him in so many words what I thought of him. I took a deep breath … then, mumbling some barely audible inanity, I scuttled on.

Strictly speaking, the next director doesn't belong here. He was an amiable enough man, who treated the company of actors with respect, initially firing them with enthusiasm and interest in his innovative production. However, the rehearsal period slowly turned into a farce, then a nightmare. The play was based on a legend involving mythical and supernatural beings, and we were given an unprecedented four months' rehearsal time. The first three were spent having endless seminars about evil, ghosts, ESP experiences and the like, and it became rather like having to attend endless tedious dinner parties without the food. A couple who professed to be white witches (naughty but nice) were invited to give us a talk, from which we developed some good company jokes, and a pair of 'spell-casters' who put the fear of God into our leading actor, so much so that he would send up a quick prayer on stage before each performanace to protect us, and indeed the audience, from any evil spirits we might inadvertently raise.

We were cajoled into watching endless videos of any similar production ever recorded, and were swamped with books ranging from high philosophy to low black arts. Time wore on and on until finally, with only three weeks to go, the director decided it was time to stage the production … and didn't. We began to panic and work thirteen-hour days. Choreographers came and went, and we all began to chip in with ideas until the entire cast seemed to have taken on the role of director and tempers began to fray. Tears were shed by almost everyone at one time or another, and then came the alarming joke of the costumes and the fittings thereof. Ann Summers catalogues had been casually left amongst the other literature, and we were encouraged to leaf through them with an eye to choosing how we wished to appear in the orgy scene.

"Don't worry about nudity," said the misbegotten female designer reassuringly. "You can wear clothes like the crutchless tights"!

She wasn't having a good time, and at one of my fittings said tearfully, "I can't wait to leave this production!"

To which I countered, "At least you CAN leave … we can't!"

But the cast did worry about the rumoured nudity. An Equity representative was called in, a meeting was held, the director announced that he couldn't work with one hand tied behind his back, and the company's artistic director supported him. The actors had no choice but to get on with doing what they were told to do. I opted to play an old woman with a severe limp, wrapped in an anonymous cloak, who sold unmentionables off a tray hung around her neck. Others were not so lucky, and the two that stick out (if you'll pardon the pun) are the young actress wrapped in cling film, and the actor wearing a thong supporting an alarmingly huge prosthetic penis.

The epic finally opened, playing in two long parts. It must by now be fairly obvious that I am not an ensemble player, and with my sense of humour it was difficult to perform my several (and hopefully well disguised) allocated parts. I played a dancing Citizen in peasant wear, and part of a Greek Chorus in drapery. Roped together with other members of the cast, we trudged around the stage following our Leader. At one point we had to feign sleep, waking up to the sight of an actor being lowered from the flies in a large (and some nights revealing) nappy. Aching with embarrassment, I played a Large Mythical Bird wearing egg-yellow tights stuffed with knee pads, and a black feathered body with wings that flapped when the strings were manipulated. Mercifully, I can't recall the headdress, but whatever it was I know I pulled it as far down over my face as it would go.

When we opened, the notices were generous though not

particularly positive. However, Charles Spencer of the *Daily Telegraph* castigated the production and the director mercilessly:

It's a dirty job but someone's got to do it, and after hours of crass gimmickry, putting the boot into this dire production becomes a duty as well as a pleasure ...
... Suffering is what this production is all about. The cast suffers, the audience suffers, and the author suffers most of all as this director wreaks havoc on a classic.

A somewhat personal attack? That's show business.

The only time that I worked with an actor who was as intransigent as I can be, was in a play written by a celebrated American playwright, in which I featured opposite the star of a popular TV sitcom. He also happened to be a fine English character actor. The play was set in an apartment in New York. The raucous, randy husband is fraught with frustration because his wife is frigid and hates being touched by him. To add to his woes, his eldest son is a transvestite cop and his youngest son has just climbed out onto the ledge of their apartment building, threatening to jump. We began rehearsals but they were sticky. Apart from anything else, I was miscast and too young for the part, a point made later in several of the reviews. When we opened out of London, it was clear that the play wasn't going to be the success we had hoped for, and the leading man was particularly unhappy. Still, in spite of misgivings, it was thought that the line-up of names would carry the play, and we opened in London on Shaftsbury Avenue.

The curtain went up on an apartment with pink quilted walls, six television sets, five telephones and ranks of electronic toys, and there I was, delivering an endless speech on one of the phones, when the star entered to an enthusiastic round of applause. As he began to speak, instead of the character he had rehearsed, to my dismay he was playing his television persona, but with an American-Jewish accent! He sustained it through the whole of the first act, to quote one critic, "slapping his sides, blowing oy-yoys, stuffing his hands deep in his pockets, and padding around the stage shouting imprecations and obscenities at all concerned."

When the interval came, he disappeared into his dressing room and I went to mine. After the twenty-minute break the stage manager called act two beginners, and I went back on stage to wait for my fellow actor. I waited long enough for it to become obvious that something was amiss. The stage manager assured me that he would be ready soon, but as the interval stretched into thirty minutes there was a distinctly restless murmur coming from the auditorium. An apology was about to be made over the tannoy when he joined me and the curtain went up. His performance was now somewhat muted, but his TV character was still pretty much in evidence. At the end of a difficult week the play closed, and I was told what had happened that fateful night. The author had been watching the play from the back of the dress circle and, horrified and enraged by the leading actor's personality switch, had knocked back several large gin and tonics. When the interval came he had stormed backstage and burst into the star's dressing room, bellowing, "What the hell are you doing to my play?" It had taken the director, the producers and everyone else concerned (bar, of course, the playwright himself) to persuade him back onto the stage. Later I received a postcard from the author:

Dearest Sheila
Thank you so much for your opening night gift - and thank you even
more for your valour in the face of enemy action onstage every night.
Love

THE VISIT

"You should be lying here dying, Harold, not me. I deserve some happiness after all these years of misery with you."

My mother's voice is low, rasping with rage, the bitter lines entrenched in her face confirming the harshness of her words. She is eighty nine years old and dying of cancer of the bladder, and this verbal thrust is all the ammunition left to her. She lies straight and angry in one of the twin beds pushed together for the sake of space, the other, covered with a faded bedspread, unused since my father was banished to the small bedroom that had been mine before I left for England to pursue a career in the theatre. And Eda lies here now in this house with its miserable memories and bleak atmosphere, the house that had imprisoned her life. I stand beside my father, watching the final act of this tragic misalliance. She had called us into her bedroom from the sitting room where I had been trying to comfort him as we sat on stiff-backed chairs at the dining table that had hosted so many silent, uneasy meals. And now he is here at her bedside, red-eyed, confused, an old man of ninety four, stubbornly fighting the approach of Alzheimer's and stunned by the venom of her words.

I had been given a week off from the Royal Shakespeare Company in Stratford-upon-Avon to fly to South Africa in response to a phone call from my mother. She had gone into hospital to have, she assured me, "a simple operation to have some nodules removed from my bladder". When she called me from the ward she was distraught and confused.

"They haven't done what they said. They stopped the operation halfway through. They said my heart isn't strong enough. They promised to put everything back inside me, but now I have this awful bag thing."

Two weeks later I was there in the bungalow in which I was raised, with its corrugated tin roof that heats with the sun and drums with the rain, the house dismally similar to the others squatting along the dusty tarmac road. Reluctantly there once more in the home I had fled when I was seventeen, there in Berea, middle-class suburb of this ugly city of Johannesburg that sits on the flat, dry veldt of the Transvaal in this vast and troubled country of South Africa.

Three months later my mother died of a stroke. Exactly two weeks after, in spite of his expressed determination to live to at least a hundred because he had so much left to do, my father died; without my mother he simply lost the will to live. It came as no surprise to me. I had always known that neither could exist without their fierce, misplaced loyalty, and the fuel of their perpetual rage.

BRIAN

"Oh Lord, it looks like he's really coming this time!"

I was speaking to my cousin Geoff about an imminent visit from my brother Brian. For more years than I care to admit, the threat of his coming over from South Africa had hung over me. We hadn't met since my last visit to Johannesburg fifteen years earlier when my mother Eda was terminally ill, and I had been appalled at how little he'd done towards sorting out details that would have made life for both my parents under those difficult circumstances easier. When I arrived my mother hadn't seemed pleased to see me. She had, in fact, persuaded Brian to call me in Stratford-upon-Avon to say that she was fine and I wasn't to disrupt my performances with the RSC. This didn't altogether surprise me. Our relationship always had been difficult and, although I think she loved me in her own way, I was very like my father whom she feared, and I suspect her fear of him had filtered down to me. But I knew she wasn't 'fine', and so, ignoring his request, I duly arrived at her hospital bedside. She sat bolt upright, her silver hair, of which she was so inordinately proud, now out of perm and severely straight.

"How much did it cost you to get here?" she asked, after a peremptory greeting.

"Not a lot. It doesn't matter," I told her.

She turned to my father. "Harold, go to the bank and get out some money."

He was old and he was confused. "How much?"

Without hesitation the answer came, "A lot!"

I put my hand on his arm and imperceptibly shook my head.

"Where's Brian?" she asked anxiously. Then, "You know I don't have any favourites, don't you?" And then, "Where's Brian?"

"Coming soon," I answered, and hoped I was right.

The following day Eda was sent home. Arriving with an agency nurse I had booked that morning, I found her in a chair in front of a small electric fire in the sitting room, looking ashen and frightened, my father sitting by her, helpless. The colostomy bag hanging by the side of her leg was full, and the nurse quickly began attending to her needs.

"I want to go back to the hospital!" she whimpered.

"You're going straight to bed," I told her, and soon she was back in her bedroom, pleading yet again for Brian.

I stayed on for a week, contacting Jewish associations, booking round-the-clock care, and trying to organise their immediate and future needs with the indispensable help of a cousin who ferried me around the city and tolerated my frustrations. Eda was angry at the new electric heaters, angry at the crisp new bed linen, and enraged at the appearance of a small television set I had bought for my father, knowing how avidly he had watched TV when he had visited me in London. All the while she asked for Brian and, much to my chagrin, Brian seldom came. He lived alone and wasn't working, so as far as I could see he had no commitments to keep him away and was simply being stubbornly uncaring, and I was angry that he had allowed the house to deteriorate and its elderly occupants to muddle along as best they could. Looking back, I realise now that my mother was his best, if not his only, friend, and I think his failure to visit stemmed from a reluctance to face up to her deteriorating health. It is also certain that my own presence, along with my father's, deterred him.

Before I left for Stratford-upon-Avon a week later, my mother made me promise to keep in touch with my brother, and apparently she made the same request to him, and so we did, at first by the briefest of letters, very occasionally by phone (although there was embarrassingly little to say), and finally by short, uninformative emails. Not long after I returned, Brian phoned to tell me that my mother had suffered a stroke that had paralysed the left side of her face, adding that she had lost her power of speech. I remembered an incident in my teens when she and I had visited a great aunt who had been similarly affected by a stroke, and spoke with difficulty out of one side of her mouth. When we left, my mother was visibly shaken.

"It sounds so awful!" she had said. "If that were to happen to me I would never speak again!"

Six weeks later Brian phoned again, this time to tell me that my mother had died that night of a second stroke.

"And do you know," he said, "she looked marvellous, absolutely marvellous!"

Perhaps she had finally released the tight rein that she kept on her emotions, let the bitterness and misery of her past drain away, and found peace. I wish I had seen her like that.

The years passed with sparse contact between us, but from what he wrote it was clear that Brian's health was deteriorating, and having lost faith in conventional medicine he was turning to any and every alternative cure he could find. It was difficult to gauge his physical condition. At one point he wrote to say that a doctor had told him he must have a leg amputated but a Chinese potion had made it unnecessary. At another he was told that he had two extra vertebrae in his spine and that was the cause of his problems. He was convinced that he had been given a vasectomy when he was only nine (he didn't know why) and was impotent. At the same time he was writing a thesis, studying the Old Testament and finding more and more clues to corroborate his theory that Darwin was wrong and we were descended from aliens. Based on all this, he wrote asking for my help to find him a documentary maker or a publisher, but when I suggested that he send some chapters, or at the very least a synopsis, he angrily refused, emailing that his unique work would be appropriated and copied. Only in the broadest terms was he prepared to tell how his research would amaze scientists and change the direction of space research and the history of mankind. He was certain he was right and the rest were fools. The more we corresponded, the more I recognised our dreaded Family Flaw, and the more I distanced myself from him.

Brian often wrote of his intention to 'come over', and, although I knew it was unlikely he would be able to raise the fare for a return flight, I worried guiltily about whether he might manage a one-way ticket. Of course he would stay with me, and I imagined that he would see no reason not to stay on indefinitely. The prospect filled me with dread. I had always played down my achievements to him, aware that my successes might trigger jealousy, or bitter memories of his disadvantaged childhood. What would he think when he saw my large house, my smart car, my comfortable lifestyle? And wouldn't he have every right to be bitter? I had once tried to redress the balance when my debts were sorted and I had some capital left over, by offering to buy him a flat in a better and less dangerous and disreputable part of Johannesburg. He had hesitated and then declined, saying that the apartment on offer wasn't as sunny as his own and he preferred to stay where he was.

Then, one day in early 2007, an old acquaintance of his, an Italian woman who had lived in the same block of flats for several years before returning to Italy, invited him to visit her at her own expense. Delighted, he had accepted, and he emailed to say that on his return journey he would be spending a week in London and wondered if I could put him up. Of course I could put him up ... but could I put up with him? We were both Family Flawed, and I remembered his dogmatism, his arrogance and his intransigence. I imagined that he would be difficult to feed and to entertain. If his legs were a problem, would he manage the stairs to his bedroom? And what to do with him for a whole week? How could I possibly introduce him to my friends? In company he was uncooperative and taciturn, a shyness misinterpreted as arrogance and indifference, and his general appearance had always been unprepossessing. His beard, I guessed, would be wild, and having once sent him a sweater only to have it returned with a note saying that the clothes he had were more than adequate, I knew that he would look shabby. I opened a fresh pack of Prozac and waited.

He arrived on Easter Monday, and in spite of leaving in what I thought was plenty of time the traffic to Gatwick was a nightmare, and I was over an hour late. I saw him leaning on a stick at the information desk with a luggage trolley at his side, and my heart sank. He was hidden behind the biggest, roundest pair of dark glasses, and wearing a baseball cap, a crumpled pale blue jacket, baggy brown trousers and trainers. An embrace was out of the question, and I was grateful that the lateness of my arrival made my greeting easier.

"So sorry I'm late. Awful traffic!" I blurted out, and I put a hand on his arm, the only physical contact I could manage.

His walking was painful and slow, and as I steered him towards the car park conversation was awkward.

"Lovely car," he said admiringly as he got in. "Whose is it?"

"Mine," I answered, half apologetic, half proud, adding to salve my own conscience, "it's second hand."

But I had misjudged my brother; there wasn't a jealous bone in his body. The week I had been dreading was revealing and pleasant and passed surprisingly quickly, with the Prozac blisters staying unburst. Brian's constant battle was walking, but he insisted on climbing up and down the stairs ("It's good for me!") and ventured on a trip to the West End on his own which knocked him out for the next few days. The only painkiller he would take was a foul-tasting concoction he had brought with him, quoting, "The worse the taste, the better the cure." He would sit on a tall stool in my kitchen, watching me cook, and the silence between us was comfortable, as were the silences between us that we had both understood as siblings. I noticed that he would pause before answering any question, and when he answered it was as if he were dredging up the words from somewhere deep within him. I understood this loss of verbal agility. Having lived alone myself, sometimes not seeing or speaking to anyone for days at a time, conversational skills can become rusty.

At last, one expansive day, he talked of his beloved manuscript, telling me of his theories, his belief in aliens, and his determination to get his thesis published. His theories were a total mystery to me, but I was getting to know him for the first time and finding his straightforward simplicity endearing.

One day, with nothing better to say, I asked, "What would you choose to eat if it was to be your very last meal?"

He looked at me in surprise. "I've never considered that," he said. After a moment he smiled apologetically. "No idea."

He went on a shopping trip and bought himself an M&S dressing gown, and when I asked to see it he was shyly delighted.

"Not used to this sort of thing," he said, as he paraded self-consciously in front of me.

As I became aware of his physical disabilities, I tried to adapt things to make his everyday life easier without being too obvious. He had developed a severe tremor, which made cutting his food difficult, so I would only serve him manageable portions, and I made sure that his cup was only half filled. As I listened and watched and stopped being judgemental, I saw a childlike quality and an unexpected gentleness in him that really moved me, and some of the remarks he made saddened me.

"I don't understand what love is," he said once, and another time, "I hate my looks." But perhaps for me the most telling was, "Mom was afraid of you, you know."

Yes, I knew.

Here we both were, handicapped by the characteristics of our parents, my brother looking so very like the father he reviled. When I asked him what he thought about his father, his reply was not at all what I expected.

"He once taught me a brilliant algebraic theory," he said. "I've passed it on to others and it never fails. I owe him for that." He paused for a long while, and then added quietly, "He wasn't a very nice man."

That was all he said.

For Brian, life was an adventure, and although even in his seventies he still hadn't quite decided what course to follow, whatever he did, he was certain he would succeed. I began to wonder whether, having failed to win his father's affection, he was still trying to earn his respect.

So he sat on my lawn in the sun, accepting coffees and snacks, doing his crosswords and smoking (not permitted indoors), and by the end of the week he looked noticeably better than when he had arrived. The Sunday before he left I invited members of what small family we had in London to join us for lunch. To my surprise and delight. Brian was quite outgoing and animated, and when they eventually left late in the afternoon, uncharacteristically, he embraced the women. As I closed the front door behind the last visitor, I turned to find him standing in the hallway.

"Well ..." I said with a sigh, and as I walked towards him he held out his arms. And we hugged. For the first time in our lives we hugged one another. Tears welled up, my throat was tight, and I knew that I was about to weep copiously, interminably. Barely able to speak, I pulled away and managed, "Stop it or I'll cry!" aware that, after decades of misunderstandings and evasions, in this one brief moment I had found a brother, and he a sister.

We emailed our mutual delight, Brian referring to our moment of discovery as THAT hug, and after phoning for a chat he vowed he would call more often.

A month or so after his visit a late night phone call came to say that Brian had died. It seems he'd had difficulty in breathing, and had called the building's security officer for help. He, in turn, had roused a friend of Brian's from a neighbouring flat, and she had been with him at the end. The cause, they said, was a heart attack.

I am not a great believer in Fate, but our reconciliation meant so much to both of us that his visit does make me wonder.

As I drove him to the airport, I remember him saying, "Do you know, I've had a wonderful life," and, knowing the tribulations and harsh times that life had thrown at him over the years, I felt humbled, and ashamed of my own small-minded dissatisfactions.

ONE WOMAN AND HER SHOW

I would have felt much the same had I been about to be wheeled into an operating theatre for major surgery with no guarantee of survival. This, however, was no operating theatre: this was a small room over a pub in Ealing, and I was about to do my first one-woman show. So great was my terror that rather than face them en bloc, I had wedged myself onto a bar stool next to the piano, greeting the enemy as they came in, one by one, in an attempt to disarm them. Paul Maguire, without realising how much of his future life and time it would consume, sat at the keyboard playing standards, while I joined in now and then, hoping the more outgoing members of the audience would sing along and help thaw the ice in my veins.

The idea of doing a one-woman show had lurked at the back of my mind for some time, but the creative Everest of finding the material and learning it so thoroughly that nothing could frighten it out of my head, was enough to make me scuttle back into the kitchen and clean the oven as never before. One day I overheard a couple of fellow-thespians discussing the Edinburgh Festival. It was January, and now was the time to apply if you wanted to be in it the following August. If I were to book myself in I'd be committed, I'd panic, and I'd be forced to put a show together. So I did. All four.

I decided to base it on different characters (my forte), playing up the comic side, and include a bit of singing, some rather amateur dancing, and any other odds and ends that took my fancy. I approached several writers that I knew from *Frost* and *Week Ending*, and the material eventually included such luminaries as Keith Waterhouse, David Nobbs, Andy Hamilton, Christopher Matthew, Paul C. Davies and Nigel Planer. Barry Cryer and Dick Vosburgh, two of my closest friends, were incredibly generous with their time and talent. (A few years ago when Dick was diagnosed with cancer of the colon, I was angry; it was unthinkable! He fought fiendishly and hung on remarkably longer than seemed possible, determined to draw a line under each unfinished project. And then he was gone. His cremation was full of laughter and with not a sign of religiosity, the battered, beloved brief case he was never seen without, sitting staunchly on his coffin. Beryl, his widow, was strong and witty about his last days (during radio-therapy 'If I was a Marx Brother I'd be 'Keemo'; coming round from an anaesthetic 'Nurse, can I see the baby now?' and during a scan when the consultant asked if he'd like to view the screen, 'No thanks, I never watch daytime television'). We devastated friends and family were there for him, and love for the man was palpable).

Hunting for material, I can't believe how wide or how cheekily I spread my net. I collaborated with Dennis Kiley, an erstwhile foreign editor of the FT, to create 'Auntie Kitty', a stinging attack on white prejudice in South Africa. I asked Stephen Fry (who was yet to hit those dizzying heights) over a drink in a Hampstead pub, but he politely refused. I even knocked on Richard Curtis's door (well before his mega successes), but he, too, declined, possibly because my ignominious reputation might have reached him. I asked Alan Coren, who turned me down, but as compensation invited me to one of his exclusive Punch lunches where, once the dishes had been cleared, literary guests were expected to provide erudite and witty conversation. I particularly remember Ann Leslie's contribution, whilst I, overawed and incapable of adding anything of worth, overcompensated by drinking far too much wine.

I contacted Victoria Wood, whose career was beginning to head skyward, and she invited me to visit her in her seaside town. When I arrived at her flat she introduced me to her friend Julie Walters, and the two girls huddled in a corner giggling together conspiratorially while I stood in the doorway waiting to take her to lunch. The food at the local hotel was memorably unpleasant (the fish I ordered was dry and smothered in vivid orange breadcrumbs), but Victoria was warm and friendly and offered me one of her sharp, funny songs, which I gratefully accepted but never actually used.

I wrote to Arnold Wesker, and to my great astonishment and delight he expressed an interest. This was to be the beginning of a strong and lasting friendship, not only because we shared a Jewish heritage as well as the star sign Gemini, but also because we genuinely respected each other's talents. The piece needed to play for only four or five minutes, but the script Arnold sent me would have played for at least ten, and we agreed it wouldn't edit down, but could certainly be extended. That became his 40-minute one-woman play, *Yardsale*.

Instead of using costumes in my show, I searched for appropriate shoes for each character; after all, they say that once you get the feet right, the rest of the character falls into place. And I needed a pianist. Heaven knows why Paul Maguire said yes, but I shall be eternally grateful that he did, and it was the beginning of a long and happy alliance.

I hadn't really considered the cost, and when the harsh fact hit me I tried frantically to find a backer. The more desperate I became, the more reckless I was in whom I targeted, scavenging names of likely 'angels' from everyone. Then someone suggested a well-known company director. Over lunch at his large and sumptuous house he expressed an interest, and suggested I hire a room somewhere cheaply and hold a drinks party for the writers. To cover the costs he handed me a cheque for £50, which I accepted, deciding to say nothing and make up the deficit myself. The cheapest place I could find was a room in the Arts Theatre Club. I bought the least expensive drinkable wine I could, and explained to the writers that it would be a quick drink to meet the prospective 'angel'. It was an embarrassingly meagre affair, with our absent benefactor arriving just as it was about to break up. He had ordered his chauffeur to wait because what he had to say would be brief.

Waving his cigar for silence, he said, "So you're the a... h...s who're going to write this tosh, are you? Well, get on with it!"

As he left he handed me an envelope. In it was an extraordinary contract for me to sign. Here are a few of the clauses:

I intend but do not guarantee to finance a revue to star SS.

SS will devote reasonable time to the preparation of the show and agrees to appear in the show as requested when required subject only to the completion of such professional commitment as SS may be undertaking at such time as I call for the services of SS for the show. (Pardon??)

3. SS will provide her services without fee until such time as the show has recouped for the investors the amount of their investment plus a sum equivalent to one per cent over bank lending rate, at which time SS will further receive seven and a half per cent of the gross box office takings (less VAT) it being understood that if such additional payments bring the investors back into deficit then such additional payments will cease until the investors are repaid as above.

I sent a note thanking him and returning his £50. Instead I remortgaged my house, vowing that if the show ever came to anything I would, however ineptly, handle it myself.

It occurred to me that there must be stacks of delightful Victorian Music Hall songs in the British Library that would never again see the light of day, and I applied for a reading room ticket. My hunch was right, but as I waded through the huge volumes it became apparent that the Victorians were obsessed with death and disaster! I was intrigued. I found titles like 'How Did You Lose Your Arm?', 'I Wish I Had Died in My Cradle' and 'Are There Any Coloured Angels?' Sometimes the heavy tomes I ordered up offered nothing special; it was a case of pin-sticking and hoping for the best. Then, to my dismay, I discovered that the library wouldn't allow photocopies to be made without the publishers' permission, and since most of the publishing houses no longer existed it meant no permission, and with no permission, no songs. Fortunately, I discovered that Francis, Day and Hunter had bought up many of these small companies, so I wrote to them, and thankfully they sent a covering letter releasing almost all the songs I wanted.

I needed a critical pair of eyes to oversee the project, and Jon Plowman (Head of BBC Comedy, no less) agreed to sit in on rehearsals. His input was invaluable and, to my everlasting shame, unremunerated, as were many of the contributions made by some of the writers, because of my ridiculous and unworkable system based on percentages. It hardly endeared me to the writing fraternity, and it still makes me shudder with shame. Nonetheless, with Jon's wit and faultless eye, the show was honed and ready to be tried out. But where? Someone suggested the pub in Ealing, so we booked it and, apart from a hiccup or two, the evening went well. Two talented and ambitious young men, Andre Tuchinsky and Martin Bergman, offered to produce the show in Edinburgh, and things were looking distinctly positive except for one thing: ad-libbing on stage terrified me and I knew I couldn't do it. I asked Barry Cryer and Christopher Matthew for their help.

"I won't even be able to say 'Good evening, ladies and gentlemen' unless it's written down!" I told them pathetically. "And what's more, I've no idea of how to start the show!"

Christopher wrote an opening monologue, in which I said: "I suppose I could do *Oklahoma* in three minutes, or maybe tear a telephone directory in half."

"Do you mean that?" I asked, incredulous.

"Good Lord, no!" he replied. "They were just the silliest things I could think of."

The silliest they may have been, but they were inspirational. Paul and I do *Oklahoma* in one minute twenty (including a ballet sequence and an interval), *The King and I* in two minutes thirty (well, banging the gong takes up time), *West Side Story* takes two minutes and *My Fair Lady* just over two and a half. The props had to be adaptable. *Oklahoma* was easy, as I happened to own a hat that adapted into different shapes for each of the characters. For *The King and I* we put a gong on a stand next to Paul for him to strike between scenes, but I had to think of a prop that would do for Anna, the Prime Minister, the King's favourite wife, as well as the King himself. Inspiration struck. I cut the bristles off a hairbrush, glued on a curly black hairpiece, and bent it into a U shape. Held downwards over my upper lip, it made a luxuriant moustache for the P.M., held downwards from my forehead it gave Anna curls on each side of her face, and when I held it the other way up on my forehead it became an exotic hairdo for the King's wife. The King, a man with a shaved head who wore earrings, was proving a problem. Maybe if I could find an old-fashioned chamber pot that fitted over my head, I could attach a curtain ring to the handle. That would do the job! If you'll pardon the expression. The only 'potties' available in Boots looked like short top hats leaning to one side, but at last I tracked down a manufacturer in the Midlands who did a line in good old-fashioned 'gozunders'. Unfortunately, when I asked, "Is it big enough to fit over your head?" the line went dead. Not long after, I happened to notice a row of large strainers hanging in John Lewis's kitchen department. What is more, they had little metal ears sticking out on either side, ideal for attaching a large gold curtain ring. The King was cast. And I did indeed finish the show by tearing a telephone directory in half. I tracked down a friend's secretary, who did this as a party piece, and she showed me the knack, so, in spite of what audiences may have thought, it wasn't 'fixed'. Unfortunately, because of their laminated covers, the current directories cannot be subjected to this feat, so I needed a stash of those good old pastel-coloured phone books with soft covers. I asked a clerk at one of the main GPO depots if they had any to spare.

"What d'you want them for?" he enquired.

"I tear them in half."

He looked at me long and hard.

"Bert," he called, "come 'ere a mo."

Bert came.

"Tell 'im," he said, jerking his head in his mate's direction.

I told him.

Without a moment's hesitation, Bert pushed up his shirtsleeves.

"'ow many?" he asked.

But sadly, once I had used up my supply of oldies I could no longer demonstrate my amazing prowess.

We had booked an old church as our Edinburgh venue and rented a basement flat that slept three officially and ten unofficially. I had a 50-minute show, we called it *The Late Sheila Steafel* because it went up at 11 p.m., with Paul Maguire as my accompanist. On stage was a hatstand, from which a dozen or so pairs of shoes were suspended by metal butchers' hooks; I called it my Shoe Tree. On the first night only eighteen people turned up, on the second we had an audience of about thirty, and by the end of the week the queue stretched around the block. The show was a success, but once again The Family Flaw reared its ugly head. For no coherent reason I treated my young producers Andre and Martin with some antipathy, even though their involvement and help were invaluable, and by the time the Festival was over I was, unsurprisingly and deservedly, well out of favour.

Because of our success in Edinburgh, Dan Crawford engaged us to appear at the King's Head Theatre in London's Islington, a venue that only seats about seventy. We called it *Steafel Solo*, and although we were booked for a three-week run we stayed on for three months! Through the years the show played twice in the West End. First *Steafel Variations* in the Apollo Theatre in Shaftsbury Avenue, where I saw my name up in lights for the first thrilling time. But the theatre was far too big, the publicity almost non-existent, and the proposed six-week run ran all of six days. There's nothing quite as salutary as moving your personal effects out of a 'star' dressing room a few short days after you've moved them in. But my bruised ego was soothed by a couple of positive notices:

She is a wide-ranging revue soloist with bite ... Her own talent and timing are irreproachable. (Jewish Chronicle)
There are thumbnail sketches that are moving and delicate, and moments when joshing turns into burlesque. The range is astonishing. (The Guardian)

During the oh so short run, we played to some ridiculously small houses, and one evening I found this cheering letter at the stage door:

Dear Sheila

I was in the audience at your 6 p.m. performance this evening, as a result of which I feel compelled to write - not to commiserate, but to congratulate and thank you for a superb couple of hours. Many performers would not have gone on. Not only did you go on but you won - you beat 780 empty seats and created an intimate atmosphere within which you so thoroughly entertained.

I have to confess it was a bizarre evening. I wish you had been in the bar when the manager, the barman, the usherette, your deputy pianist and 4 of the audience (includes me!) hatched plots to fill the Apollo. It felt like a few friends together for some fun, and it certainly was as much fun as I've ever had with my clothes on!

If success is measured in ticket sales - OK, you lose. But measure it in terms of creativity, entertainment, and above all, the challenge - boy, what a success this evening. You should be more proud of that performance than any packed houses, rave reviews and sellouts.

Sheila, my thanks for a lovely evening.

Gareth James

So that was nice. A few years later we made up for it by running to capacity at the Ambassador's theatre with *Steafel Express*, but, wisely, only for a week.

Paul and I have had extraordinary times together doing the show, some good, some awful, and some real bonuses, like going to Australia to take part in the Adelaide Festival. And when Arnold Wesker recommended us we were invited to Istanbul as guests of the Turko-British Association to provide entertainment for the ex-pats at their annual ball, and we stayed in the Consulate, a beautiful, old, square building constructed around a central courtyard and surrounded by a high wall guarded by armed police. We were chauffeured in a long limousine with a small Union Jack attached to its nose, and when we alighted bodyguards walked closely around us.

I decided that it might be fun to deliver a short message at the ball in Turkish from our then Prime Minister Mrs Thatcher, an impression I had learned to do in *Week Ending*. I asked one of the Turkish secretaries if she could think of a word that, if mispronounced, would mean something entirely different. She thought for a moment.

"Yes, I can," she said, blushing.

"What is it?"

"No, it is too much. Too rude!"

"What?" I insisted.

"Well, there is a word that means 'friendly relations'," she said, "but if you put the emphasis on the wrong syllable, it means ..."

She stopped.

"It means VERY friendly relations?" I guessed.

She nodded.

"You couldn't say it!" she said.

But I did.

"I hope," I said, reading phonetically in Turkish, "that your people and mine will in the future enjoy 'very friendly relations' with one another."

There was an audible intake of breath followed by a pause long enough to make me wonder whether I had gone too far. Then, like a distant approaching train, the laughter grew. Reprieved!

David Donabie, a lovely man and entrepreneur who shared his time between the UK and Saudi Arabia, invited me to perform the show in Riyadh and Dhahran for the large community of Brits living and working there, and Instead of taking a pianist I took a recorded tape and drew up a detailed script for volunteers to follow. I stayed in a large, modern compound surrounded by a high wall, an armed guard at the entrance, and no matter how frequently we drove in, in the same car, it was stopped and thoroughly searched. The morning sun blazed bright and early. All the residents worked outside the compound, and by 7 o'clock I was left alone until my early evening pickup, when a car would sweep me off to whichever hall in whichever compound I was to entertain. With nothing to do, I read every book on the shelves and watched NBC news endlessly on the television. Sometimes I wandered through the empty streets where the silent Filipino gardeners, eyes averted, brushed dust from the whitewashed stones that defined each immaculate plot. I got into the habit of taking a short swim each day in the nearby lukewarm pool with its neat stacks of faded canvas deckchairs. I considered hiring a taxi to take me into the town, but I had been warned not to venture anywhere on my own, and in any case I couldn't have given an address because I didn't know where I was. The evening entertainments were well received, the British folk charming and welcoming, and although alcohol is strictly forbidden I never did a show without being offered a drink, sometimes distinctly raw, but welcome all the same.

Back home, so many people told me how fascinated they were by the Victorian songs of misery and misfortune that I devised an entire evening of Victorian entertainment, which included monologues, poems and other bits and pieces from the period, and called it *Victoria Plums*. I had tremendous fun making costumes from bits and pieces gleaned from theatre companies with overstocked wardrobe departments, picking over torn skirts, blouses fraying at the edges, worn satin shoes and ragged high-buttoned boots. The Players theatre let me ferret through their bulging drawers and crowded rails, and I salvaged a stunning wine-coloured satin evening dress ruined by a long splash of white paint down its front. I retrieved a crumpled piece of ecru lace, which, once washed and lovingly restored, turned out to be a genuine delicate Victorian bolero. I made velvet brocade waistcoats and frilly shirt fronts for whichever pianist might be accompanying me, and so that I could change on stage, had a screen made that would break down into sections so that it could travel.

With this new show we were able to revisit theatres we had played before, and a year after my last visit to Rhyadh David Donabie invited me back for a week to perform *Victoria Plums*. It was close to Christmas, and I decided to take our host a Fortnum's Xmas pudding to remind him of home. When I handed it to him he looked at the ingredients and flinched.

"Did you know there's brandy in this?" he asked. "You're very lucky. If customs had looked at the label it would have been confiscated, and you might have been detained or sent home!"

The pianist I took with me was Paul Smith, and we both stayed with David in his town house - a brave risk on his part, as unmarried guests are forbidden to stay in the same residence, not even in separate rooms. I had been warned that I would need to 'cover up' in public. Apparently, if any part of a woman's anatomy was visible, the police vigilantes would swipe at the offending flesh with their sticks, so in London I had bought a dark brown full-length linen coat. One day, as David, Paul and

I walked to the nearby shops, me wearing my coat of all covers, a passing car slowed down and the man at the wheel, a Saudi, made a distinctly salacious gesture at me.

David was unnerved and asked, "Are you covered up?"

"Of course!" I replied.

He started scrutinising me.

"No," he said. "Look, the top button of your coat is undone."

Back in London I was approached to do a late-night performance of Solo at The Subway Club in Leicester Square, one of the most popular gay clubs in London. I was apprehensive, Paul even more so! We were greeted by the club's manager and walked across the crowded floor into his office. Black leather seemed de rigueur: heavy boots, bomber jackets and peaked caps, accessorised with studded bracelets and neckbands, and topped (or should I say bottomed) off with the teeniest of leather thongs. It turned out to be one of our most successful evenings. Every point and nuance was picked up, the audience was demonstrably appreciative. To my delight we were immediately booked for a second appearance.

The other gay venue we played was on a Sunday night at The Dog and Fox in Battersea, where the theme was 'Uniforms' and the pub clientele had dressed in every permutation imaginable. Tables had been pushed together to make a stage, with Paul somewhere below me sitting at a dodgy upright. After my short act, barely audible in the noisy strobe-lit room, I climbed clumsily from my perch and pushed my way through the crowd to the comparative safety of a nearby corridor. Four schoolgirls in gymslips and panama hats followed hard on my heels.

"We've got a bet on," one of them panted. "Tell us, are you a bloke?"

We were invited to appear in a midnight cabaret at the opening of a French restaurant in a grand residential block in Dolphin Square. Barry Cryer had written me a sketch as a French chanteuse who, somewhat the worse for drink, forgets the words of her song, ideal for this particular bash. When we arrived, the noise of happily overindulged people trying to make themselves heard above the pounding beat and painfully loud speakers was deafening. We pushed our way in through a side door, wedged open by rows of thick electric cables and manned by a fraught security guard. Looking up at him was a tiny woman, a resident of the building, wearing a mink coat over her nightdress, tearfully pleading with him to have the sound turned down!

The restaurant was vast and high-ceilinged, with tables packed around the edge of a central dance floor, and on it a crowd of celebrities were indulging in one of the best freebie evenings of their careers. The last chords from a pop group reverberated around the room and the musicians shambled off the small platform, heading in the direction of what we assumed must be the bar. A breathless man put his hand on my shoulder.

"There you are at last!" he said accusingly. "You're on!"

Once we were on the platform, with the clutter of abandoned electric paraphernalia, it seemed even smaller. Paul sat down at the synthesiser and began to play, and I picked up the nearest microphone.

"Good evening, ladies and gentlemen," I slurred in a French accent. "Good … good evening!"

One or two people looked at me, then returned to their conversations. I tried again, louder.

"Good evening, ladies and gentlemen. My name is Yvette, Yvette Herriot, and it is wonderful to be over here …"

No response. I decided to continue - after all, that was what we were there for - and exaggerated my drunken swaying and slurring.

One of a group of guests standing close by turned to look at me, then said loudly, "Don't look now, but Sheila Steafel's got hold of the microphone and she's pissed out of her mind!"

To make matters worse, an actor I vaguely knew detached himself from the crowd, dragging his very pretty girlfriend behind him. They had dressed appropriately for the evening, she in short skirt and fishnets, he in waistcoat and spotted scarf, both sporting black berets, and both more inebriated than I was pretending to be.

"Quiet, you lot!" he bawled. "This is Sheila! Hooray for Sheila! Now come on, shut up!" And then "Tarah!" he yelled, flinging his arms wide.

"What do we do?" I hissed at Paul.

"Finish the chorus and get out of here!"

As we hurried out through the side door we passed the group's drummer, who was leaning against the wall smoking a joint.

"Tough bunch, eh?" he nodded sympathetically. "Still, it's a living."

"Not even!" I responded as we fled, leaving our little brown envelope behind.

I can remember a New Year's Eve when we were booked for a restaurant near Crystal Palace. As we began, the customers looked at us momentarily, and then got on with their banter, balloons and bevvies. We persevered gamely until a scuffle broke out and a bottle winged its way past my head. We saw the New Year in at a traffic light in Clapham.

We were invited to be the first performers in a newly built theatre in Warwickshire. I decided to look as glamorous as I could, and instead of my usual jeans and shirt I wore very high heels, tight pink satin pants and a very chic, beaded, pink chiffon top. We waited in the wings, the lights went down, then came up again, I ran on stage ... and slipped on the highly polished floor, skidding on my bottom, legs flailing. Paul rushed onstage and grabbed me just before I landed in the laps of the horrified front row.

"That entrance took weeks to rehearse!" I quipped, trying not to show the pain.

Eager to believe me, the audience laughed, and, through gritted teeth, so did we.

"Do you know," said the proud owner of the theatre after the show, "one of our cleaners has been working on that floor ever since it was laid. It's her pride and joy. Would you like to meet her?"

"It depends," I replied, "on how much you need her."

Victoria Plums was due to play for a week in a small theatre in Hampstead. The audiences were embarrassingly thin, and one evening, in desperation, I headed for a nearby pub and handed out free tickets for that night's performance. Two men and a woman appeared at curtain up, all in various stages of inebriation, to join the few genuine punters. Having sat through the first ten minutes, one of them staggered to his feet and declared loudly that this sort of entertainment wasn't for him and he was off. His chum agreed, but the woman argued that she wanted to stay, and a noisy altercation followed. They clattered down the auditorium steps and headed for the exit, but, instead of following her companions out, the woman staggered onto the stage, oblivious of the small audience.

"I know your face," she said, standing in front of me as though

271

we had just met in the street. "I've seen you in something on the telly, haven't I? What was it, now? No, don't tell me!"

She continued her guessing game as, feigning polite interest, I cajoled her towards the exit and ushered her out with a helpful hand in the small of her back. There was nothing for it but to discuss this bizarre interruption with the few remaining members of the audience, and, with an atmosphere not unlike that of a family drawing room, it was one of the most authentically Victorian evenings I have ever played.

Richard Cook, an executive of Polygram Records, was an enthusiast and connoisseur of Victorian artistes and music hall and owned a sizeable collection of records by, and photographs of, all the stars of the genre. He suggested that I make a CD of *Plums*, which he would produce, and within a few months it was done. I was delighted with the result, and so was Richard. "It will be an antique of the future," he said - prophetically, as it happens, because it's no longer available! I treasure it, not only as a reminder of the show but also of Richard himself, who became a dear and good friend, and tragically died much too young.

In 2002 I put together a third show, *Steafel Xposed*, which, as the title suggests, is autobiographical, telling personal truths both good and not so good, and throwing in some of my favourite characterisations.

In amongst my cuttings I came across this:

If an American actress got the kind of rave reviews S.S. has picked up for her one-woman shows, she'd have been whisked onto the comfortable conveyor belt of the great hype machine, with agents taking the strain and deals dropping like confetti. Back in Britain the comedienne is still having to run her career like a cottage industry.

Recently I counted up the number of theatres I've visited with my shows over the years; the total is 95, and the actual performances amount to 316. And still, I hope, counting!

TV OR NOT TV
During the 1960s and '70s I appeared with almost every comedy star on television, either in one-offs or as a regular in

their series. Some were delightful, some difficult, and some a mixture of both. Les Dawson proved to be surprisingly different from his persona as a comic. He was genial, highly intelligent and engaging, and was one of the nicest people I have worked with. Another was Kenneth Horne, with his series *Horne A'Plenty*. He was warm-hearted, humorous, interested in others and generous to a fault. Duirng the series, he and a few VIPs were invited by a government minister to an exclusive gourmet dinner at the Savoy Hotel. Kenneth enjoyed the cuisine so much, he decided he'd like to share the experience with us, and ordered a repeat performance for the production team and the members of the cast. On another occasion I happened to admire a shirt he was wearing, joking that I thought it would look better on me. The next day he handed me a package. It was the same shirt in my size.

Spike Milligan's genius made him eccentric and temperamental. I was in two series with him, first *Beachcomber* and then *Q7*, which he starred in and wrote. It was directed by Ian McNaughton, Harry's best man all those years back, and he dealt admirably with his star's idiosyncrasies. During rehearsals bizarre ideas and one-liners bubbled out of Spike so fast it was impossible to grasp one before it was superseded by another. In one show, for no particular reason, he insisted that everyone should wear large prop noses and funny hats, and in another the wardrobe department was told to leave the large name tags on the actors' costumes for the public's edification. Each episode usually featured big-breasted, scantily clad Julia Breck as a 'glamour stooge', and there was always a musical interlude of some sort. The Mike Sammes Singers appeared one week, and at the end of their contribution Spike surprised them by throwing well-aimed custard pies. If things went wrong during a recording he would fly into an uncontrollable rage, and the next day everyone would be castigated mercilessly. On these occasions there was no reasoning with him, and the only thing to do was sit quietly and ride out the storm.

BBC2 had just started up, and I worked *Some Matters of Little Consequence*, a regular late-night show with David Nobbs as script editor. There were only three in the cast, myself, Frank Thornton and Kenneth Griffith. Because it was topical, the sketches were short and the rehearsal period brief. Kenneth found this difficult to handle and at one point, when the

273

pressure got too much for him, lost his temper, shouting, "It's all very well for you and Frank, you're comedy people. I'm a real actor!"

As for Frankie Howerd, although I worked with him several times I never got to know him. He was very much a loner and barely spoke to any of the cast during rehearsals. On the day of recording this suddenly changed and, possibly feeling in need of some reassurance, he became friendly and chatty. I also got to work with the great Tommy Cooper, who was notorious for being late, and although it didn't matter too much when we were rehearsing it did matter on studio days when time was at a premium. No matter how much he was cajoled or threatened, Tommy would be late, and as everyone hung around waiting for him tempers shortened and the atmosphere became brittle. Then just before lunch Tommy would appear, larger than life and beaming, throwing out apologies like confetti, and everyone instantly melted and forgave him again.

Tommy would never do his tricks or tell his jokes during the rehearsal. Instead, he would do the moves so that the camera would know where to find him, substituting the gag with the words, "Patter, patter, patter," followed by, "Woof!" where the laugh would come, and punctuating the whole bizarre performance with those trademark thrusts of his hands. The rehearsal was as funny as the performance itself, and we felt a true affection for the big man with the big feet and the red fez.

Although the three series of *The Ghosts of Motley Hall* were made as children's programmes, they attracted viewers of all ages, probably because the director Quentin Lawrence and the writer Kip Carpenter, as well as the cast, never played down to the lowest common denominator. To us the series was a serious, if somewhat eccentric, drama. A good deal of its merit was in the casting. It is impossible to think of anyone but Freddie Jones playing the blustering Victorian military ghost of Sir George Uproar, and who but Nicholas Le Prevost could have brought the young, swashbuckling Restoration blade 'Fanny'... I nearly said, '... to life'! Arthur English was ideal as the Shakespearean jester Bodkin, as was Sean Flanagan as Matt the stable boy, and the team of regulars was rounded off with the estimable Peter Sallis as the nervous yet determined janitor. I still wonder at my luck being cast as the anonymous White Lady who wailed, "I'm not a ghost, I'm just a description!" It was a part to die for, which I suppose, in a way, I did. I loved wearing the wispy white robes and flowing tresses, but the long, false fingernails became the bane of my life, on and off screen. They had to be glued on each morning and were inclined to come off under the slightest pressure, so I tried to avoid using my fingertips. As a result, ordinary activities such as dressing and eating demanded innovative manual skills and a deal of patience. Peeling the nails off at the end of the day's shooting soon began to weaken and discolour my own, so I tried leaving them on overnight. More often than not I would be woken by a painful jab from a fugitive nail lurking inside the bed, and in the morning the few that remained would be hanging off at alarming angles.

I once asked the writer Kip if the White Lady actually knew who she was, and he pointed out that whenever it looked likely that her identity might be revealed, she manipulated the situation so that the enigma remained. As for me, I'm sure she did know who she was, and I'm fairly certain I know who she was too. But I ain't telling.

In 1987 I was sent a script that featured an elegant, egocentric literary agent, a dyed-in-the-wool snob, Miranda Shaw. The series was *You Must Be the Husband*, written by Colin Bostock-Smith, and I couldn't wait to play her. Apart from the fact that she was a character I could really get my teeth into, she was ultra-glamorous, and it meant I could put aside the usual dreary clothes and funny wigs, and appear at last in high fashion and false eyelashes. The storyline was based on a couple, Tom and Alice Hammond (played by Tim Brooke-Taylor and Diane Keen), who have been happily married for twenty years until she writes a best-seller. Tom and Alice's agent, Miranda, are constantly at loggerheads over issues arising from her success, and poor Tom seeks support from his best friend Gerald, played by Garfield Morgan.

The general consensus from the press was that the programme was "not exactly bad, just distinctly unmemorable," while I came out smelling of roses:

Were it not for S.S., who could get laughs out of a house brick, YMBTH could be passed off as a serious drama. (Sunday Times)
(S.S.) is by far the star as overpowering Miranda with a tolerance level as high as the Grand Canyon. (Observer)
S.S. is superb, as ever. What a boon she is to any comedy show bright

and lucky enough to get her. (Daily Mirror)

It was 1987, and in an interview I did at the time I'm quoted as saying, "This will be my first TV series for seven or more years." The journalist observed:

It is a sad comment from a lady with more talent in her little finger than the entire cast of some comedy shows.

It was depressingly true that in spite of the mountain of cuttings crammed into four fat ring files in my loft, eulogising my talents, work had slowly tailed off; no offers were coming in. All I could do was perform my one-woman shows, and that source was drying up because I wasn't been seen on TV, and without TV you are soon forgotten and can't attract an audience.

In 1968, when *Horne A'Plenty* was being televised, a notice appeared saying:

Sheila Steafel has tremendous potential and is one of the biggest assets Kenneth Horne has got. By the end of the year she will almost certainly have her own series.

In 1974, on reviewing a series I was in called *How's Your Father*, a critic wrote:

S.S., one of our few first-rate comediennes, managed to steal the show. She has long merited her own series, and perhaps after this someone will at last have the good sense to showcase her.

I never did get my own series, so what went wrong? The answer became startlingly clear to me when I happened to read the following, written by John Simms, an astute critic on the *Somerset County Gazette*, after he had seen my one-woman show *Steafel Xposed* in 2002:

… you began to wonder why exactly the woman on stage who is possessed of a heavy duty talent hasn't seen much more success down the years and is doing a one woman number to a half-full house in Taunton? There are a surprising number of gifted performers who carry an anti-success mechanism with them to a greater or lesser degree …

Putting my files of cuttings to good use at last, I was brought face to face with the raw and painful truth: I had, and hopefully still have, a God-given talent that was recognised and should have assured my future, yet for no accountable reason I managed to chip away at it and ruin a flourishing career. I seem to have deliberately kyboshed many of the opportunities that came my way, often backing off when stardom was almost a foregone conclusion. The anti-success mechanism made perfect sense.

TRUTH TO TELL

My actor friend Hugh Paddick once quipped, "You're not difficult to work with, you're impossible!" It was said in jest but he had meant it. I didn't suffer fools gladly. If actors fooled around at rehearsals I showed my impatience, and it did me no favours when I sat silently glowering while fellow artistes laughed and joked during recording sessions wasting studio time, though that was none of my concern. When directors didn't understand the nuances of comedy I showed my disdain, maintaining that I knew more about the technique of my craft than they did. I couldn't help making suggestions when I saw better alternatives, and when opportunities for laughs were missed it was hard not to interfere. I thought I was invincible, that whatever I did, my talent would conquer all. But nobody likes a smart-arse. Nor do they care for amorality, and I was being blatantly promiscuous, overplaying my hand in return for the slightest indication of interest or affection. What I neglected to consider was the toll that my liaisons might take on my self-respect, not to mention the respect of others for me.

Unlikely as it may seem, I was painfully insecure and shy, reluctant to socialise and more comfortable in my own company. I still find small talk difficult and wonder whether my father's view of it as a waste of time, along with our family's insularity and the enforced silences, accounts for these traits. Often I would avoid fraternising with fellow actors, choosing to sit alone in rehearsal rooms or on train journeys. Greeting people often took courage, and I would say nothing as I passed, fairly sure in my mind that they wouldn't know who I was, thus adding to my reputation for being arrogant and aloof.

Yet, when presented with the opportunity, I was unable to resist countering a good feed line with a witty remark, however hurtful. Staunch friends warned me against indulging this habit, but I was riding high and laughed them away. Heaven knows how many I upset with verbal barbs that were bound to wound, and many were the friendships I lost in consequence. I offended Jane Glover, the talented and respected conductor under whose baton I performed Walton's *Façade*, with some crass and uncalled-for observation about her private life. Wanting to appear 'smart', I made some specious remark about the glorious voice of counter-tenor James Bowman to his partner after a performance I'd been invited to, thereby losing two valued friends. Doubtless there were others left smarting after I found some comeback irresistible, and even now I spend the odd restless, guilty night considering how to make reparations. Dawn logic, tells me it's too late.

Ever since I missed getting my own series after *The Frost Report*, I hoped for a script to turn up that I might feature in. Then out of the blue I received an offer to play Miranda in *You Must Be the Husband*. Here was a character so strongly written, that I foolishly assumed it would be a starring role alongside Tim Brooke-Taylor. I sat in the producer's office along with the writer and, in a proprietary way, pointed out some changes I thought would improve my characterisation. They looked a little surprised but said nothing. Much the same happened during rehearsals, and I irritated Tim by making suggestions about restructuring lines and adding bits of business. Of course I shouldn't have interfered. I should also have kept quiet when, to my huge disappointment, the credits rolled for the first time and Tim and Diane Keen were featured but not me. As ever, lemming-like, I headed for the precipice, creating a deal of fuss and adding another twist to my downward-spiralling reputation.

John Kilby directed the first few episodes and was then replaced by Richard Boden. For some inexplicable reason, as rehearsals progressed, I began behaving like a diva. In one episode I made a huge fuss when the script called for Miranda to be photographed by another character as she inadvertently sat on a new toilet being delivered to the Hammonds'. At the time I said it was literally 'toilet humour' and I was protecting my character's image, when the truth is that I was probably protecting my own. So uncooperative was I that one evening Richard phoned me at home. He was at the end of his tether.

"I've noticed you don't seem very happy," he said, admirably understating his case.

"I'm not," I answered.

"Why is that?"

"Well," I said tartly (and my reply still haunts me), "because you don't know anything about comedy, and I do."

Richard, by the way, went on to direct, produce and win awards for the hugely successful *Black Adder* series. I can't imagine why I was never offered a part in it!

Having made myself thoroughly unpopular in the BBC Light Entertainment department, I decided that if my acting career were scuttled I would do a director's course (and show 'em!), proclaiming loudly that "It was time someone knew how to direct comedy." The powers that be accepted my application, and at the end of the first period of study the tutors decided I had potential, and recommended that I carry on. But I pulled out; my heart wasn't in it. Each time I passed actors in the corridor on their way to rehearse or record, I wanted to be with them, rather than directing them.

But before I blame myself entirely for the ruination of my prospects, there is an ingredient in the mix that's missing, and it's this: it's possible that some fellow performers found me a threat because I was too funny. I can certainly recall two occasions when this proved to be the case. The first was when the star of a popular sitcom petulantly insisted some of my lines should be cut after I had garnered appreciative laughs from the crew during the dress run, on the grounds that they impinged on his own laughs. On the second occasion I happened to pass a well-established star on a staircase in the BBC who pointed at me, calling out, "I'll never work with you, darling, you're much too funny!"

I should, by now have developed some sort of behavioural maturity, or, at the very least, learned to keep my feelings in check. But I did neither, and thus it was that I was taught the most salutary lesson of all. At the time I was yet again wallowing in self pity at the end of yet another unhappy affair with yet another suitably unsuitable lover. Almost all the lovers I chose were suitably unsuitable, guaranteeing that any potential for a long lasting relationship was scuppered from the start. The misalliance would inevitably end, and I would find myself desolate, miserable, and, of course, free. Free to start again.

These entanglements often intruded on my career, and in spite of my professed dogged ambition, more often than not I followed my fickle heart.

I was mooching about in the depths of despair when my agent phoned to tell me she had a job for me. I was to appear in an episode of *Fry and Laurie*, in a short sketch playing an Italian mamma. I hadn't worked for the BBC for a long while, and although I was used to playing major roles I was more than grateful for this opportunity, however minor. At the first rehearsal in Acton we sat around a table reading through the very funny script, and although I appreciated the humour, so choked up was I with my woes that I couldn't raise a smile. We got up to block the moves and I did as I was told, feeling bereft and trailing clouds of gloom, so it was hardly surprising that my agent called me later that afternoon to tell me they had recast the part. I had been sacked! Good God, I had been sacked! It shook me to the core. I was appalled and genuinely frightened for my future.

"But they can't!" I blustered, my heart racing.

"They can and they have. What did you do, for Christ's sake?"

How could I explain? I begged her to ask them to reconsider, but I knew it was too late and hopeless.

Mortified and ashamed, that night I wrote a letter addressed to Stephen and Hugh explaining that a long personal relationship had just ended and had left me devastated. I apologised as best I could for being self-indulgent and unprofessional, adding that I was deeply disappointed at having missed the opportunity to work with them. Early the following morning I drove to the rehearsal rooms and left it at the reception desk. Stephen, elegant man that he is, sent me the following letter by return:

Dear Sheila

Thank you so very much for your letter, which made me go quite pink about the ears. Believe me, I am terribly sorry that you should be upset - doubly so as it all seems to have come in a bad week for you. La, isn't life a bitchy thing? It would have been delightful to have had you in the show; you know what an admirer of yours I am. Why, do you remember, we met in the Flask Inn to talk about your Edinburgh show, which I so loved.

Anyway, here's till the next time. Please be cheerful and don't hate

us too much.
Lots love
Stephen

Lesson learned? Family Flaw permitting, you bet!

CALIFORNIA HERE I COME

I was sitting on a plane, thinking: why on earth am I leaving a perfectly good career in England to start again in Los Angeles? A perfectly good career? I had barely worked for the past three years and my future looked bleak. I should, of course, have gone to the States when I had the opportunity. I had featured in a comedy series in 1974 called *How's Your Father,* playing a character called Ivy Watkins, who had the catchphrase, "Yes, Mr Cropper," which caught on. Unfortunately, the series didn't, but I came out of it remarkably well with quotes like: "The greatest waste is that of the tremendously talented SS," and "S.S's sense of timing would bring out the humour in a Gas Board training manual." This performance netted me an invitation to repeat it with an American cast in Los Angeles, where, unlike the British at the time, they loved and promoted funny women. I declined, a decision I've regretted ever since. But why? I made up spurious excuses, telling myself I couldn't leave my newly acquired house in the hands of builders without being there to oversee the alterations, and how unfair it would be to abandon my rescue dog Crispin to the care of others. I was probably enmeshed in the web of one of my emotional predators, but my memory thankfully refuses to surrender which of them it may have been. Excuses, excuses. But what really made me back away from this opportunity? After all, it would have consolidated my career and fulfilled the future I had always dreamed of. Probably that cankerous anti-success mechanism was working overtime, but, whatever it was, it was clear that now, seventeen years on, I had little to lose by crossing the Atlantic. I sipped my second vodka and tonic, courtesy of American Airways, and smiled wryly: too late now! With my limited resources but infinite determination I was finally setting off to conquer America, and although I knew I'd have to start at the bottom of the ladder I felt reasonably confident.

I had no money for the venture, but I did have a diamond

solitaire that my mother had given me. It had been given to her mother by my grandfather, but she had never liked it nor attached much sentimental value to it. My mother wore it from time to time and happened to have it on her finger when, on my arrival in London, we visited some distant relations in their large mansion flat in Maida Vale. They were an odd old couple. Aunty Esther was a lugubrious soul, who was in permanent mourning for their son, not departed to a Heavenly Haven but to Australia after a serious brush with the law. Aunt Esther was also paranoid about the theft of her three expensive fur coats and, as a result, took them with her wherever she went. Uncle Henry had been a jeweller in the diamond market and was, as a result, wealthy.

That afternoon Uncle Henry had admired my mother's ring and had offered to clean it for her. She handed it over reluctantly, and he disappeared into the next room. He seemed to be gone for an inordinately long time, and, somewhat agitated, my mother went to see what the delay was.

"The phone," he explained apologetically, quickly handing back the ring. On the bus ride home she examined it carefully and discovered that the diamond was loose in its setting.

Having a diamond ring worried me. I couldn't afford to insure it and seldom wore it. It was worth, I was told, about £4,000, and, after much heart-searching and a consultation with my mother, we agreed to put it to good use to subsidise my trip to Los Angeles. I decided to ask a theatre impresario, a good friend of mine, whether he would consider giving the ring to his wife, whom it would suit so much better than me. We met for lunch, and he generously offered not only to buy it but also to keep it in his safe for a year, during which time, if I wanted to, I could redeem it. I never did.

I had persuaded friends to move into my house and look after my family of four dogs. My American fellow drama student, Dan, now a good friend of many years standing, had rallied splendidly and found me a bedsitter in a house in Brentwood, a green and hilly suburb of Los Angeles. He had also organised a hire car for me to pick up at the airport and sent instructions on how to get to my new accommodation. I found the hazards of driving on the right side of the road less stressful than trying to use a payphone at the airport to let Dan's cousin Sergio know that I was on my way. The girl in the car hire office laughed a lot as she watched me struggle for a good ten minutes with dimes and cents, but eventually, seeming to hear my sobs, she came over and showed me what to do. It was nice to discover early on that Americans have such a healthy sense of humour. The journey along Sunset Boulevard from the airport took me two hours, during which time I lost heart and made several stops to make sure I was still in LA. Somehow I did manage to locate the 'Very Des. Res. With Glorious View over the Brentwood Hills towards Distant Ocean'. A young man, whom I assumed to be cousin Sergio, opened the door and thrust a key into my hand. Then he rattled off some sentences peppered with Italian, which I later came to recognise as 'Italio-Americano-Show-Offo', pointed me at my basement bedsit plus shower, and disappeared. It was 10 p.m. local time, which made it 6 a.m. my time, and I needed some food, not to mention a large drink. I climbed back into the car, somehow found a vast local supermarket and, more by luck than judgement, found my way back. As I unpacked I comforted myself with slurps of Californian wine and munched on a large German sausage, while the small, chattering TV set kept me company. Exhausted, I fell into bed and woke with the sun blazing through the windows and the television announcing that this was the NBC news at 1 p.m. It was time to brave the streets of LA.

"You're a manic depressive!"

I freeze. Did he really say that? It's hard to tell over the music blaring out of the CD player on the floor in a corner of the room. I smile nervously.

"Sorry?" I try to project my voice over the sound.

"I said your résumé's impressive!" he shouts, waving my CV at me across his desk.

I breathe a sigh of relief and watch Larry as he continues to read. He isn't the first agent I've seen in Los Angeles. The others had also said they were impressed by my CV, or 'résumé', as the Americans will have it. They also said that they didn't want to represent me. Some told me that there were no parts for women of my age, others that it was an ideal time for women of my age - but not, it seemed, for me. Either way, I was getting nowhere fast. And then, after my first frustrating week in LA, I had found a message on my answering machine from Larry T. asking me to come and see him in his new offices. In fact, I'd met him once before in my London agent's office, when he had spent the interview telling me of his high and envied status in New York and LA without asking me a single question about myself or my career. He was on my list of possibles, but somewhere towards the bottom. Now here I was, having handed over sheaves of my biography, my lists of credits, and my hopes for future success in the USA.

Larry looks up at me and says something. I try to lip-read. Useless. I point at the CD player and mime turning it off.

"Hell, no!" he yells. "I have a Very Important Actor recording a Very Important Pilot of a Very Important TV series tonight. I need music or I get Very Nervous, which puts me in A Very Bad Mood!"

It's no wonder Larry is hyperventilating - I'd been told what large amounts actors here can earn in successful series, even in minor roles.

Suddenly he gets up, beaming. "Come meet the team."

I follow his big hulk as, shoeless, he pads ahead in tracksuit and socks, kicking a path through the 'Welcome' balloons that bounce around on the new-smelling fitted carpet. The 'team' are all charming, encouraging, and play interested. Short, broad Becky, in vast baggy trousers and an XL Snoopy T-shirt, jokes her way through a phone call while she waves me into a chair. I like her. Then there's NicolIe (Nico for short, because, I'm told, she chain-smokes). She kneels on the floor of her untidy office, hair cascading, huge glasses balanced on the tip of her nose, surrounded by stacks of paper and being nuzzled by a small, anxious dog. And finally Stefan, who, as far as I can see, is dark-haired and smiling, though it's hard to tell in the gloom of his windowless office, the only dim light coming from a single lamp facing into a corner. And at last I have an American agent! Now all I have to do is sit back and wait for the work to roll in – that is, as long as I can get a Green Card.

Ah, that elusive Green Card, the work permit without which you are snookered. I was told that it could sometimes be acquired on payment of about $2,500 to the right, or perhaps 'wrong', lawyer, although this can be dodgy because it's a dodgy thing to do. One alternative is to go to an interview and omit to mention that you haven't got a Green Card. If the company want you badly enough they'll acquire it for you, and if you're very lucky, they'll even pay for it. But this also means they will have to convince some clerk, whose knowledge of showbiz is probably based on the American equivalent of *Hello* magazine, that there is no actor alive anywhere other than you who can play the part. The usual way is to make your own application. To do this you have to supply another plodding office clerk with a pile of commendations that will gobsmack him into thinking that the American world of entertainment would be deprived of a major talent without the benefit of your services. Somewhat shame-facedly, before I left London I had touted for letters of recommendation from every 'name' I had ever worked with - actors, producers, writers and even companies, just for their impressively headed notepaper! The response had been surprisingly generous - even Dudley Moore had sent a flattering credential - and I had tucked these trophies into a big Manila envelope, along with photocopies of posters, snapshots of me with anyone vaguely famous, and a clutch of glittering notices culled from my bulging scrapbook. I handed my precious package over to Larry, exhorting him to put it somewhere safe. He did. So safe, that it was never to be found again.

It was late January, and I had been told that now was the time to be in LA, when the pilot season began. Scripts galore are written, cast, recorded and dumped, and here I was, tail held more or less high. But at least I was confident about one thing - my gift for comedy. And those people who knew my track record had assured me that so long as I was prepared to sit it out, I couldn't fail.

At first the days passed quickly. I drove around, finding my way, discovering places, and learning the city. Journeys between locations always took so long that one or two trips took up most of the day. I couldn't afford to splash out on sprees; my budget just about allowing me to try out different takeaways and feed petrol into my hungry car. Of necessity I bought an answerphone, and each evening when I returned I prayed that its ruthless red light would blink. It didn't. I still hadn't seen anyone socially, even though several British actor chums who lived in LA had sent messages to me in London saying that they would be in touch. Instead, I found myself thankful for the comforting telly, and apart from missing my dogs it was much like being at home, on my own and waiting for the phone to ring.

With no interviews, no chums and no 'fun' money to spend, I took to going into Larry's office and wandering from room to room just to make contact with other human beings. If an opportune moment came, I would try to persuade one or other of 'the team' to phone a casting agent on my behalf, and by the middle of the second week the "Hi's" in the office were distinctly low, and smiles were wearing thin. I had become a pest. Then one morning I noticed a large, ugly glass vase with flowers haphazardly stuck into it on the table in the reception area. I've always had a flair for flower arrangement and I was itching to get at it. I put my head timidly around Larry's door and asked if he'd mind.

"Fine," he said, delighted that my attention was fixed on something other than the office switchboard. "No problem. Go ahead."

Visibly cheered, I decided to push my financially restricted boat out and buy a decent cheap vase for the office as a gesture of goodwill. Hopping into my little car, I headed for Santa Monica Boulevard, where Becky had told me I would find a florist shop. The 'shop' turned out to be a huge open yard filled with life-size animals, elephants, camels and donkeys, all of them made of straw. To one side was a glass-domed building filled with buckets of brilliantly coloured flowers and shelves of vases of every shape and size. I found a young man standing at a long trestle table, working on an elaborate flower arrangement, and explained that I was looking for an attractive but reasonably priced vase, "because," I explained, smiling (I hoped, winningly), "I'm a bit on the broke side."

"Broke, huh?" he said. "I know the feeling. Talking of broke, how would you feel about a chipped vase? Nothing wrong with it that a careful arrangement couldn't hide."

He bent down and pulled out a tall, cylindrical glass vase with a small chip on its rim.

Perfect!" I said, as I reached for my purse. "How much?"

"Forget it," he said, getting back to his work.

I thanked him profusely, and as I turned to go an idea struck me.

"I'm looking for a part-time job," I said. "Need any help here?"

"Maybe," he answered. "Valentine's Day is pretty soon. Ask the boss."

The boss was at the front desk checking the till.

"I'm an actress from England," I told him, "and I need a part-time job."

He didn't seem surprised. In LA everyone - waiters and petrol pump attendants, cleaners and shop assistants, chambermaids and traffic wardens - is an aspiring actor waiting to be discovered.

"Okay," he said, "come in Sunday ten o' clock and show me."

Back at the office I spent a happy half-hour arranging what I thought was a pretty nifty vase full. I felt distinctly cheered; after all, I had Sunday to look forward to.

"Use anything you like!"

The boss waved his arms expansively around the exotic blooms. It was Sunday morning, it was ten o' clock, and I was so nervous, you would have thought I was about to audition for a leading role in a movie. Stepping carefully between the flower-filled buckets, I hardly knew where to begin. They were all so beautiful … and so expensive! Frugality got the better of me. After all, it wasn't as if he was going to sell my creation, and he was bound to be impressed by my considering the cost. I found a plain, round, dark blue vase, selected some delicate pink and white lacy sprays, a bunch of darker pink carnations and, bravely, a few high-priced deep purple blooms. Then I set to work. Half an hour later I stood back to view my efforts. I decided it was pretty enough, but something was lacking. Then I noticed a sheaf of the palest mauve blooms with stiff spiky heads lying by me on the floor. Just the contrast I needed!

"I've finished!"

The boss walked slowly around my arrangement, then stood back rubbing his chin.

"It's pretty … er … Victorian."

"Oh yes," I simpered, not knowing if he meant it was pretty or just Victorian, or both. "Well, being British …"

Then he pulled out one of the spiky mauve stems.

"These," he said, "we don't use. These," he said, "are dead."

I had failed my first audition in Los Angeles.

RIGHT BACK WHERE I STARTED FROM

It had been a marvellous comfort having Dan and his wife, Audrey, there to call on if I needed advice or support when I was flagging. Dan had given up his career as an actor very early on, a loss to the profession in my view, and was now an established film and TV director, while Audrey had a successful writing career. I loved being with them in their home, the only place of sanity in this competitive environment. One night, at a small dinner party they hosted, I met Michael Douglas's mother, a beautiful, elegant woman, who mentioned that her son was looking for a long-term house-sitter. I was more than tempted, but with my future plans so uncertain I dared not commit myself to anything long term.

And then there was Miriam. I had known Miriam Margolyes in London since way back when. We had grumbled to each other about the lack of work for such talented actors as ourselves.

"What we should do, Sheila, is go to the States, make a name for ourselves, and then we'll get all the work over here that we want."

It sounded like a good idea, but I didn't have the courage. Needless to say, Miriam did. By the time I arrived in LA she had appeared on the Johnny Carson show, got herself an agent, and was about to do her brilliant one-woman show of Dickens characters in a smart little theatre on Sunset Boulevard. She invited me to lunch in her Santa Monica apartment, where I met her hugely proud father. She exuded the sort of unequivocal confidence that I lacked and envied as I watched her wade through a vast number of answerphone messages and tell her agent in no uncertain terms what she would and wouldn't do. She did her hasty best to get her agent interested in me and tried to get her friends to take me on, but they were busy and the agent wasn't interested. Miriam, however, was kind and supportive, and I was grateful.

I had had a course of therapy in London with a highly qualified and sympathetic psychotherapist, Rita Lynn, wife of Jonathan Lynn who co-wrote the reputable TV series *Yes Minister*. He was now directing films, and they were living in a fine house in the Hollywood Hills. They invited me round and were more than generous, wining and dining me, listening to my fears and woes, and even lending me their spare car (a little old Austin) when my hire car failed.

I'd been sitting it out in LA for five long weeks when at last a call came: could I get myself to Columbia Studios that very afternoon? I sure could.

"And don't wear too much make-up," I was instructed. "You're reading for the role of a 76-year-old grandmother."

I was sceptical of my chances.

"Now come on, Becky," I said, "I realise anxiety may have left its mark, but ..."

"They start shooting tomorrow and they're desperate," she interrupted shortly. "You never know. Go."

I went.

The receptionist pushed a large notebook at me across her desk and I added my name to the list of actors, filling in my agent's name, the time of my arrival, the name of the character for which I was to read, and leaving a noticeable blank against the Green Card social security number. She handed me a résumé of the plot, a brief description of the character and a page of dialogue (for some strange reason they're called 'sides'). There were two other actresses in the waiting room, who both greeted me as though I were a long lost friend, nerves and desperation drawing us together. This was a pleasant surprise and the opposite of what mostly happens in London, where actors go to inordinate lengths to avoid meeting one another at auditions, and if they do cross paths the embarrassment is palpable. I scrutinised my American counterparts: both seemed nearer the age of the character than I was.

"I don't really know what I'm doing here," confided the older looking of the two. "I'm much too young for the part."

The other actress took a hefty drag on her cigarette.

"You may be too goddam young!" she countered, puffs of smoke punctuating her word. "Me, the way I feel right now, I'm too goddam old!"

Just then a candidate emerged from the inner sanctum, raised her eyes to heaven and, with a hefty sigh of relief, said, "She wants whoever's next," adding as she crossed to the door, "And boy, are you welcome!"

I hissed, "Good luck!" as the older actress hurried through the door, only to emerge in what seemed a mere minute later.

"How was it?" I asked.

"Just fine!" she beamed. "Oh, just fine. Next!" And she sailed happily out of the room.

My second new-found friend stubbed out her cigarette and winked at me.

"It is a far, far better part I want than I will ever get," she intoned, and the casting room door closed behind her.

Five minutes passed ... six ... seven ... She was doing well! Then she emerged.

"Well?"

"Who knows? Who the goddam knows?" she shrugged, digging into her handbag for the cigarette pack. "We must be out of our tiny goddam minds, you know that? Good luck, honey." And the door slammed behind her.

I sat on the other side of the desk opposite an immaculately coiffured, perfectly made-up black girl with the longest, reddest fingernails. She looked all of 16.

"You ready?" she asked briskly. "Let's read."

"Who with?" I asked, looking around the empty room.

"Me. Who else?" she said irritably. "Got your sides? Let's go."

We began. She read 'her' lines (a man's part) and then looked up quickly, eyes focused narrowly so that she didn't miss an eyelash flicker. I tried to concentrate, but this scrutiny was disconcerting and my sense of the ridiculous was getting the better of me.

Halfway through the first page she leaned back and, slapping the script down on her desk, said, "Nope. You ain't it."

"But if you tell me exactly ..."

She stood up sharply. "Look, dear, I've got to cast this yesterday! Just send the next one in, OK?"

I sent the next one in and fled to the car park, telling myself that, however humiliating, at least I knew the bad news immediately. As I drove towards the exit I passed the older actress, who waved at me cheerfully.

"Didn't even get to read," she called. "Like I said, much too young!"

The second job I was sent for was much more up my street: a few lines in a German accent either selling or serving cheese, dressed as a 'Cheese Maid'. It was in a sketch show starring a popular American comic, and it was just the sort of cameo that had got my career in comedy going in the UK. The anteroom was crammed with actresses with ages ranging from seventeen to seventy, and they had almost all made some sort of effort to look the part. There were rough-woven skirts and ethnic sandals, embroidered blouses with big puffy sleeves, shawls wrapped around shoulders or heads, and hair in bunches or plaits or coiled around the ears. On a chair in the corner sat a wrinkled old woman, who was so small that her dangling legs didn't quite reach the floor. She wore a pair of lederhosen, an embroidered waistcoat, and Alpine boots with thick woollen socks that left her bony knees exposed. On her head was a wig with two fat plaits made of thick yellow wool. Had I been casting, I would probably have given her the part. The door to the audition room was paper thin, and hearing each attempt at a convincing German accent boosted my confidence no end.

My turn came, I was ushered in, and a bored blonde sitting beside the video camera said, "Stand there and say your name, then say something or other, it doesn't matter what, in a German accent."

"I'm Sheila Steafel," I said, and then, thinking it might be amusing, I went on in a heavy German accent, "and I am saying something or other, it doesn't matter what, in a German accent. Ja wohl!"

I didn't get that job either.

A week later Larry sent me to read for a part in an episode of a crime series. The role was that of a widow who blames the leading man for the death of her husband. She threatens to throw his ashes in the leading man's face, and slowly unscrews a suspicious-looking thermos flask, gets it open and - wait for it - pours herself a cup of coffee. It was so awful I loved it, but unfortunately they didn't love me, and the next day I found out why. Larry phoned and asked me to call in at the office. I sat and watched anxiously as he pushed the chair away from his desk and leaned back, eyes closed, hands clasped behind his head.

"Sheila," he said, "about yesterday. From what I'm getting, you're snooty."

"Snooty?"

"That's what I'm getting, Sheila," he repeated. "You're snooty."

It's true that I have to make a conscious effort to be confident and outgoing, but I had forced myself to be as jolly and friendly and have-a-good-day-ish as I could at that interview. Clearly I was failing.

"Maybe it's your English accent. Makes you sound kinda uppity, like you was talking down to people."

I was at a loss. "What can I do?"

"Listen, next time I send you to meet these people you speak with an American accent, okay?"

291

"How can I go in with a résumé full of English credits from the BBC to the RSC, and talk with an American accent?" I asked, on the verge of tears.

"Believe me, they won't notice. Next time, do it!"

I was worried about the authenticity of my accent, so on my way home I decided to stop off at the local supermarket and try it out. I wandered along the aisles, wire basket in hand, gathered one or two odds and ends, and searched for a likely looking assistant to use as a guinea pig. A large, friendly-looking woman in a blue overall was stacking tins on a shelf. She looked as American as apple pie! If I could fool her, I could fool anyone.

"Pardon me," I drawled, "I wonder if you could possibly help me. I have this really darling little jacket that I just love and it's gotten a little dirty. Know what I mean?"

She didn't seem to, so I tried again.

"Well now, the reason I'm asking is I don't know the stores around here any too well, and I want to take it to a really good dry cleaning establishment. Do you happen to know if there's one someplace hereabouts at all?"

She frowned, and then smiled apologetically.

"No comprendo, signora," she said. "Plisa you speaka my fren."

If you're going to succeed in Hollywood, you must believe in yourself absolutely and pursue your ambitions relentlessly at any cost, and it was dawning on me that I was out of my comfort zone and floundering. The more success I saw around me the more insecure and inadequate I felt. I confided in Rita Lynn and she suggested that if I felt that way there was no future for me in LA's uncompromising world of entertainment. I was torn between returning home or gritting my unwhitened teeth and playing the waiting game.

Then, out of the blue, I received a letter from my solicitor. Back in London I had been suing a builder for removing all the roof supports in my house when he converted my loft into a studio for me to paint in - and presumably get crushed to death in. It had been a long and miserable four years since litigation began, and the letter stated that the date of the court hearing had been set and that it was essential I return immediately for a meeting with my barrister the following Monday afternoon. I phoned and begged for a postponement, but my solicitor was intransigent; the barrister was a busy man and if the meeting was postponed there was no guarantee that it would be reassigned. I had no choice. Reluctantly I arranged to leave two days later, changed my air ticket, forking out the $70 penalty I could ill afford, and determined to return, left a suitcase full of clothes with the Lynns. I was booked to leave for London early on Sunday morning, but meanwhile I had one more interview on the Friday. This time the casting director thought that I was ideal for the part and asked me to meet the producer and director on the Monday.

When I got back to London I found a message on my answerphone telling me that the unalterable and desperately important meeting with the barrister had been postponed. Once my tears of rage were spent, I began to wonder if it had been a blessing in disguise - perhaps this was no time for beginnings. Finally daunted, I decided that I would give up attempting to become a major star, and stick to being a minor celebrity. I dropped a line to Rita Lynn, apologising for giving her the added irritation of sending me back my suitcase.

EXITS AND ENTRANCES

Of course, nothing could have been further from the truth. Unlike old soldiers, actors never fade away; they cling on, refusing to relinquish their hopes and dreams and aspirations. Besides, mine were deeply embedded, the seeds sown at the age of four, and, seventy years on, still intrinsic to me. It's amazing how the mind can choose to ignore the blindingly obvious: that the glory days are over. But even the evidence of a CV whittled away to almost nothing fails to douse the small, flickering flame of belief in chance, and with good reason, for without it nothing would remain but the bleakest of outlooks and a future with no purpose. From time to time I'm asked, "Didn't you used to be an actress?" It still hurts like a jab in the solar plexus. Then again, someone, usually of a certain age, will say, "You're an actress, aren't you?" and for a short while I'll walk taller.

I decided I should face up to the fact that performing my three one-woman shows again was unlikely, and that it was time to clear out the paraphernalia stored in the loft. It took some determination, and I began by heaving the weighty brown paper packages holding hundreds of posters, flyers and programmes, down the steep ladder, then dragged them into my car and headed for the recycling centre. It was quite a load, and a chirpy young lad in overalls helped me to turf them into an enormous skip, commenting as he did so on how surprisingly heavy the neat packages were.

"As heavy as my heart," I joked, and, as he reached for the last bundle, for no accountable reason I said, "Leave that one."

I took it home and struggled it back into the loft.

Now it was the turn of the costumes, the props and the bits of stage furnishings, all in place, ready and waiting for the next outing. 'Never again' loomed over me like a dark cloud. I opened the wicker skip that had travelled with me through such rich and fulfilling times, carrying the familiar treasures I had collected for *Victoria Plums*, and took out the elegant white ostrich feather fan that had belonged to my grandmother, and possibly her mother before her. It's only a fan, I told myself, a prop you used in your show. You've no children to hand it on to, you've no need for it anymore, and it might fetch something on eBay. Then, quite unexpectedly, I cried. I cried soundlessly from somewhere deep within me, crouching on the floor beside the open skip. After a long while I put the fan back carefully in its tissue-papered box. I'd clear the loft out some other time, but not now, not just yet.

Meanwhile, as I wait for the call from my agent about that long-delayed script, I reassure myself by paging through past performances. There are five plays in particular that have made all the sacrifices and all the struggles worthwhile. The first may seem an odd choice, but there was a plus side to this salutary tale: I managed to realise two lifelong ambitions. One was to sing with the backing of a full orchestra, and the other, to fly, suspended by a Kirby wire. Surely, thus fulfilled, a girl could die happy. And I did, on stage, every night!

1983, *Hansel and Gretel*, opera by Engelbert Humperdinck
Short run at the Bloomsbury Theatre

When my agent phoned and asked if I'd like to play the Witch in *Hansel and Gretel*, thinking she meant the pantomime, I said yes, I'd love to. She said, "They're sending you a tape." I said I thought that was rather grand for a panto. When I played the tape I laughed so hard, I fell off my chair: it was Elisabeth Schwartzkopf singing the role of the Witch in Humperdinck's opera. I phoned back to tell her that they'd got the wrong lady, but it seemed that the assistant director, Chris Pickles, had heard me sing the part of one of the ugly sisters in a Players pantomime, and he and the producer, Christopher Renshaw, both of whom became staunch friends, were sure that I could hack it. As it turned out, I did - to pieces.

I took a course of singing lessons and worked for several months on the score with the patient and encouraging conductor Christopher Fifield. By the time we got to rehearsals I knew my part thoroughly, and the two Chris's encouragement and belief in my abilities boosted my confidence. As the opening night approached I had a few sessions hooked up to a Kirby wire, learning how to fly. Apart from the discomfort of the leather harness, and the terror of sailing dangerously close to the huge arc lights overhead as I swung towards the opposite wall, flying was a glorious experience.

Then came the first rehearsal when, for the first time, I sang with the support of a fifty-piece orchestra. It sent shivers down my spine. Seeing the set, though, brought me down to earth with a jolt. It was a metal box made of mesh and suspended a few feet above the stage. The 'floor' was sharply raked, making walking hazardous, exacerbated by the narrow heels of my Witch's boots, which kept catching in the wire. What with that, the harness under the padded clothing, the wig, the hat and the false nose, moving about took more concentration than my singing, and it showed. The rest of the cast were trained opera singers with splendid voices, and although I sang the correct notes in the right order my voice was, to say the least, small and inadequate. The two Christophers pleaded with the management for some sort of amplification, but they refused on the grounds that this was opera, and opera would never countenance any such calumny! Not true, of course, but by the time we found out it was too late.

On the opening night all went reasonably well until my solo, to be sung whilst in full flight. The orchestra played the introductory notes that anticipate the famously thrilling aria to come, I stood astride my broomstick ready for take-off, and ... nothing. I was manifestly thoroughly earthbound. I began singing and headed towards the wings, where a member of the crew stood tugging at the wire meant to hoist me heavenward. He shook his head at me, spraying beads of sweat. There was nothing for it. I climbed off the broom and sang on, sweeping the stage vigorously from one end to the other until the aria was done. Shrugging my shoulders, I raised the broom aloft and shook my head apologetically, hoping that the audience would understand my dilemma. They seemed to, except for one critic who thought my gesture vainglorious.

Once, when my profile in comedy was riding high, I asked my father if he was pleased with what I'd achieved, and his answer was, "Yes, but I would have preferred you to have been a second Janet Baker." Knowing this, I made the fateful mistake of inviting him over from South Africa to see me in the role. The poor man came anticipating great things, and I cannot begin to imagine how disappointed and outraged he must have felt seeing me out of my depth and struggling. But my father said nothing about the production or my part in it, neither before, nor during, nor after. Absolutely nothing. In hindsight, perhaps it was as well that he kept his counsel.

Here are a few of the reviews, so bad (and deservedly so) that they still make me laugh!

… Hisses all round for S.S's Witch. The insistence on having a 'star' name on the bill results in a central character who can hardly sing, and whose Dr Strangelove-style depiction of evil goes over children's heads and to adults seems clichéd.
- HAM & HIGH

The Bloomsbury Theatre's Hansel and Gretel requires not so much a notice as a post-mortem. What took to the stage should not have been put before a paying public.
… Worst of all S.S had to sing the first half of the Ride off-stage while being hitched into flying apparatus, which then failed to work when she came onstage. The poor woman jigged about a bit, sloped off to be unhitched, and then expected sympathetic applause on her re-entry. … She is modestly gifted as a comic, even more modestly as an opera singer, having about four useful notes in the middle of the stave and virtually nothing elsewhere. I wish I could suggest with confidence that it will all improve during the run. But I can't.
- FINANCIAL TIMES

1979, *A Day in Hollywood, A Night in the Ukraine*
New End Theatre and Mayfair Theatre
" … and I think you'd be ideal as Harpo."

Dick Vosburgh had just told me of his project to collaborate with composer Frank Lazarus and write a stage version of a Marx Brothers movie. I had seen most of the Marx Brothers films and, coincidentally, had always felt an affinity with Harpo, aware of the sensitive man beneath the foolery as he rendered his harp solos. But no one, and certainly not a woman, could get away with playing him.

"Me play Harpo? That sounds great, I'd love to do it!" I replied, knowing it would never happen. But it did.

Dick called to say that the writing was done, a production management had been found and a script for *A Day in Hollywood, A Night in the Ukraine* was on its way. The first director that Dick approached had firmly vetoed the idea of a woman playing Harpo, but Dick was intransigent, and it was Ian Davidson who eventually directed it.

The first half, *A Day in Hollywood*, reviewed films and the stars of the thirties, and the cast had a chance to sing some of the songs, tell anecdotes and recall those satisfyingly trite film clichés. Although I had no lines to learn for the second half, *A Night in the Ukraine*, there was much work to do incorporating Harpo's classic comedy business and seamlessly devising new ones. I can't whistle, and Harpo whistled constantly to replace speech or attract attention. I tried using a 'swizzle', a small disc used by Punch and Judy animators and kept under the tongue, but I was paranoid about swallowing it and gave up. Instead, I used a little brass horn with a rubber ball attached, and when I squeezed it, it hooted. I wore a chequered shirt and tie, men's two-tone shoes, a large raincoat with pockets both inside and out, deep enough to hold a collection of unlikely props, and, of course, a crushed top hat perched drunkenly on a curly blonde wig.

Dick had a brilliant mind for verbal jokes but, as he was the first to admit, not visual gags. When it came to playing the harp solo, Dick suggested I use the back of a chair, the window blinds, a waste-paper basket, and anything else on the set that looked likely, but I balked at the idea. In fact, I balked at doing it at all; the whole concept unnerved me, and it seemed a step too far. But Dick and Ian were insistent. We had already opened at the New End and the audience were asking about the anticipated harp solo. Reluctantly I puzzled over it, and eventually came up with the idea of playing the back wheel of a bicycle. The bike would have to be upside down on the floor, but why would Harpo turn it over? To inspect it, because … because it wasn't feeling well! How could he tell that the bike was feeling low? It wouldn't eat when he offered it … a carrot, fished up from the depths of a coat pocket. Slowly, the routine took shape. I asked a harpist to teach me the basic fingering, put together a short tape of incidental harp music culled from the BBC sound department, and learned it very precisely so that playing the wheel would look thoroughly genuine. I begged an old unwanted bicycle from a friend, turned the handlebars upside down, giving it a hangdog look, cut several spokes out of the wheels, flattened the tyres, twisted the torn saddle to one side, and spattered the whole sad creation with bird droppings of white paint. My partner and I were ready to roll:

The entertainment was a huge hit, and moved from the New End to the West End. Soon there were rumours of interest from America, and this was confirmed when the following appeared in *What's On*:

Dick Vosburgh's brilliant comic tribute to the Marx Brothers is to open off-Broadway, but because of an American Equity ruling not one of the cast Dick hand-picked will be allowed to accompany the show. Even greater treachery, though its American sponsors delight in the novelty of a female Harpo, they are to deny Sheila Steafel the glory of recreating her spectacular 'coup de theatre' in this role over there. Dick is distraught.

A video had been made of our production, which, of course, included my harp solo, and a friend who saw the show in New York reported that the actress playing Harpo had repeated my performance exactly. She won that year's best actress Tony award for her performance in *A Day in Hollywood, A Night in the Ukraine*.

At this point I should say that the inclusion of any of the following notices favouring me should not be read as self-congratulatory. Well, not entirely.

… Dick Vosburgh gives it the funniest script the brothers never wrote.
- *DAILY MAIL*

You rub your eyes in disbelief. There on stage are the Marx Brothers cavorting in a comedy as funny ... often funnier ... than anything they did on screen.
- WHAT'S ON

... Perhaps best of all S.S joyfully brings the mute Harpo to life, and after attempting to feed a dejected bicycle with a carrot, turns the machine over and plays the back wheel as a harp. Miss S. gives us a comic routine that Harpo would have been proud to have created.
- THE TIMES

S.S. brings Harpo brimmingly to life, illuminating him from the inside. To watch her trying to feed a carrot to a bicycle is to risk a hernia.
- PUNCH

1985, *The Merry Wives of Windsor*
Stratford-upon-Avon
1986, The Barbican; 1987, Revived at the Barbican
Bill Alexander's concept was to set the play in the early Thatcher years, 1959, and this much acclaimed production is still well remembered. Bill had previously directed me in Pinter's *Old Times* at the Bristol Old Vic, and I was surprised when he offered me the part of Mistress Quickly. At first I declined; the prospect of joining the illustrious Royal Shakespeare Company daunted me, and frankly I didn't think I was up to it. Bill talked me round, although during rehearsals he may well have wondered if he'd made a bad mistake: always one of my problems, I had no idea how to play the part. I'm a 'bad rehearser' and don't really resolve my performance until I get in front of an audience. It bothers me as much as everyone else, and finally Bill called me to one side with an ultimatum: I really had to decide which way the character was going to go. I'd had a notion that Quickly might be a secret tippler, getting more inebriated as the plot progressed, and he agreed that it might be an idea worth pursuing.

... and in a superb performance S.S makes Mistress Quickly into a dotty flask-toting eccentric.
- DAILY TELEGRAPH

… The abiding delight of the production is S.S's Mistress Quickly, a down-at-heel little figure of faded and bibulous gentility, incorrigibly helpful, touchingly delighted with any rewards that may come her way, succoured through life's trickier passages by a hip-flask, bemused by the antics of the stage furnishings, and finally a squiffy Fairy Queen who has lost her way to the party. Miss S.'s performance leaves us in no doubt that Mistress Quickly is one of the greatest gifts to comic actresses in English drama.
- TIMES LITERARY SUPPLEMENT

S.S's Mistress Quickly simply reconfirms her as our reigning female clown …
- THE TIMES

There were several more such notices, but modesty (what's left of it) forbids.

2006, *The Birthday Party*
The Bristol Old Vic

After too many years a phone call came from Simon Reade, artistic director of the Bristol Old Vic, inviting me to play Meg in his production of Pinter's *The Birthday Party*. It was a part that I had always coveted, and to play it in such a prestigious theatre was a huge boost to my flagging morale. But after such a long gap, could I still hack it? It so happened that there was a delay of a month before rehearsals began, by which time I was nigh-on word perfect - until we started to work, when every syllable disappeared into a black hole! Fortunately, this was just a blip, and as we rehearsed the lines slotted back into place. Simon was witty, sharp and innovative. Where other directors might have curbed my comic tendencies, he encouraged me to be bold within the confines of the play, paring down my performance until it was razor sharp. The part of Meg fitted me like a glove, and at the end of the run I dropped Harold Pinter a line to thank him for writing the part for me.

The great star, though, is S.S., her ditsy landlady Meg note-perfect and her body language the sign of a seasoned actress.
- BRISTOL METRO

300

No one does comedy better than the marvellous S.S. as the landlady Meg.
- *THE BATH CHRONICLE*

S.S.'s Meg is stunning.
- *THE BRITISH THEATRE GUIDE*

Steafel is worth the price of admission alone.
- *THE INDEPENDENT*

2008, *Funny Girl*
Minerva Theatre
Chichester Festival

A mere two years later the phone rang again, this time asking if I'd be interested in playing Rosie Brice, Fanny Brice's mother in the musical *Funny Girl*. Would I? Ever since I had stood on the dining room table as a little girl and sung and danced to our wind-up gramophone, I had dreamed of being in a musical. Now here, only 70 years later, was my chance, not only to sing and dance, but to play a role that was dramatic and funny and moving, in spades.

From beginning to end, the Chichester experience was everything I could have hoped for. Samantha Spiro, talented, down to earth and a brilliant Fanny Brice, led a flawless company that quickly developed a family feeling, and once we were up and running this filtered through to the orchestra. The production was a sold-out runaway success and, with the glorious venue, the attentive theatre staff and the idyllic country digs, where I smuggled my dogs in and out for fear of complaints from the other residents, life could not have been sweeter - except for one thing: I seemed to be physically weakening. I hadn't time to be ill and determinedly ignored the symptoms, but they persisted, and it was only when I could barely make it to the theatre for a midweek matinee that I was forced to face up to the fact that something was seriously amiss. An MRI scan revealed that I had developed arthritis in the vertebrae in my neck and the bone was constricting my spinal cord. I needed emergency surgery or risked paralysis.

In spite of having an understudy, there was no way I was going to let myself or the show down. It was the last week of the run, there were five performances to go, and somehow (Doctor Theatre never fails to work his magic!) I still managed to jump onto tables and tap my way through a song-and-dance routine. On Saturday night I was onstage in the theatre, the following Monday morning I was on a table in an operating theatre. But, hey, I stayed the distance! And, to quote Mister Sondheim, I'm still here.

During the run I often remarked that if *Funny Girl* was the last job I ever did it would have been worth it. I only wish that Whoever is Up There hadn't taken me quite so literally!

… Best of the pack is perhaps Sheila Steafel as Fanny's mother, who provides a wisecracking homespun Yiddish backdrop to the Broadway glamour.
- SUNDAY TELEGRAPH

… the doughty Jewish mother, played with glorious timing and insight by Sheila Steafel. It is a mystery how she manages to play simultaneously deadpan and with a flourish. But she does.
- PORTSMOUTH NEWS

Sam Spiro, a considerable actress, is expertly supported by the divine Sheila Steafel.
- WHATSONSTAGE.COM

DETAILED CV

1954-56	Amateur theatre in South Africa
1957	Webber Douglas School of Drama: Repertory: Lincoln – Hunstanton – Blackpool
1958	Schools' tour of Wales: Understudied Old Vie
1959	First appearance at Players Theatre: Tour of *Landscape With Figures* by Cecil Beaton, with Donald Wolfitt and Mona Washbourne
1960	Tour of *Milk and Honey* with Maggie Lockwood, Derek Farr and Patrick Cargill
1964	Took over Barbara in *Billy Liar* with Tom Courtenay; Director Lindsay Anderson First TV role: *Kipps* (Granada), Kipps' first girlfriend First comedy role: *Justin Thyme* (BBC), Miss Pennypacker; Director Joe McGrath
1965	*Close Prisoner*, secretary (scene with Patrick McGoohan) *Time and the Conways* (Granada), Joan *Comedy Playhouse* (BBC), 'The Exploding Whoopee Cushion', with John Bird *Splits on the Infinitive*, revue at Hampstead Theatre Club, with Julian Chagrin *TV Armchair Theatre*, 'A Headful of Crocodiles', with Donald Churchill *TV Armchair Theatre*, 'The Man with the Iron Chest, with Bernard Cribbins *Anyone for England*, revue at Lyric Hammersmith, with Paul McDowell *It's Dark Outside*, TV serial (Granada), with Oliver Reed and William Mervyn *The Way of All Flesh* (Granada)

The De Maupassant Stories (Granada),
with Anton Rogers
A Fat Woman's Tale (Granada), by Fay Wheldon
Close Prisoner, with Patrick McGoohan
Z Cars (BBC)
The Liars (Granada), playing a girl who imagines
she's a bicycle, with William Mervyn, Ian Ogilvy
and Isla Blair
Troubleshooters (ATV)

1966 Frost Over England (BBC) 13 episodes with David
Frost, Ronnie Barker Ronnie Corbett and John
Cleese (the series won the Golden Rose of
Montreux)
Danger Man, with Patrick McGoohan
Daleks' Invasion Earth (film), young woman
(villainess!)

1967 Just Like a Woman (film), Isolde
Quatermass and the Pit (film), journalist
Monsieur Lecoq (unfinished film), with Zero Mostell

1968 The Bliss of Mrs Blossom (film), pet shop assistant
Baby Love (film), Tessa Pearson, with Dick Emery
Otley, ground stewardess, with Tom Courtenay
Dickie Henderson Show (ATV)
Frankie Howerd Show (first, BBC)
Illustrated Weekly Hudd (BBC series),
with Roy Hudd
Horne A'Plenty (ABC series), with Kenneth Horne

1969 Beachcomber (series), with Spike Milligan
Hugh and I (BBC), one episode, with Hugh Lloyd
and Terry Scott
The Guardsman (play), by Frank Marcus,
Theatre Royal Watford
Goodbye Mr Chips (film), Tilly, with Peter O'Toole
Not Only … But Also (BBC series), with Peter Cook
and Dudley Moore
The Fabulous Frump, (BBC Weds play), title role
Several episodes in series with Eric Sykes and
Hattie Jacques, Bob Monkhouse and
Jimmy Tarbuck
The Troubleshooters (BBC series), one episode,
Dr Yvette Leduc

1970	*Some Will, Some Won't* (film), Sheila Wilcox, with Michael Hordern
	Tropic of Cancer (Paramount film), Tania, with Rip Torn 2nd
	How the Other Half Loves (play try-out), with Hugh Paddick, Leicester
	Cribbins (ABC TV series), with Bernard Cribbins
	Who Goes Bare? (farce try-out), with Leslie Darbon and Richard Harris, Windsor
	Three Sisters (Chekhov play), with Hayley Mills, Leicester
1971	*Percy* (film), Mrs Gold, with Hywel Bennett
	S.W.A.L.K. (aka *Melody*) (cult film), Mrs Latimer, David Puttnam's first production
	The Val Doonican Show (ATV series), with Val Doonican and Bernard Cribbins
	To Catch a Spy (film), woman in lift, with Kirk Douglas
	Some Matters of Little Consequence (late night BBC series)
	Who's Who? (play by Waterhouse and Hall), try-out, Coventry
	Jump (play by Larry Gelbart), with Warren Mitchell, tour and short run at Queen's Theatre, West End
1972	*How the Other Half Loves*, with Robert Morley, 9 months Lyric Theatre, 4 weeks Alexandra Toronto
1973	*The Sebrof Story* (ATV play), with Alfred Marks
	Go for Gold (BBC play)
	Digby, the Biggest Dog in the World (film), TV control operator
1974	Unreleased movie, playing Harpo and paranoid murderess, producer Ray Starke, director Bob Kellett
	Old Times (Pinter play), Bristol Old Vic, director Bill Alexander
	Old Time Music Hall, several appearances, Players Theatre
	How's Your Father (Granada series), Ivy Watkins (catchphrase "Yes, Mr Cropper"), with Michael Robbins and Arthur English

	Second Time Around (BBC series), with Michael Craig
1975	*The Good Old Days*, Emmaline, Popsy Wopsy, etc., hosted by Leonard Sachs, director Barney Colehan
	The Ghosts of Motley Hall (Granada, first series), White Lady
	Sykes (BBC series), 'Xmas Party', Clara
	No Room for Sex (play), tour with Thora Hird and Hugh Paddick
	The Goodies, 'The Goodies Rule - OK?', guest
1976	*You'll Never Be Michelangelo* (play), with Robin Bailey, Hampstead Theatre Club
	Salad Days, Elizabeth Seale, Windsor and Duke of York's
	The Ghosts of Motley Hall (second series)
	The Waiting Room (short film for Bob Kellett)
	The Good Old Days
1977	*The Good Old Days*, Jubilee programme
	Let's Make A Musical: The History Of Mr Polly (BBC), with Roy Castle
	The Ghosts of Motley Hall (third series)
	Week Ending (Radio 4), member of team 1977-1983
	Are You Being Served?: The Movie, hat customer
	The Goodies, guest
1978	*The Good Old Days*
	Q7 (BBC series), with Spike Milligan
	The Bluebird (Players' panto), ugly sister
	The Perishers, voices for Marlon and Maisie
	What's Up Superdoc? (film), Dr Pitt
	Balmoral (play by Michael Frayn), Enid Blyton, Guildford try-out
	The Jason Explanation (BBC Radio 4 series), with David Jason
	Motley Hall, Xmas Special
	Beryl Reid Show (BBC), guest
	Leslle CROWTHER SHOW (BBC), guest
	My Sainted Aunt (BBC Radio 2 show)
	Diary of a Nobody (BBC serialisation), Carrie
	Quiz Kids (ATV play), Brenda
1979	*A Day in Hollywood, A Night in the Ukraine* (play by Dick Vosburgh), Harpo, New End and Mayfair
	In Loving Memory (Yorkshire Television series),

Nelly Asquith, with Thora Hird
Honky Tonk Heroes (trilogy by Ray Connolly), with
Denis Quilley and Helen Mirren

1980   *The Jason Explanation* (second series)
Rainbow (Thames Television children's TV series)
Give Us a Clue (ITV panel game show)
Jackanory Playhouse, wicked TV director
Frankie Howerd Reveals All (BBC special)
3-2-1 (Yorkshire Television game show with
sketches)
Can We Get On Now, Please? (TV series),
Myrtle Prior, with Hugh Paddick
Cowboys (Thames TV series), two episodes, with
Colin Welland and Roy Kinnear

1981   *The Good Old Days*
3-2-1 (Yorkshire TV game show)
Q7 (BBC series), with Spike Milligan
Towers of Babel (short film), with Brian Pringle
Jackanory Playhouse, Supergran
Saturday Night at the Mill,
promo for Edinburgh Festival
Live On Two, two interviews, first one with dog
Crispin, second Edinburgh promo
The Late Sheila Steafel,
New End and then Edinburgh Festival
Punchllnes (ITV panel game show)
NatWest (promo film), with Kenneth Williams
Steafel Solo, King's Head

1982   *Steafel Solo*, King's Head, extended from 3 to
11 weeks
Call My Bluff (BBC panel game show),
first appearance
The Kenny Everett Television Show (BBC),
regular guest
Legal, Decent, Honest and Truthful (BBC Radio 4
series), with Martin Jarvis
Steafel Solo, Adelaide Festival
Steafel Plus (BBC Radio 4)
Steafel Revisited, second Edinburgh Festival
Sheila (Channel 4), version of one-woman show
Steafel Variations, Apollo Theatre

1983   *Babble* (Channel 4 panel game show)

	Call My Bluff (BBC panel game show)
	Celebrity Squares (ITV game show)
	Punchllnes (ITV panel game show)
	Steafel Lately, third Edinburgh Festival
	Twelfth Night, Maria, Young Vic
	The Duenna (comic opera), title role, Young Vic
	Keep It In The Family (Thames TV comedy series), one episode, Aunt Kate
	Cabaret in Istanbul
	Hansel and Gretel (Humperdinck opera), the witch, Bloomsbury Theatre
1984	*Steafel With An S.*, (Radio 4), three shows
	Cabaret in Istanbul (second)
	Starbreakers (Tyne Tees series), Bea Lillie
	The Diary of Adrian Mole, mother, Leicester try-out
	Blood Bath at the House of Death (film), with Kenny Everett
	Dramarama (ITV series), Fowl Pest(play), with Irene Handle
1985	*Yardsale*, 40-minute one-hand play written for S.S. by Arnold Wesker
	'Pizza on the Park' show, January
	Steafel Xpress, Ambassadors Theatre
	Merry Wives of Windsor, Mistress Quickly, RSC, director Bill Alexander
1986	*Merry Wives of Windsor*, transfer to Barbican
	Façade, Q.E. Hall, with London Mozart Players, conductor Jane Glover
1987	*Merry Wives of Windsor*, revived January to March
	You Must Be the Husband (BBC TV sitcom), Miranda Shaw, with Tim Brooke-Taylor and Diane Keen
	The Kenny Everett Show (BBC), guest appearances
	Crosswits (Tyne Tees quiz show)
	Call My Bluff (BBC panel game show)
1988	*The Musical Comedy Murders of 1940* (play), with Tom Baker, try-out in Greenwich
	The Gingerbread Lady (play), Watford
	Blankety Blank (BBC game show)
	Wogan (BBC chat show), interview
	Minder (ITV series)
1989	*Much Ado About Nothing*, with Alan Bates and Felicity Kendall, Strand Theatre

Ivanov, with Alan Bates and Felicity Kendall,
Strand Theatre
Wogan, second interview
Bluebirds (BBC children's series),
with Barbara Windsor
Paris Match (play), with Stephen Moore and
Sian Peters, Garrick Theatre
Month of Sundays, four one-woman shows,
King's Head
Woof! (Central Independent children's TV series)
Minder (ITV series)

1991	Trip to USA
	Sailor Beware (play), Edie, Lyric Hammersmith
1992	*Happy Family* (play), Farnham
	Good Sex Guide (TV series)
1993	*Minder* (ITV series)
	Cinderella, first panto, Fairy Godmother, Oxford Playhouse
1994	*Displaced* (BBC radio play), lead role
	Babes in the Wood, second panto, Good Fairy, Bromley
	Laughing Aloud/Reading Aloud (BBC radio), written and read by S.S.
	Letters from the Greenroom (BBC radio), written and read by S.S.
1995	*Victoria Plums*, new one-woman show
	The Relapse (play), Nurse, RSC, Stratford
	Faust, Martha, RSC
1996	Continued RSC productions at Barbican
	The Eleventh Commandment (play), Hampstead Theatre Club
	Whizziwig (CITV children's TV series)
1997	*The Eleventh Commandment*, extended
	The Importance of Being Earnest (BBC World Service), Miss Prism
	Robin Hood, first commission to write Xmas panto, Chipping Norton Theatre
	Victoria Plums, Polygram CD
1998	*Rab C. Nesbitt* (BBC sitcom), one episode
	Grange Hill (BBC children's TV series), one episode
1999	*The School for Wives*, West End, director Peter Hall

	Parting Shots (Michael Winner film),
	president's wife
2000	*Back to the Secret Garden* (TV film),
	with Joan Plowright
	The Mrs Bradley Mysteries (BBC drama series),
	with Diana Rigg
	Get a Life, Harry (interactive video film on Internet)
2001	*Tenth Kingdom* (TV series), Dr Horowitz
2002	*Steafel Xposed*, new one-woman show
	The Attractive Young Rabbi (BBC Radio 4 series)
2003	*Grease Monkeys* (BBC TV series), Magda Lovitt
2005	*Doctors* (BBC TV series), one episode,
	Dorothy Maples
	Victoria Plums, New End Theatre
2006	*The Birthday Party*, Meg, Bristol Old Vic
2007	*Holby City* (BBC TV series), one episode,
	Olivia MacBain
	Doctors (BBC TV series), one episode, Doris Dooley
	Frost Report Reunion (BBC Radio 4)
	Rocking Horse (BBC Radio 3),
	new Arnold Wesker play
2008	*Funny Girl*, Mrs Brice, Chichester Festival

VOICINGS:

The Perishers
SuperTed
Legoland
Stretch and Slim
Snailsbury
Beatrix Potter animations
Schools' animations

READINGS:

Three *Women's Hour* serialsed stories

AUDIO BOOKS:

The Poppy Chronicles, by Claire Rayner
For Love and Duty, by Maisie Mosco
The Deep Well at Noon, by Jessica Sterling
The Gates of Midnight, by Jessica Sterling
The Blue Evening Gone, by Jessica Sterling